DATE		

LEARNING FROM PALLADIO

LEARNING FROM
PALLADIO

BRANKO MITROVIĆ

W.W. Norton & Company
New York • London

For information about permission to reproduce selections from
this book, write to Permissions, W. W. Norton & Company, Inc.,
500 Fifth Avenue, New York, NY 10110

Book design and composition by Abigail Sturges
Manufacturing by Quebecor World/Kingsport
Production Manager: Leeann Graham

Library of Congress Cataloging-in-Publication Data

Mitrović, Branko.
    Learning from Palladio / Branko Mitrović.
    p. cm.
    ISBN 0-393-73116-2
    1. Palladio, A. (Andrea), 1508-1580—Criticism and interpretation.
    2. Architectural design—Methodology. I. Title.

NA1123.P2m58 2004
720'.92—dc22   2004041483

ISBN 0-393-73116-2

W. W. Norton & Company, Inc., 500 Fifth Avenue, New York, N.Y. 10110
www.wwnorton.com
W. W. Norton & Company Ltd., Castle House, 75/76 Wells St.,
London W1T 3QT

0 9 8 7 6 5 4 3 2 1

Title page: Rotonda (Vicenza). Facade by Ottavio Bertotti-
Scamozzi. (Collection Centre Canadien d'Architecture/Candian Center
for Architecture, Montréal. M7616:2, 1786, Tavola 2).

Page 188: Villa Cornaro. Author's photograph.

Photographs by author unless otherwise credited.

The following figures are from the Collection Centre Canadien
d'Architecture/Canadian Centre for Architecture, Montréal: 1-4, 1-6,
1-8, 1-10, 1-12, 1-14, 1-17, 1-18, 1-19, 1-21, 1-22, 1-19, 1-35, 1-44,
1-46, 1-50, figure on page 82, 2-1, 3-1, 3-2, 3-9, 3-15, 3-16, 3-17, 3-
19, 3-20, 3-29, 3-30, 3-31, 3-32, 3-33, 3-34, 3-35, 3-36, 3-37, 3-38,
3-39, 3-40, 3-46, 3-47, 3-50, 3-51, 4-1, 4-5, 4-8, 4-9, 4-10, 4-11, 4-
12, 4-13, 4-14, 4-15, 4-16, 4-17, 4-18, 4-20, 4-21, 4-22, 4-27

Portions of this text have been previously published in the following
articles by the author:

"Palladio's Canonical Corinthian Entablature and the Archaeological
Surveys in the Fourth Book of I quattro libri dell'architettura."
Architectural History 45 (2002), 113–127.

"A Palladian Palinode: Reassessing Rudolf Wittkower's Architectural
Principles in the Age of Humanism." Architectura 31 (2001),
113–131.

"Palladio's Theory of the Classical Orders and the First Book of
I quattro libri dell'architettura." Architectural History 42 (1999),
110–140.

"Palladio's Theory of Proportions and the Second Book of I quattro
libri dell'architettura." Journal of the Society of Architectural
Historians 49 (1990), 279–292.

Has he realized that he is not alone,
and that Apollo, arcane and unbelievable,
has revealed to him an archetype...?

Jorge Luis Borges[1]

CONTENTS

PREFACE

THE WRITING OF THIS BOOK took nine months—and fifteen years of preparation. I cannot say precisely how it came about that, as an architecture student at Belgrade University, I became interested in Palladio. All I remember is that once, accidentally, I went to a lecture on Palladio in a course which I was meant to take the following year. At that time I could not read Italian but—again by accident—at a book fair I saw Andreas Beyer's German translation of the *Four Books on Architecture*, whose price, because of the exchange rate, was astronomical for a student's budget. However, I could read German, and after a friend reproached me for not having bought the book, on a subsequent trip to Munich I obtained the German versions not only of the *Four Books*, but also Rudolf Wittkower's *Architectural Principles in the Age of Humanism*. Some time later, in Belgrade, I also managed to obtain copies of Lionello Puppi's *Andrea Palladio* and James Ackerman's *Palladio*. By the time I enrolled in the fourth year of architecture, I was as immersed in Palladian studies as the circumstances—and especially the difficulties in obtaining foreign books—allowed; a visit to Vicenza was the highlight of my carefully planned trip to Italy in 1986.

Since then, I have been engaged in studies that often had nothing to do with either architectural history or the Renaissance, but I have kept coming back to Palladio's works and reconsidering them from my newly acquired perspectives. My understanding of Palladio's oeuvre has gradually evolved around my interests. The original attraction came from my interest in proportional theories, and I was captivated by Wittkower's *Architectural*

Principles. The fact that I studied philosophy after completing my architecture degree pushed me to think about the aesthetic and epistemological implications of proportional theories. For instance, if a building should have certain proportions, are these proportions simply to be applied to the building, or should the building be designed so that they are perceived on it?

My final thesis in philosophy at Belgrade University was on Quine, the problem of universals, and the nominalist theory of language. I continued my doctoral studies at the University of Pennsylvania, where I realized that a whole set of traditional problems of architectural theory (optical corrections, the use of perspective) are specific formulations of the perennial philosophical debate about universals. As a result, my dissertation on Daniele Barbaro's commentary on Vitruvius leaned towards the reconstruction of the philosophical framework of Barbaro's views. While working on the dissertation, I taught architecture at the University of Notre Dame, a classicist school of architecture. In teaching there, I became aware of the importance of the classical orders for Renaissance architects and the inadequacy of attempts to reduce Renaissance theory of design to a pure proportional theory or to the narratives that contemporaries related to architectural works. A rectangle and an ellipse may have the same length/width ratio, but their aesthetic impact will be different. Renaissance architectural theorists may have described Ionic volutes as representations of female hair, but that narrative cannot explain why architects preferred a certain shape of the volute since it can apply equally well to other shapes.

I have always had formalist inclinations, but arguments of this kind gradually pushed me more and more in the formalist direction, which eventually resulted in my works on Vignola and Geoffrey Scott. Gradually, formalism also prepared the ground for my skepticism and ultimate rejection of Wittkower's interpretation of Palladio's design theory.

My approach to Palladio is also largely formed by the fact that I have never studied art history. The interest in "meanings," which dominates contemporary writing in English on art and architectural history, is a direction I have never developed taste for. Such research is surely very important; buildings certainly acquire "meanings" in the sense that people think conceptually, talk, or write about them. Treated this way, works of architecture indeed present an important aspect of social history. But buildings also possess formal, spatial, and visual properties, which are not reducible to the study of the narratives that individuals historically associated with architectural works. As an architect and later a teacher of architectural design, I wanted to learn how Palladio designed. I cared little about the narratives of architectural works he and his contemporaries produced unless those discussions revealed aspects of his design procedures. Moreover, my background in philosophy has made me extremely doubtful about the search for "meanings." From my first contact with the approach, I recognized in it the methodology of nineteenth-century Romanticist historiography whose epistemology I did not regard as credible. From my perspective as a former student of philosophy formed on Quine and Davidson, the search for "meanings" relied on a theory of meaning and language that seemed significantly outdated, in spite of its prevalence in contemporary architectural history. Its epistemological premises were incompatible with the interest in visual mental processes in post-behaviorist cognitive psychology, a field I believe to be of paramount importance to architectural theory. Worst of all, the ontological commitments implied by the exploration of "meanings" in architectural history tend to go far beyond anything I could accept: if you believe that there are individual humans' thoughts and actions, but no such thing as *Geist*, then the whole project of *Geistesgeschichte* is difficult to take seriously.

Formalism has thus dominated my approach to Palladio for more than a decade and ultimately determines the issues addressed in this book. The idea that the history of design theory is a valid subject of research for an architectural historian has almost died out in American scholarship, but it is very much alive in Europe. One of my goals is to summarize and present the results of research on Palladio's design theory that have been published since World War II in Europe, but are often disregarded in English-speaking scholarship.

The last chapter of the book discusses the use of Palladio's design principles in contemporary architecture. I am aware that this may raise some eyebrows, and I certainly know that this kind of material is sometimes regarded as a topic inappropriate even to mention in modern scholarly work. Knowing the controversy surrounding the subject of modern classicism, I was originally hesitant to include late twentieth-century material, but I was strongly encouraged to do so by my editor at W. W. Norton. From the beginning, my interest in the discussion of contemporary Palladianism has focused on the potential for reasoned arguments (both for and against) to yield interesting insights into the theoretical basis of each view. In the past, uncritical enthusiasm or arrogant dismissal has often obscured such insights, but I believe these insights are vital if we want to understand our modern situation and the problems we face today. The fundamental question that needs to be addressed is what can be learned from the great architects of the past, including Palladio. What has fascinated me are not only the questions of how and on which premises to construct an argumentational system that would justify the use of Palladian design precepts today, but equally the theoretical implications of the standard arguments used to dismiss their use. In order to avoid the impression that I am merely a nostalgic old fogey, I have intentionally placed the discussion of modern Palladianism in the context of some very recent debates in contemporary aesthetics. Insofar as I believe that Palladio's design principles are worthy of studying and reconstructing, this is not in order to praise the past over the contemporary, but to change the contemporary for the better by learning from the past. This means seeing in Palladianism, and in classical architecture generally, with genuine optimism, the architecture of the future. This is a proposition that will probably be alien to some, but it merely means that if we agree that something looks good, then we should not hesitate to improve our designs by learning from it. And, indeed, I believe that we will.

ACKNOWLEDGMENTS

A BOOK WHICH REFLECTS the development of one's ideas over a period of fifteen years accumulates many debts. An acknowledgement can only mention the most direct ones. My gratitude must first go to my Belgrade professors: Jovan Nešković and Branislav Milenković, who taught me the craft of writing architectural history and encouraged my early Palladian interests, and professors Joseph Rykwert and James Ackerman, under whose influence—even if sometimes in opposition to whose views—the conceptual framework of the book was formed. Professors Rykwert and Ackerman have provided careful guidance and immeasurable help at many difficult moments, as well as with the smaller projects which have led to the formulation of this book.

Many friends colleagues and professors have helped on numerous occasions with encouragement, important insights, and thoughtful consideration of problems which were troubling me. I have to particularly express gratitude to Marco Frascari from Virginia Tech, Lothar Haselberger and Christle Collins Judd from the University of Pennsylvania, Nadja Kurtović Folić from Belgrade University, Thomas Gordon Smith, John Stamper, and Samir Younés from the University of Notre Dame, Mark Wilson Jones from the University of Bath, Cristof Thoenes from the Max Planck Institute in Rome, Bruce Boucher from the Art Institute of Chicago, Mark Jarzombek from MIT, Joseph Connors and Margaret Haines from the Harvard Center for Renaissance Studies (Villa "I Tatti"), Phyllis Lambert and Mario Carpo from the Canadian Centre for Architecture (CCA), Christine Smith from Harvard University, Nick Zangwill from Oxford University, Stephan Wassel from Sweet Briar College, Wolfgang Wolters, Adrian von Buttlar, and Robert Suckale from Technische Universität Berlin, and Andreas Beyer from Rheinisch-Westfalische Technische Hochschule. Outside academic circles, Count Lodovico di Valmarana and Mr. Carl Gable have kindly allowed me access to their properties as well as insights into aspects of Palladio's buildings, which are not normally accessible to visitors. Substantial sections of the book were previously published as articles and I have received much help and encouragement from the respective journal editors in which the articles first appeared: Patricia Waddy from the *Journal of the Society of Architectural Historians*, Andor Gomme and Judy Loach from *Architectural History*, and George Hersey from *Architectura*. I also owe gratitude to these journals for allowing me to reproduce material that has already been published.

In an acknowledgment like this one, one can hardly do more than mention the names of people who have helped in the order in which I came to know them, but behind each name is a long story of intellectual exchange, goodwill, and patient consideration of my doubts. Yet, the names of some of the people who have helped most directly for the past fifteen years—the anonymous reviewers of my articles—will always remain unknown to me.

Different stages of the project were supported by generous grants from the University of Pennsylvania, Harvard University, the Canadian Centre for Architecture, and the Humboldt Foundation. Special gratitude must go to my home institution, Unitec Institute of Technology, and my Heads of School, John Sutherland and Tony van Raat, Dean John Boon, and the President of the Institute, John Webster, for their strong encouragement to work on the project and for tolerating my long absences for so many years. Centro Internazionale di Studi di Architettura "Andrea Palladio" (CISA) in Vicenza has helped by providing numerous illustrations and its Director, Guido Beltramini, as well the staff members—I should particularly express my gratitude to Maria Vittoria Pelizzari, Daniela Tovo, Elena Poli, and Remo Peronato—have provided infinite support in addressing numerous problems which needed to be resolved as the work progressed. The Canadian Centre for Architecture and the Royal Institute of British Architects (RIBA) have also provided help in obtaining illustrations. Thomas Gordon Smith, John B. Murray, Durston Saylor, Marc Bailly, Quinlan Terry, Robert A.M. Stern, Robert Adam, Anne Fairfax and Richard Sammons, David Schwartz, Peter Pennoyer, John Blatteau, Ferguson & Shamamian Architects, Daniel Parolek, John Malick, William Baker, and Jonathan Lee have kindly permitted me to reproduce pictures of their works. My exceptional gratitude must go to Marc Bailly who has helped select, collect, and organize illustrations of modern work included in the book.

Not a native speaker, I am fundamentally dependent on copyeditors for my written English and I should express my gratitude to Ivana Djordjević and Karen Wise for patient help with different sections of this book. Tim Ross performed the most labor-intensive part of the project in retyping over and over again the corrections to my writings; without his drawings, this book would be much poorer. Lastly, Bojan Vučenović has kindly provided the particularly complex drawing of the staircase on page 79.

I-1 Andrea Palladio,
portrait according to
Loukomsky, *Les villas*.
CISA

INTRODUCTION

ANDREA PALLADIO: LIFE AND WORKS

ANDREA DI PIETRO DALLA GONDOLA was born in Padua on November 30, 1508.[1] His father, Pietro, was a mill worker who probably transported grain by boat, giving him the nickname "dalla Gondola." His mother, Marta, mentioned in the sources as *zoppa* (lame), seems to have died when Andrea was still a child. Almost nothing is known about the childhood and adolescence of Europe's most influential architect, but the scant documentation does suggest that he grew up as an ordinary working-class youth of his time. At thirteen, Andrea was apprenticed to the Paduan stonemason Bartolomeo Cavazza. Two years later, in a breach of contract, he left to join his father in Vicenza. Cavazza followed him to Vicenza and brought him back.

A year later, Andrea finally parted with Cavazza, and in 1524 he was enrolled in the Vicentine guild of stonemasons. He trained under Giovanni di Giacomo da Porlezza and Girolamo Pittoni, owners of a shop known as Pademuro bottega from the section of Vicenza where it was located. During the 1530s, he was gradually entrusted with responsibility for individual projects. By 1534, Andrea was confident enough of his income to marry, and he and his wife, Allegradonna, ultimately had five children.

It was probably in late 1537 or early 1538 that Andrea, who was about to turn 30, joined the entourage of Giangiorgio Trissino, a Vicentine aristocrat who had retired to his native city after a long and successful diplomatic career.[2] A humanist, poet, and scholar, he assembled talented young Vicentines in a sort of private academy, similar to a boarding school, at his estate in Cricoli near Vicenza. There his disciples received instruction in literature, classics, and perhaps some elementary philosophy. How and why Andrea attracted the attention of Trissino is a mystery; legend has it that Trissino was impressed with the young stonemason during work on his villa. In any case, during the years with Trissino, Andrea learned some Latin and acquired some general education. In the 1540s, he traveled to Rome a number of times, with and without Trissino, spending long periods there, studying and measuring ancient ruins.

The education that Andrea gained through Trissino, the study of classics, especially his exposure to Vitruvius, and the trips to Rome transformed the talented young stonemason into an architect. In 1540, aged 32, he officially began to use that title and, in 1545, he took the name Palladio. How he acquired this name remains a mystery; the most common explanation refers to Trissino's epic *Italy Liberated from the Goths*, in which the angel Palladio comes to rescue the Byzantine general Belisarius. It is possible that Vicentine aristocrats saw Palladio as the architect who would transform their town into a city built according to the principles of the ancients and liberate it from the barbaric architecture imported from the North.

I-2 Villa Godi. *CISA, F0000947F*

I-3 Villa Forni Cerato. *CISA, F0005747*

I-4 Villa Gazzotti.

I-5 Villa Pisani (Bagnolo).

Palladio's first major commission was the Villa Godi in Lonedo, which he received through the Pademuro bottega in 1537 (I-2). During the 1540s, he built a series of villas for Vicentine patrons in the towns surrounding Vicenza: Forni Cerato in Montecchio Precalcino, Gazzotti in Bertesina, Pisani in Bagnolo, Saraceno in Finale, Caldogno in Caldogno, and Poiana in Poiana Maggiore (I-3–I-8). These projects do not exhibit the refined use of the classical orders that characterizes Palladio's work in later years. Orders begin to appear on the urban work in Vicenza in the 1540s. In the early Palazzo Civena (I-9) their use is still tentative, limited to pairs of Corinthian pilasters between the windows on the piano nobile. There has been considerable debate about the authorship of Palazzo Thiene (I-10). The building is included in the *Four Books*, but, in 1614, Vincenzo Scamozzi, the architect who completed many of Palladio's unfinished buildings, told Inigo Jones that it was designed by Giulio Romano and that Palladio merely supervised the construction. Palazzo Iseppo

I-6 Villa Saraceno.

I-7 Villa Caldogno.

16

I-8 Villa Poiana.

I-9 Palazzo Civena.

17

I-10 Palazzo Thiene.

I-11 Palazzo Iseppo Porto.

I-12 Palazzo Iseppo Porto. Facade detail.

Porto (I-11 and I-12), dated in 1549, has all the characteristics of Palladio's mature style in the detailing of the ornament of the facade, but the width of intercolumniations excludes it from Palladio's high style of the next decade.

During the last years of the 1540s, Palladio established himself as the leading architect in the Veneto. The decisive moment came when he won the commission to complete the facade of the Palazzo della Ragione, more commonly known as the Basilica, in Vicenza. The Gothic structure had lacked a proper facade for almost a century. The city council consulted prominent architects of the time—Jacopo Sansovino in 1538, Sebastiano Serlio in 1539, Michele Sanmicheli in 1541, and Giulio Romano in 1542—but the complexities of the task seem to have been daunting. The council finally adopted Palladio's proposal in 1549. Work on the Basilica progressed for decades, and the structure was finally completed in 1614, after Palladio's death (I-13 and I-14).

Palladio's mature style emerged during the early 1550s. The first major commission after the Basilica, and the first to demonstrate his full mastery of classical language, was Palazzo Chiericati in Vicenza (I-15 and I-16). For the first time, the orders are used not only to ornament the facade, but also to define the internal spatial system of the building. Palladio applied Vitruvian

I-13 Basilica.

I-14 Basilica. Facade detail.

I-15 Palazzo Chiericati. *CISA, F0004149*

I-16 Palazzo Chericati.
Facade detail.

I-17 Palazzo Antonini.

I-18 Villa Cornaro.

I-19 Villa Pisani (Montagnana). *CISA, F0002205*

precepts for the intercolumniations, which gave a new, highly balanced shape to his designs, in a manner that had not previously been achieved in Renaissance facades. Other buildings from the 1550s that mark this high point of Palladio's style are Palazzo Antonini in Udine (I-17) and a second group of villas: Cornaro in Piombino Dese, Pisani in Montagnana, Badoer in Fratta Polesine, Chiericati in Vancimuglio, and Foscari (Malcontenta) on the Brenta Canal outside Venice (I-18–I-22).

By the time Trissino died in Rome in 1550, Palladio was an established architect in the Veneto. Within the next year or two, he came under influence of another

major intellectual figure of the day: Daniele Barbaro.[3] Six years younger than Palladio, Barbaro was the scion of a highly ranked Venetian family renowned for achievements in the world of letters. It is very likely that the two men first met in Padua in the 1540s. Since Barbaro was in London as the Venetian ambassador from 1548 to 1551, regular contact between the two can be confirmed only after his return to Venice. In 1551, Barbaro was appointed to the post of Patriarch-elect of Aquileia, a position of significant political importance for the Venetian Republic but without specific duties. From then on, Barbaro dedicated himself to studies and intellectual work. Before leaving for England he had

I-20 Villa Badoer. *CISA, F0000662*

I-21 Villa Chiericati (Vancimuglio).

I-22 Villa Foscari. *CISA, F0002007*

already published a commentary on Porphyry's *Isagoge* and prepared editions of the works of his great-uncle Ermolao Barbaro and Sperone Speroni.[4] In 1556 he published a commentary on Vitruvius that is regarded as the highest achievement of Renaissance Vitruvian exegesis. Among his other works, the commentary on Aristotle's *Rhetoric* and a treatise on perspective should also be mentioned.

Palladio collaborated with Barbaro on the commentary on Vitruvius and prepared a number of its illustrations.[5] It seems that Palladio and Barbaro traveled together to Rome and spent substantial time there in 1554 studying ancient remains. That year, two small books by Palladio, about Roman remains and churches of Rome, were published. After the publication of the commentary on Vitruvius, Palladio designed a villa in Maser for Daniele and his brother, Marcantonio Barbaro (I-23). The villa, which was occupied by 1560, is somewhat of an anomaly in Palladio's work, and its

mannerist elements suggest that Palladio's design instincts yielded to the influence of his architecturally sophisticated patron. Daniele Barbaro helped Palladio secure important commissions and even after Barbaro's death in 1570, the family continued to advocate for Palladio. During the 1570s, Marcantonio Barbaro occupied the highly influential position of Procurator of St. Mark's and played a major role in securing projects such as the Redentore for Palladio.

The complex collaboration between Palladio and Daniele Barbaro leaves many questions open. Palladio's contribution to the commentary on Vitruvius was not limited to the preparation of illustrations, and we may assume that he supplied much of the material in the sections about the classical orders in Books Three and Four. But it should by no means be assumed that the two agreed on everything. It is very difficult to assess Barbaro's influence on Palladio or to identify specific points on which they agreed or disagreed. Nevertheless,

25

I-23 Villa Barbaro.

many of the differences can be reconstructed by comparing Palladio's theoretical statements in *Four Books on Architecture* with those made by Barbaro in his writings. Barbaro's theoretical statements should be read in the context of his other (especially philosophical) writings, which are deeply rooted in his Paduan Aristotelian education. In contrast, a strong and systematic Platonist line permeated Palladio's approach to design, leading to a number of differences between their theoretical views.

During the 1550s, Palladio assumed an active role in the intellectual life of Vicenza. In 1556, he was one of the founders of the Accademia Olimpica, a local learned society that organized public lectures and theatrical performances. Also among the founders was Silvio Belli, a Vicentine mathematician and engineer who supervised Palladio's work on the Basilica and was the author of a small treatise on proportions published in 1573.

As his reputation grew, Palladio began to receive commissions for ecclesiastical projects in Venice. In the early 1560s he received commissions for the facade of the Church of San Francesco della Vigna and the Convento della Carità (I-24 and I-25), as well as commissions for different sections of the complex of San Giorgio Maggiore (I-26). Three major villa projects from the 1560s are the Rotonda on the outskirts of Vicenza, Villa Emo in Fanzolo, and Villa Sarego in Santa Sofia (I-27–I-29). In the second half of the decade, there were also a number of commissions for major buildings in Vicenza—the Loggia del Capitaniato and the palazzi Valmarana, Barbarano, and Porto Breganza (I-30–I-33).

The year 1570 brought a number of significant changes in Palladio's career. With the death of Sansovino towards the end of the year, Palladio became the first architect of the Venetian Republic. His treatise, *Four Books on Architecture*, came out the same year. He moved to Venice, where he worked for the last ten years of his life. The most important project of that period was the Redentore (I-34); many other projects remained unrealized. In the last year of his life, he was occupied with the Teatro Olimpico in Vicenza and the Tempietto

I-24 San Francesco della Vigna.

I-25 Convento della
Carità. *CISA, F0003306*

I-26 San Giorgio Maggiore. *CISA, F0002901*

I-27 Rotonda.

I-28 Villa Emo.

29

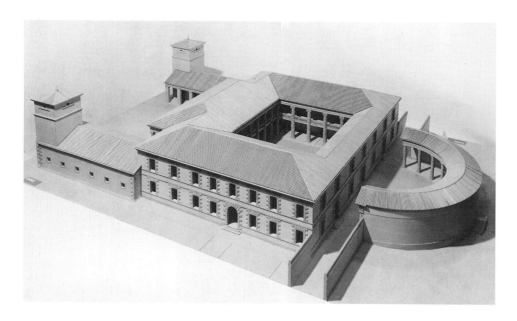

I-29 Model of Villa Sarego, Santa Sofia, based on the original design, which was never completed. *CISA, F0002778*

I-30 Loggia del Capitaniato.

in Maser, a small church next to the villa he had built for the Barbaros (I-35). According to tradition, he died in Maser while supervising work on the Tempietto, on August 19, 1580.

SOURCES FOR THE STUDY OF PALLADIO'S DESIGN THEORY

In terms of the number of buildings he designed and built, Palladio was the most prolific of all major Renaissance architects. His built works, his treatise, *Four Books on Architecture*, as well as his preserved drawings provide a wealth of information for the study of his approach to design. Theoretically, Palladio's executed buildings should be the most reliable document of his design procedures, but reliable surveys exist for only a few of them. The most extensive corpus of surveys is the one made by Ottavio Bertotti Scamozzi in the eighteenth century. Scholars have occasionally dismissed Bertotti Scamozzi's work as inaccurate, but his plans can be a valuable tool if they are used carefully. Although the information they provide is incomplete, they do present very stimulating material for formulating hypotheses about Palladio's design practices. However, verification

I-31 Palazzo Valmarana.

I-32 Palazzo
Barbarano. *CISA,*
F0003995

I-33 Palazzo
Porto Breganza.

I-34 Redentore.

of these hypotheses will require modern and detailed surveys. A number of buildings were surveyed in the twentieth century and published predominantly in the *Corpus Palladianum* series. Those books provide a wealth of general art-historical information related to Palladio's works, but they tend to omit detailed surveys of buildings and their ornamentation, especially the orders used on the buildings. Some of the results presented in this book are based on surveys made by the author in collaboration with Stephen Wassell, Tim Ross, and Melanie Bourke during the summer of 2003. These surveys, unpublished thus far, include a detailed survey of the Villa Cornaro in Piombino Dese as well as surveys of the orders on the Basilica, Palazzo Chiericati, and Villa Pisani in Montagnana. Relying on executed buildings has its dangers; Palladio's buildings were often modified after they were completed, and it is not always clear which portions were done under the architect's supervision.

Palladio's preserved drawings are interesting material against which to test interpretative theses. Major collections are in the Museo Civico in Vicenza and the Royal Institute of British Architects in London. A substantial group pertains to Palladio's own projects, the development of his architectural ideas, and preparatory drawings for execution. However, they usually present buildings at one stage of the development of the design, which may not be the final version of the project. When drawings differ from the built work, it is often difficult to say whether they document stages in the development of an idea or whether the final version was incorrectly executed. Palladio's archaeological surveys of Roman buildings comprise another large group of drawings. Since Palladio selectively surveyed aspects of Roman buildings that could inform his own designs, this material is also very interesting for the study of his design theory.

I-35 Tempietto (Maser).
CISA, F0001736

Palladio's treatise is one of the most influential architecture books of the Renaissance. It has been well studied, but it has numerous internal inconsistencies and leaves many questions unanswered. Palladio spent more than a decade preparing the treatise, but in the end he finished it for publication hastily. It is probably because of this final haste that so many important aspects of his architectural theory are left vaguely defined. The first book contains, among other important issues, an account of the theory of the classical orders, but there are contradictions between the text and illustrations, which may indicate different stages of the preparation of the treatise. While the description of the orders refers to the account Barbaro provided in his 1556 commentary, the illustrations step out of the Vitruvian tradition and clearly show the influence of Giacomo Barozzi da Vignola's *Canon of the Five Orders* of 1562. The second book presents more than forty buildings designed by Palladio. Not all of the drawings were prepared with equal care and the descriptions leave many things unsaid. The third book presents bridges and some public buildings, among which Palladio's idealized project for the Basilica in Vicenza is particularly important. The most thoroughly prepared part of the treatise is the last book, which contains Palladio's archaeological surveys. Arguably, this fourth book of Palladio's treatise is the most significant Renaissance publication on Roman archaeology. The sheer size of Palladio's project, which included surveys of twenty-five Roman temples, far exceeded any similar works by his contemporaries, such as Antonio Labacco or Pirro Ligurio. It is probably the most ambitious project in the history of Roman archaeology. Similar projects by Antoine Desgodetz or Edward Cresy and Lidwell Taylor were much more limited in scope.

Working with a variety of different sources necessitates working with a variety of systems of measurement. All modern surveys have employed the metric system. Its use is a well-established practice among architectural historians and archaeologists, even those from countries where the metric system is not in everyday use. Bertotti Scamozzi's eighteenth century surveys, however, were made in Venetian feet. Where it was necessary to compare them with modern surveys, these data were converted to the metric system; otherwise, they were left in their original form. A problem arises, however, with the dimensions stated by Palladio in his treatise. In the opening of the second book, Palladio says that the measurements he provided are in Vicentine feet. The actual size of the Vicentine foot of his time has been a much-debated question for decades.[6] Moreover, in spite of Palladio's statement, there are very good reasons to doubt whether all measures stated in the treatise are indeed expressed in Vicentine feet.[7] As a result, when quoting dimensions from Palladio's treatise, one can only repeat what he says and, where necessary, carefully explore what his measurements may mean in the modern metric system. One should thus bear in mind that when this book refers to feet and inches, this is never a reference to modern feet and inches—but to measurements stated by different authors (Vitruvius, Alberti, Palladio) in the systems they were using. This approach is the established practice in modern scholarship.

Individual scholars have advanced arguments in favor of some of these sources on the study of Palladio's design theory (his buildings, drawings, or the treatise) over others. It is fair to say that contemporary scholarship is inclined to take all these sources seriously but cautiously, noting that the information they can provide needs to be combined and carefully checked. Some questions about Palladio's designs can be answered by careful collation of different sources; in other cases, it is possible to predict that a question will be answered through future research, especially when accurate and complete surveys of Palladio's buildings become available. Ultimately, Palladio has much to teach us and it is appropriate to look at his works not only to learn about his times, but also to learn how to apply his design principles to the architecture of the present.

STUDYING PALLADIO'S DESIGN THEORY

There are two principal approaches to architectural history. According to one, architectural historians study how works of architecture were designed and built, focusing on the way they were shaped through history. This approach rests on the belief that it is possible to accumulate knowledge about good design, that there is much to learn from great architects of the past, and that the study of their works can contribute to modern design. In the alternative approach, the goal of the historian is to reveal the role of architecture in culture and society and to study the ideas associated with works of architecture through history. The first approach studies formal properties, how and why buildings were designed in a certain way; the second concerns itself with the narratives associated with architecture, or, more precisely, enumerates the acts of verbal behavior that architectural works prompted through history. The former is best described as the history of architectural design; the latter is commonly referred to as "the study of meanings."

This divergence of interests among architectural historians reflects the fact that the mind responds to the properties of the objects both in words and in pictures, concepts and images. Some properties must be described in words while others can be conceived only with visual imagery. It is, for instance, seldom possible to fully describe the shape of a building in words without the use of drawings, and it is impossible to refer to abstract concepts using visual imagery. Debating the relative merits of one approach to architectural history over the other is therefore unproductive: the two simply study different properties (visually or verbally definable) of architectural works. However, in contemporary English-language art and architectural history, the study of narratives is by far the dominant approach, to the point that some scholars have openly complained about the hypercontextualization and devisualization of the discipline.[8] By contrast, in Palladian scholarship, the study of design theory is a very well established approach. The importance of formalist methodology in the study of Palladio's work has been repeatedly asserted by leading scholars in the field. Erik Forssman, for instance, stressed that Palladio's employment of architectural types provided them with their own life, independent of their original function, which was subsequently "forgotten or denied in order to make their aesthetic and space-defining qualities applicable for new purposes. The lack of historicity and the emphasis on purely artistic values is the essential aspect of Palladio's typology."[9] Manfredo Tafuri similarly observed that in order to import classical language into contemporary use, Palladio had to destroy its conceptual content; in order to be able to use it, Palladio had to disarticulate the symbolism of the language of classical architecture. The operation Palladio performed, Tafuri emphasized, is precisely the opposite of that which the philological exploration of meanings can achieve.[10] Lionello Puppi similarly pointed out that Palladio's procedure relied on semantic transposition of a sacral symbol into a civil one, and its celebration as such.[11]

The arguments of these leading Palladian scholars can hardly be more convincing: the adoption of formal systems of Roman religious architecture for use on Renaissance civil buildings is a central aspect of Palladio's approach to design. To apply a Roman pedimented temple facade on a villa, one must first bracket any religious associations one may have with it—and the only plausible motive which could explain such a design decision would be formal, i.e., aesthetic. The reconstruction of meanings ascribed to Roman pedimented facades in Roman or Renaissance times simply will not help us to explain the way Palladio applied them—a serious challenge for any methodology of architectural history which limits its interests to the study of meanings.[12] For this reason, the emphasis on the study of design theory is an approach well entrenched in modern Palladian studies. This book focuses on the formal properties of Palladio's architectural works and how they developed. It is a historical study of his design theory that will try to elucidate the principles and the process through which the shapes of his architecture were achieved. The narratives that were or could have been attached to Palladio's buildings at the time they were built will be discussed only in the context of the way they affected the formal properties of his designs.

The first chapter discusses the morphological and typological systems of Palladio's buildings, including the principles of proportioning spaces according to Palladio as well as specific design problems, such as that of the staircase. The second chapter presents an alternative interpretation of Palladio's use of proportions, based on Wittkower's *Architectural Principles*. The third chapter deals with the use of the classical orders—a central problem of Renaissance architectural design theory. Palladio's use of the orders represented a major breakthrough in Renaissance facade design and his use of Vitruvian precepts for intercolumniations introduced a new, higher level of complexity to the issue of facade composition and its relationship to interior planning. The fourth chapter discusses the way the internal coherence of Palladio's system derives from an implicit Platonist framework. Every architectural design theory is rooted in philosophical assumptions, usually pertaining to the understanding of the functioning of the human mind, the problem of universals, or the ability to make aesthetic judgments. These are perennial questions that no architectural design theory can avoid. The question is only whether these problems will be treated more or less consistently, discussed or overlooked, and whether the resolution will be part of a consistent body of theory or randomly chosen and probably in contradiction with the rest of the system. The remarkable aspect of Palladio's system is its internal coherence, derived from the application of a simplified but consistently developed Platonist program. The last chapter discusses the applicability of Palladio's design precepts in contemporary architecture. An important conclusion is that if modern use of classicist design principles is to be theoretically credible, it must be founded on the same formalist aesthetic principles that have determined much of the methodology of this book. This conclusion affirms, once again, the more general point the book attempts to make: that architectural works have spatial, visual, and formal properties, independent of any culturally derived associations, that architects have to resolve problems related to those properties, and that the study of the way architects did this in the past is not only a valid field of architectural history, but also the most significant contribution architectural history can make to modern architectural practice.

Spiral
staircase at
Convento
della Carità.
CISA,
F0003360

CHAPTER I

THEORY OF
SPATIAL COMPOSITION

BUILDINGS CONSIST OF SPATIAL PARTS: they are not merely piles of building materials, but rather building material organized into formal elements. The architect's art lies in combining the formal elements into buildings. One of the most remarkable aspects of Palladio's oeuvre is the great variety of combinations achieved from a very limited repertoire of elements, which he listed in the *Four Books*: loggias, salas, monumental entrance spaces, staircases, rooms, and courtyards.[1] External staircases also contributed substantially to his architectural compositions, but internal staircases (which Palladio often enclosed in separate rooms) rarely played an important role. He achieved architectural variety through the juxtaposition of light and shadow, wall and column, flat ceilings and various types of vaults. The simple drawings presented in the *Four Books* often require careful scrutiny to appreciate the immense richness of Palladio's imagination. Similarly, when it comes to the executed buildings, it is difficult to appreciate the complexity of relationships between spatial fragments by simply walking through the spaces. The complexities of Palladio's composition of salas or central courtyards, for instance, are best presented by means of sectional models (1-1–1-3).

A very simple plan—that of the Palazzo Antonini, for example—may contain very intriguing spatial relationships that are revealed only through an axonometric drawing (1-4 and 1-5). The Palazzo della Torre in Verona is a particularly good example of Palladio's spatial point-counterpoint (1-6 and 1-7). The building

occupies a long, narrow site with entrances on the lateral sides. Narrow corridors open into a courtyard, which is bisected by a loggia that serves as the main entrance area; this large space with columns in each corner is separated from the courtyards by colonnades. The loggia opens onto the main staircase, which leads to the sala above. The palazzo is symmetrical, and the circulation from one end to the other includes a narrow entrance, a sunny courtyard, a shady loggia defined by a double grid of columns, another sunny courtyard, and the narrow exit. Similar examples of Palladio's complex techniques of spatial composition are the two buildings for unidentified clients on pages 71 and 72 of the second book of his treatise. Complex exercises in combining vaulted spaces, both buildings are entered through halls with four columns. In the former, the entry sequence proceeds through two smaller, intermediary spaces into a large vaulted space that opens to a loggia (1-8 and 1-9). In the latter, there are two major vaulted halls, one of which serves as the entrance while the other opens to the back courtyard on one side and a tiny lateral courtyard, almost a light well, on the other (1-10 and 1-11).

TYPOLOGY

The majority of Palladio's architectural works are residential projects. These are usually divided into urban and rural residences, palazzi and villas. Simple as it may

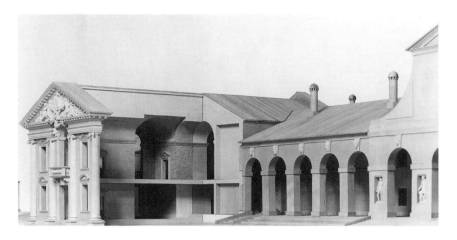

1-1 The model of the Villa Barbaro shows the position and the configuration of the cruciform sala. *CISA, F0001410*

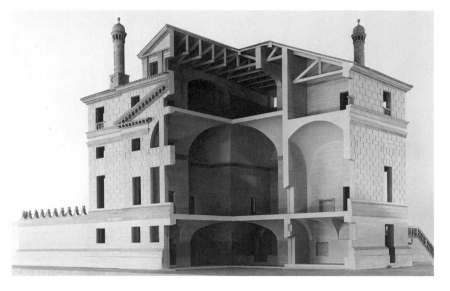

1-2 The model clearly shows the monumental composition of the cruciform sala at the Villa Foscari *CISA, F0002089*

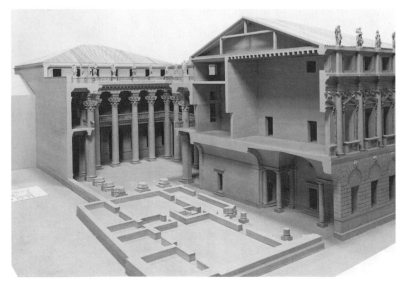

1-3 This model of Palazzo Iseppo Porto presents the courtyard in the back, which was never completed. *CISA, F00374*

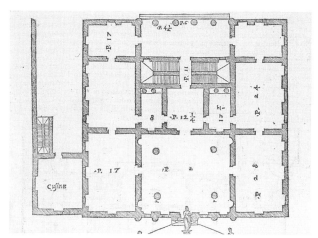

1-4 Plan of Palazzo Antonini from the *Four Books*. *CCA, NA44.P164 (W161) c.2, p. 5*

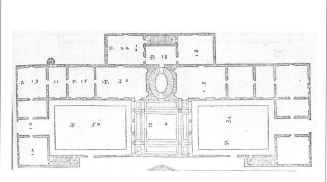

1-6 Plan of the Palazzo Torre (Verona) from the *Four Books*. *CCA, NA44.P164 (W161), c.2, p. 11*

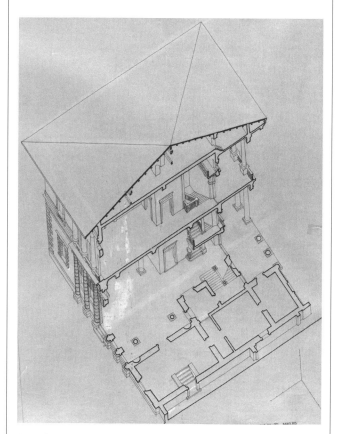

1-5 Axonometric section through Palazzo Antonini. *Rendered by M. Zocconi, 1965, unpublished; CISA, R0000211*

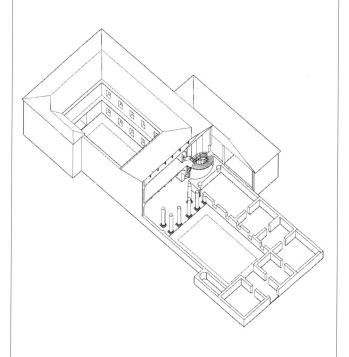

1-7 Spatial analysis of the Palazzo Torre (Verona). *Tim Ross*

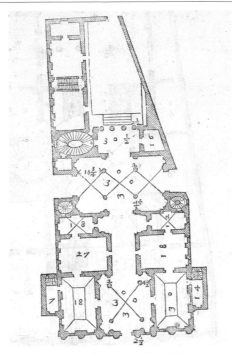

1-8 Plan of a building for an unidentified client on page 71 of Book Two of the *Four Books*. *CCA, NA44.P164 (W161), c.2, p. 71*

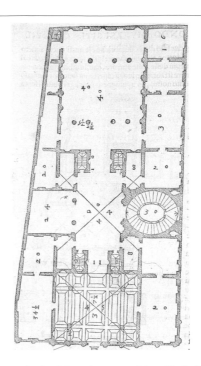

1-10 Plan of a building for an unidentified client on page 72 of Book Two of the *Four Books*. *CCA, NAP164 (W161), c.2, p. 72*

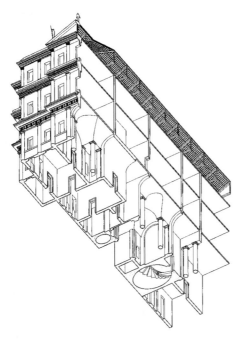

1-9 Axonometric section through the building for an unidentified client on page 71 of Book Two of the *Four Books*. *Tim Ross*

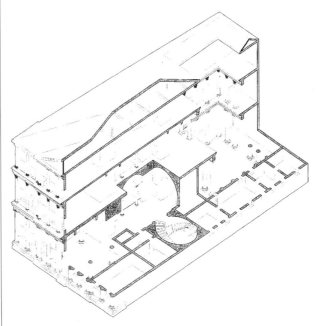

1-11 Axonometric section through the building for an unidentified client on page 72 of Book Two of the *Four Books*. *Tim Ross*

seem, the distinction between a palazzo and a villa is not always easy to draw. A palazzo is located in a city, occupying all or part of a block and organized around one or more courtyards. A villa is a residence on an agricultural estate with quarters for the owner and his family, and may include apartments for servants and workers as well as additional agricultural buildings.[2] A number of Palladio's buildings may be said to belong to both groups. In his treatise, Palladio listed the Villa Rotonda with city buildings because of its proximity to Vicenza and the fact that it was not part of an agricultural estate. Using the same criteria, however, it is difficult to say why the Villa Pisani in Montagnana should be listed among villas. The building stands just outside the city gates and is certainly more urban than the Rotonda.

Villas and palazzi can also be distinguished by their morphology. A palazzo is a bigger building, typically organized around a central courtyard (1-12). The urban residence of a wealthy, aristocratic family, a palazzo responded to many pragmatic program functions. The internal courtyard was particularly important in providing daylight, and even smaller Vicentine buildings of the period had one, at least in the form of a light well. The Casa Cogollo, sometimes referred to as Palladio's house, has a small atrium that illustrates this point well (1-13). The requirement for daylight could have seriously limited Palladio's ability to create more complex spatial compositions. In the building for an unidentified patron on page 72 of Palladio's treatise (see 1-11), the problem was resolved by the introduction of a small courtyard (*corticella*) probably not larger than the courtyard of the Casa Cogollo. A small palazzo, such as Antonini in Udine, did not require a central courtyard.

A villa is usually too small to enclose a courtyard or to need light wells. It is typically surrounded by open space, except for the agricultural buildings of its estate. Among the larger villas that do have courtyards are the unfinished Villa Sarego in Santa Sofia near Verona (see I-29) and the villa designed for Leonardo Mocenigo on the Brenta canal (1-14). Broadly speaking, palazzi are urban structures that enclose open space; villas, unless they are extremely large, have an open relationship with their environment. In his study about the use of open spaces, Mario Zocconi pointed out that Palladio care-

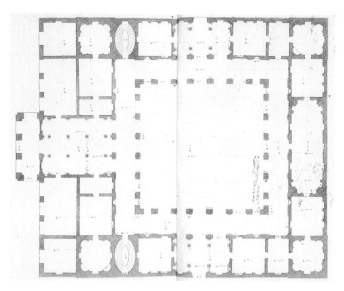

1-12 Palazzo Thiene. Plan according to Ottavio Bertotti Scamozzi. *CCA, M7616:1, 1786, Tavola XXIII*

1-13 Courtyard of the Casa Cogollo.

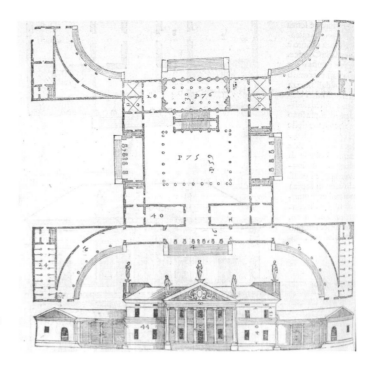

1-14 Plan of Villa Mocenigo, Brenta; from the *Four Books*. *CCA, NA44.P164 (W161) c.2, p. 99*

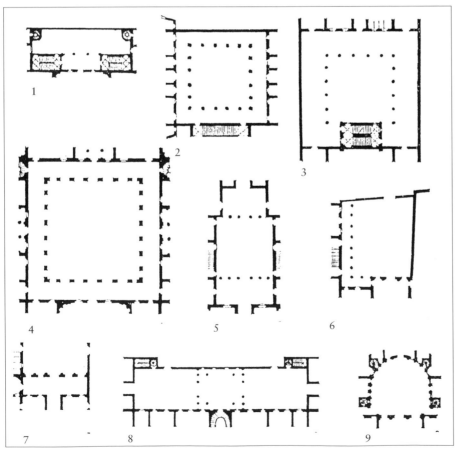

1-15 Mario Zocconi's typology of the courtyards of Palladio's palazzi, according to "I Cortili," fig. XLVII, p. 477:
1. Chiericati
2. Porto Festa
3. Angarano
4. Thiene
5. Valmarana
6. Barbarano
7. Capra
8. Torre
9. Porto-Breganza
(Palazzo Torre is in Verona; other projects are for palazzi in Vicenza). *CISA.*

fully manipulated the siting of surrounding buildings to form and control the relationship between the villa and its natural environment (1-15 and 1-16). Zocconi used the word *cortile* to describe both the enclosed courtyard of a palazzo and the open, but carefully controlled surroundings of a villa. Palladio's villas with curved side porticos are particularly good examples of this strategy. These designs are common in the *Four Books*, although only the Villa Badoer was built and survives (1-17). Palladio's use of curved porticos both to relate the villa to its surroundings and to emphasize the central block of the villa has had a huge impact on subsequent genera-

tions of architects, perhaps most famously in Bernini's porticos surrounding the piazza of St. Peter's in the Vatican. In fact, not only the form, but even the description that the colonnades of St. Peter's embrace the faithful like the arms of the Church, originates with Palladio. In the description of the Villa Mocenigo, Palladio said that the curved porticos were like arms embracing those who approach the house.[3]

Whatever the distinction between palazzi and villas, all have a central space surrounded by smaller spaces, the latter usually organized in rows of rooms. In a palazzo, the central space is obviously the courtyard,

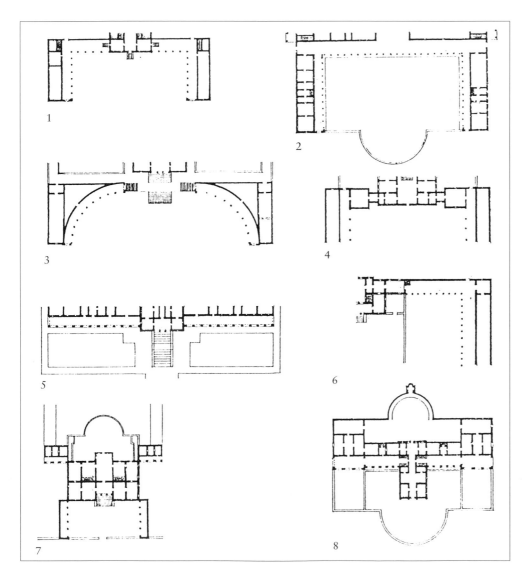

1-16 Mario Zocconi's typology of the courtyards of Palladio's villas, according to "I Cortili," fig. XLVI, p. 472:
1. Zeno (Cessalto)
2. Repeta (Campiglia)
3. Badoer (Fratta Polesine)
4. Mocenigo (Marocco)
5. Emo (Fanzolo)
6. Poiana (Pojana Maggiore)
7 Godi (Lonedo)
8. Barbaro (Maser)
CISA.

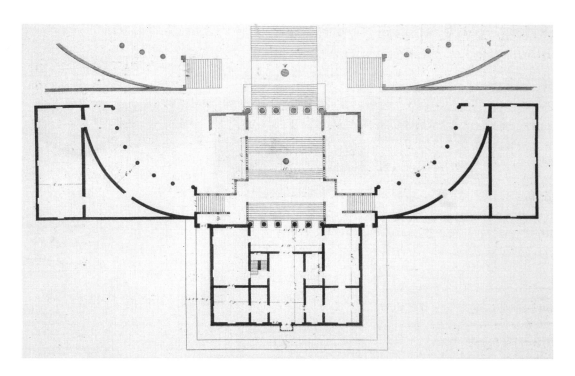

1-17 Plan of Villa
Badoer according to
Ottavio Bertotti
Scamozzi. *CCA,
M7616:3, 1786, Tavola
XLI*

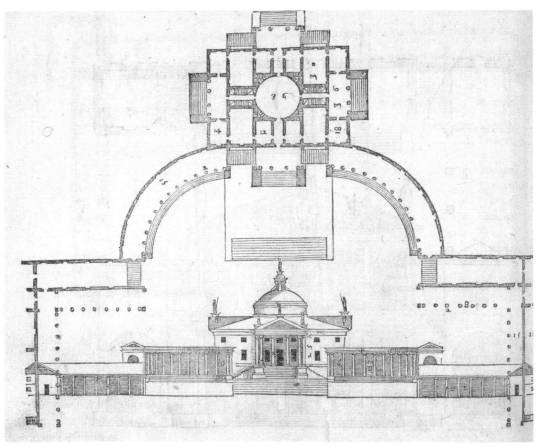

1-18 Villa Trissino,
Meledo, according to
the *Four Books. CCA,
NA44.P164 (W161), c.2,
p. 60*

but, in the case of a villa, it is the sala, the large hall, which serves as the living room. A typical villa has a sala flanked by a row of rooms on two sides. Besides the Rotonda, in the *Four Books*, only the Villa Trissino in Meledo has four groups of rooms placed around the sala (1-18). Typically, a sala will be either rectangular (square), cross-shaped, or T-shaped; a rectangular sala may have four columns, one in each corner. Figure 1-20 presents schematic plans of all villas in the *Four Books*, grouped typologically according to the shape of the sala. This typological differentiation has been made according to the plan, but one should not forget that the height and the shape of the ceiling/vault contribute to the character of the space.

Salas are often lavishly decorated with fresco paintings; they were certainly the most important part of the villas. Salas with four corner columns played a particularly important role in Palladio's design theory (1-19). The use of both salas and courtyards is rooted in the complexities of the Renaissance interpretation of Vitruvius's description of the atrium in a Roman house.[4] Renaissance architects had no access to archaeological remains which would have helped them understand Vitruvius's description of a Roman *domus*. Linda Pellecchia has presented the complex ramifications of this issue in her very thorough study, "Architects Read Vitruvius." She points out that in spite of often imaginative research, no Renaissance architect "ever conceived of the atrium exactly as it was in antiquity."[5] Renaissance architects learned from Vitruvius that the atrium was a public space that conveyed social status; in town houses it was the first space in the entry sequence, whereas it followed the peristyle in country residences.[6] From the archaeological excavations of Pompeian houses, we now know that the atrium was a rectangular room with an opening in the roof (*compluvium*) to allow rainwater to be collected in a basin (*impluvium*). Renaissance readers of Vitruvius were confused by the use of the term *cava aedium* as the synonym for atrium because it was not clear from the text that the two terms referred to the same part of a house. In his discussion of atria, Vitruvius said that their proportions were 5/3, 3/2, 1/1, or $\sqrt{2}/1$ and mentioned ceilings, roofs, and beams in this context. With respect to *cava aedium*, Vitruvius

1-19 Sala with four columns from the *Four Books*. *CCA, NA44.P164 (W161), c.2, p. 37*

mentioned five types, four of which receive rain (the *displuviate*, Tuscan, *tetrastyle*, and Corinthian), while the fifth, the *testidunate*, was fully covered. The Tuscan had no columns, the tetrastyle had a column in each corner, and the Corinthian was supported by a colonnade. Among Renaissance theorists, Leon Battista Alberti was the first to identify the *cava aedium* with the atrium and, unlike most other theorists, Daniele Barbaro expressed the same view in his commentary. Since Palladio provided illustrations to accompany Barbaro's discussion,

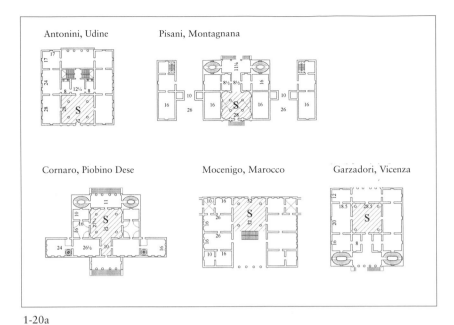

Antonini, Udine   Pisani, Montagnana

Cornaro, Piobino Dese   Mocenigo, Marocco   Garzadori, Vicenza

1-20 Typology of Palladio's central spaces.
a. Salas with four columns
b. Rectangular salas
c. Circular salas
d. Cruciform salas
e. Palazzi and with interior courtyards
Tim Ross

1-20a

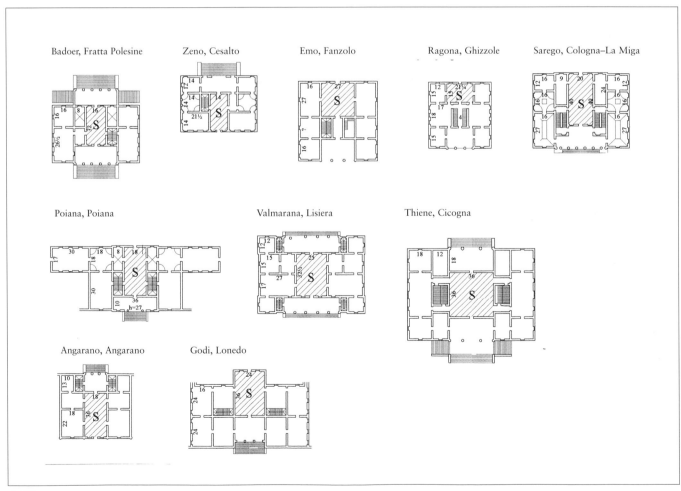

Badoer, Fratta Polesine   Zeno, Cesalto   Emo, Fanzolo   Ragona, Ghizzole   Sarego, Cologna–La Miga

Poiana, Poiana   Valmarana, Lisiera   Thiene, Cicogna

Angarano, Angarano   Godi, Lonedo

1-20b

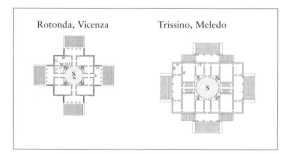

Rotonda, Vicenza

Trissino, Meledo

1-20c

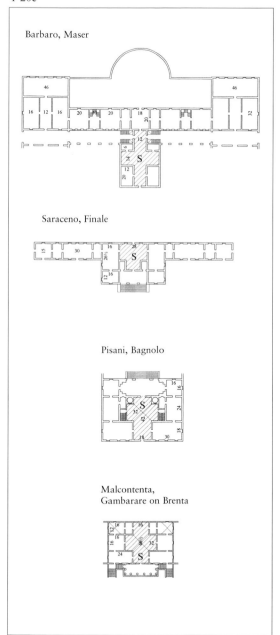

Barbaro, Maser

Saraceno, Finale

Pisani, Bagnolo

Malcontenta,
Gambarare on Brenta

1-20d

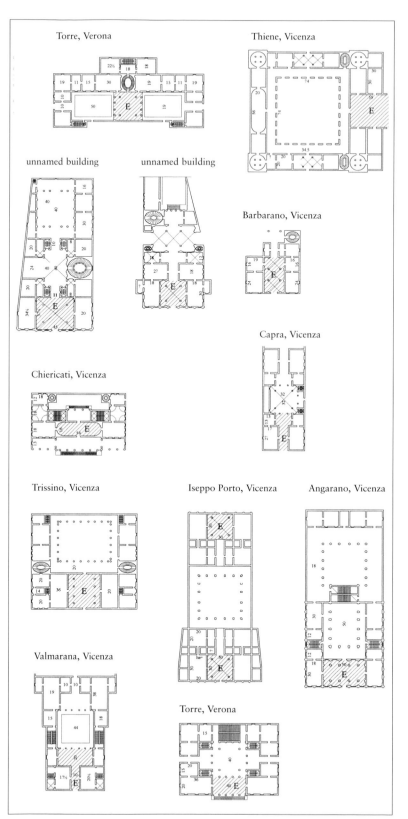

Torre, Verona

Thiene, Vicenza

unnamed building

unnamed building

Barbarano, Vicenza

Capra, Vicenza

Chiericati, Vicenza

Trissino, Vicenza

Iseppo Porto, Vicenza

Angarano, Vicenza

Valmarana, Vicenza

Torre, Verona

1-20e

49

1-21 Corinthian sala from
the *Four Books*. CCA,
NA44.P164 (W161), c.2, p. 39

1-22 Egyptian sala from the
Four Books. CCA, *NA44.P164
(W161), c.2, p. 42*

1-23 Sala with four columns in Villa Cornaro.

he was surely aware of Barbaro's interpretation of atrium as open space. Nevertheless, his own treatment of the sala, an enclosed space, reflects aspects of Vitruvius's discussion of atria, and the four-column sala clearly derives from the *tetrastyle* atrium. The advantage of the sala with four columns was not necessarily only formal or aesthetic. As Palladio mentioned several times, his motivation in placing columns in the corners was structural.[7] The thickness of the beam depends on the square of the span and the difference in size required to span seven meters and nine meters is significant. By placing columns at the corners of a room, a ten-meter span could be reduced to a six- to seven-meter span with a substantial difference in the beam thickness.

A separate section in Book Two of the *Four Books* discussed the Corinthian and Egyptian sala (1-21 and 1-22) Only the Corinthian sala, characterized by engaged columns, was presented in combination with a vaulted ceiling. The presentation of a four-column sala in this section suggests a flat ceiling as well. In Palladio's executed buildings, a tetrastyle sala and flat ceiling are used at Villa Cornaro (1-23 and 1-24) and Palazzo Antonini (see 1-4 and 1-5), but others, such as the Villa Pisani in Montagnana, have vaulted ceilings (1-25).

Vaulted salas with four columns relate to the entrance spaces of palazzi. The space through which a carriage would enter a palazzo usually received special attention in Renaissance designs. Pellechia has shown

1-24 (above) Sala with four columns in Villa Cornaro.

1-25 (right) Vaulted hall with four columns in the Villa Pisani (Montagnana). *CISA, 0002264*

1-26 (left) Entrance to the Palazzo Barbarano. *CISA, F0004059*

1-27 (opposite) Entrance to the Palazzo Iseppo Porto. *CISA, F0004502*

1-28 Side entrance
to the Palazzo
Thiene.

1-29 Drawing of the entrance to the Palazzo Farnese, by Letarouilly. *CCA, M NA44.L645.A63 1868a, vol.2, pl. 127*

that the morphology of these monumental entrances is a result of the Renaissance misreading of Vitruvius. In Palladio's Vicentine palazzi, such as Barbarano and Iseppo Porto (1-26 and 1-27), these are vaulted spaces with columns, resembling the vaulted entrance sala of the Villa Pisani in Montagnana. The entrance to the Palazzo Thiene also belongs to this group, although this is only a side entrance (1-28). A larger entrance with a loggia was intended but never built. Monumental entrance spaces were typical of Renaissance palazzi, as seen at the Palazzo Farnese in Rome, for example (1-29).

1-30 Alignment of doors in Villa Cornaro.

1-31 Alignment of doors in Villa Poiana.

SUITES OF ROOMS

Apart from the sala or the courtyard, the interior of a palazzo or a villa consists of suites of rooms arranged enfilade. In palazzi, this is obviously the most rational way to divide the longitudinal space of a wing into smaller spaces. In Palladio's villa designs two, three, four, or five rooms were grouped together on either side of the sala, each group often constituting a small apartment in its own right. A remarkable feature of these rooms (at least in the plans of the *Four Books*) is the regularity with which at least one horizontal dimension is repeated in more than one room. There are only two buildings out of forty-four in which the repetition of

room dimensions does not occur. The wing of a palazzo is likely to have a constant width, and consequently all its rooms will share one dimension. However, it is a surprising feature in villas or in those palazzi where rooms are arranged around a sala or courtyard. In these cases, the width of one room becomes the length of another. In fifteen buildings presented in the second of the *Four Books*, all rooms in a single row have at least one dimension in common.[8] Seven more buildings can be added to this list by disregarding the very small rooms with mezzanines above.[9]

A particularly interesting aspect of these rooms is the visual effect created by placing door openings along the same axis, sometimes culminating with a window or a

1-32 Alignment of doors in Villa Barbaro.
CISA, F0001754

1-33 Articulation of spaces in
the portico of Palazzo Chiericati.

1-34 Rocca Pisani by Vicenzo Scamozzi.

fireplace and visually suggesting the spatial articulation of the building in an intriguing way[10] (1-30 and 1-31). A well-known example is the alignment of doors at the Villa Barbaro (1-32). Such axial alignments of openings are a constant feature of Palladio's design; their role in articulating space can be observed not only in door placement, but also in the composition of the porticos, as at Palazzo Chiericati (1-33).

The axes along which Palladio placed openings are always part of an orthogonal matrix. It is, in fact, unlikely that their optical effects were intended at all. As an architect, Palladio was more concerned with the formal composition of spaces and architectural elements than with the way they were perceived. It is interesting to see how Vincenzo Scamozzi departed from the orthogonal placement of axes in Rocca Pisani in Lonigo (1-34 and 1-35). Scamozzi designed the Rocca Pisani while he was in his late twenties, influenced by

Palladio's Rotonda. The building is similar to the Rotonda in the internal disposition of spaces, including a central sala, but it has only one main entrance with a portico. The openings do not depend exclusively on an orthogonal matrix. Instead, Scamozzi introduced diagonal axes, thus allowing for a series of unexpected visual experiences within the villa (1-36–1-38). These axes are often not even horizontal. Scamozzi also adjusted the central intercolumniation of the main portico so that the edges of columns can be seen from the end of the circular hall (1-39).Visually, this is a way to suggest from inside that there is another formal space beyond the entrance door.

Baldassare Longhena used a similar system of non-orthogonal axes in Santa Maria della Salute in Venice (1-40 and 1-41). As with Palladio, it is unclear whether Longhena intended to form such visual axes or whether they are a by-product of his complex geometries.

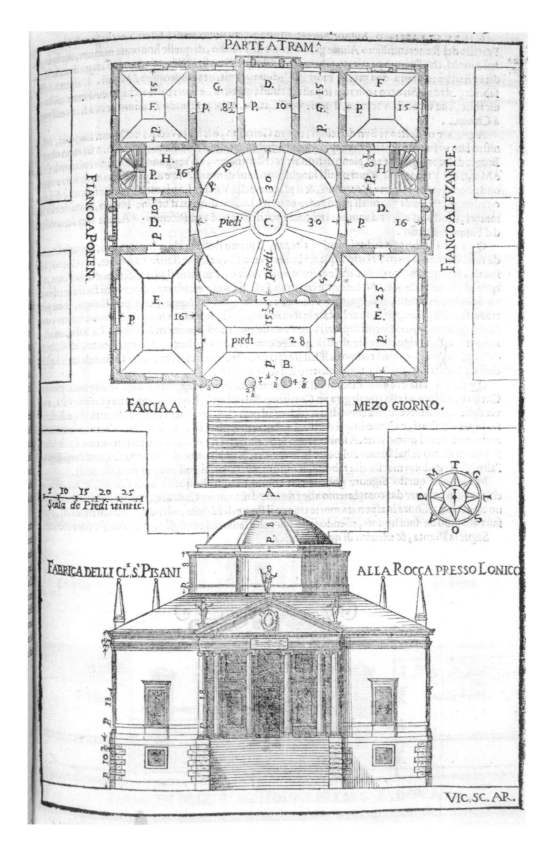

1-35 Plan and elevation of the Rocca Pisani according to Vincenzo Scamozzi's *Idea*. (CCA, cage, M NA44.S283 W190), p. 273

1-36–1-38 Alignment of openings in Rocca Pisani.　　1-37

1-38

1-39 Adjustment of the central intercolumniation to the width of the main entrance in Rocca Pisani.

1-40 and 1-41 Alignment of interior openings
in Santa Maria della Salute.

1-41

ROOM LENGTHS AND WIDTHS

In the *Four Books*, Palladio listed his seven favorite room length/width proportions: 1/1 (round or square), 4/3, √2/1, 3/2, 5/3 or 2/1. He did not insist that these ratios must be used, but simply stated that in his experience the application of these proportions gave better results.[11] Similar lists are found in the works of other Renaissance authors, and Vitruvius provided a list of the ratios suitable for atria.

Palladian scholarship has been disinclined to take Palladio's pragmatic tone and the justification of the list of his preferred ratios at face value. For the past fifty years, the dominant interpretation of this list has been the one formulated by Rudolf Wittkower in *Architectural Principles in the Age of Humanism*. Wittkower tried to explain Palladio's approach to proportioning rooms in the context of Renaissance beliefs in the underlying musical harmony of the world. Wittkower's interpretation will be presented in the next chapter. For now, one should note that it is certainly possible that Palladio derived his list of preferred ratios empirically, possibly motivated by similar lists formulated by Vitruvius and Sebastiano Serlio.

Very recently, Lionel March has provided a particularly compelling interpretation of Palladio's list.[12] March has noted that the Vicentine mathematician Silvio Belli, who collaborated with Palladio on a number of projects, discussed four kinds of means of two numbers in his treatise on proportions. While modern books on mathematics usually discuss three kinds of means—arithmetic, geometric, and harmonic—the Renaissance inherited from Nicomachus of Gerasa a list of ten different kinds,[13] four of which Belli described in his treatise on proportions. Between numbers 2 and 1, these four means (arithmetic, geometric, harmonic, and contraharmonic) produce the four ratios from Palladio's list of preferred ratios between 2/1 and 1/1 (4/3, √2/1, 3/2 and 5/3). March's explanation is elegant and very convincing, especially considering that Belli's treatise contains the kind of mathematical material that would have been delivered in lectures Palladio could have attended at the Accademia Olimpica. The additional advantage of March's thesis is that it does not assume extensive knowledge of mathematics on Palladio's part.

How often did Palladio actually use the ratios from his list in his executed buildings and in the plans published in the *Four Books*? The first systematic attempt to answer this question was made by Deborah Howard and Malcolm Longair in their influential study "Harmonic Proportion and Palladio's *Quattro Libri*." The second book of Palladio's treatise presents plans of forty-four buildings (see Table 1 in Appendix A). Palladio systematically indicated length and width, but height much more rarely. An important difficulty is that the dimensions stated in plans often do not correspond to those of the executed work. Also, the plans presented in the treatise consistently omit information about wall thicknesses, which makes it impossible to calculate the total lengths and widths of the buildings.[14]

Table 1 shows that out of 153 length/width ratios stated on the plans, 89, or 55 percent, correspond to Palladio's preferred ratios. Of these, nine ratios should be read as approximations. Approximations are in fact necessary when it comes to the irrational ratio √2/1. On his list, Palladio defined √2/1 geometrically as the ratio of the diagonal to the side of a square, but on the plans the ratio had to be expressed arithmetically, using a specific number of feet. This ratio appears rarely; there are only three rooms out of 153 whose length/width ratio can be regarded as an approximation of √2/1.[15] The ratio 21¼/15 in Villa Ragona is an exceptionally good approximation. It computes as 1.41666..., which compared with √2/1=1.414213... shows a deviation of no more than 0.17 percent. Palladio's use of a quarter of a foot when defining this ratio indicates that he did strive for a high level of precision. Elwin C. Robison has argued that a quarter of a foot is the limit of precision to which Palladio could have aspired in built masonry work.[16] We shall see later that the level of precision Palladio assumed in his formulation of the canon of the five orders goes beyond anything credible—but this pertains to stonecutting and not masonry work.

An analysis of length/width ratios in Palladio's executed buildings is presented in Table 2 in Appendix A. Because of the lack of modern surveys, this discussion must be based on Bertotti Scamozzi's eighteenth-century measurements. Over the past few decades, various views have been expressed about their accuracy, and some scholars have been inclined to dismiss them completely.[17] The greatest problem is that Bertotti Scamozzi presented buildings as completed, even if the project had not been fully executed. In these cases, he drew additions to the executed building; some were his own design but the majority conformed to the plans in the *Four Books*. The result is that it is often difficult to distinguish between the sections Palladio really built and elements derived from the *Four Books* or those of Bertotti Scamozzi's own invention. However, modern general survey books of Palladio's works—such as Beltramini and Guidolotti's *Atlante*—are very efficient tools for this. Once Palladio's built work has been identified, Bertotti Scamozzi's plans can be compared with modern surveys that are publicly available. The result is that Bertotti Scamozzi is reasonably accurate (see Table 2 in Appendix A). With executed buildings, it is necessary to accept approximations, but Table 2 contains 95 length/width ratios of rooms built according to Palladio's designs and 54 (or 57 percent) of these ratios correspond to the list of preferred ratios. A similar result has been reached by Howard and Longair, on the basis of a similar exercise of separating Palladio's built work from Bertotti Scamozzi's additions.[18]

INCOMMENSURABLE RATIOS AND TRIANGULATION

Since nearly half of the length/width ratios that Palladio used were not derived from his list, it is possible that he used other proportional systems known in the Renaissance but not directly related to the list of preferred ratios. Options to investigate include incommensurable ratios obtained through triangulation and those that relate to the Golden Section and the Delian cube. As with the preferred ratios, these can be found both in the plans in the *Four Books* and in the executed buildings, and have been summarized in Appendix A.

A good example of Palladio's use of incommensurable ratios can be found in the plan of the Villa Rotonda published in the *Four Books*. The four large corner rooms of the Rotonda have the length/width

ratio 26/15=1.7333..., which is a very close approximation of the triangulation ratio $\sqrt{3}/1=1.7325$. The deviation is only 0.07 percent.[19] (By comparison, the variation of the closest approximation to $\sqrt{2}/1$, in the Villa Ragona, is 0.17 percent.) Five other room length/width ratios in the *Four Books* can be interpreted as the approximation of $\sqrt{3}/1$, and this ratio also appears in four plans of the buildings surveyed by Bertotti Scamozzi. Palladio's use of triangulation should not be surprising; the concept was well known in the Renaissance, and Alberti had described the use of this ratio in determining room length/width ratios.

The use of ratios such as $\sqrt{2}/1$ and $\sqrt{3}/1$ raises the difficult question of the role of incommensurable ratios and irrational numbers in Palladio's architecture and in Renaissance architecture more generally. Irrational numbers such as $\sqrt{2}$, $\sqrt{3}$ or the Golden Section are those that can not be expressed as ratios of two whole numbers. However, they can often be expressed as geometrical ratios: $\sqrt{2}$ is the ratio between the diagonal and side of a square, $\sqrt{3}/1$ is the ratio between the diagonal and edge of a cube, the Golden Section is the ratio between the diagonal and side of a pentagon. It is impossible to find two numbers whose ratio would exactly express these geometrical relationships, so these ratios need to be approximated. (Irrational numbers should not be confused with those numbers which cannot be expressed with a finite number of decimal points, such as 5/3=1.66666.... The latter number is still a fraction of two whole numbers. While numbers such as $\sqrt{2}$ or $\sqrt{3}$ would also require an infinite number of decimal points, it is impossible to find two numbers whose ratio would exactly express $\sqrt{2}/1$ or $\sqrt{3}/1$—and these ratios need to be approximated.) It is, in fact, a remarkable insight that there are spatial relationships that cannot be mutually compared as numerical relationships; modern notation, which uses $\sqrt{2}$ or $\sqrt{3}$, is merely a way of avoiding the problem. However a side of a square is divided into equal units, the diagonal cannot be expressed as a whole number of the same units. The use of modules in architectural design consequently precludes the use of incommensurable ratios, unless those ratios are approximated.

Both in Vitruvius and in Renaissance architectural theory, the status of incommensurable ratios is contradictory. Vitruvius referred to the commensurability of parts as symmetry, emphasized the importance of the use of modules, and insisted that an architect should have no greater concern than to use commensurable ratios.[20] This statement did not deter him from advocating $\sqrt{2}/1$ as the atrium length/width ratio, or from prescribing $\sqrt{2}/1$ as the ratio between the width of the abacus and the lower column diameter of the Corinthian order.[21] Nevertheless, he was fully aware of the incommensurability of the ratio between the diagonal and the side of a square. In the Preface to Book Nine, where he cited the method for doubling the area of a square from Plato's *Meno*, he noted that since $\sqrt{2}$ cannot be expressed using numbers, the problem has to be resolved by means of geometry.[22]

Vitruvius's view that incommensurable ratios should be precluded from architectural designs was widely adopted by Renaissance commentators. Barbaro was keen to repeat that view and emphasize the importance of the use of modules.[23] Palladio similarly endorsed the view that all measurements on a building should be commensurable.[24] But at the same time the square diagonal-to-side ratio appears among his preferred room length/width ratios, making his position as contradictory as that of Vitruvius. The square diagonal-to-side ratio appears also in the lists of preferred ratios of other Renaissance theorists, including Serlio and Francesco di Giorgio Martini.[25]

The only systematic Renaissance treatment of incommensurable ratios by an architectural theorist was that of Leon Battista Alberti, who defined them as ratios on a cube. Alberti described $\sqrt{3}/1$ as a cube diagonal-to-edge ratio and $\sqrt{2}/1$ as the side diagonal-to-edge ratio; he mentioned the incommensurability of $\sqrt{2}$ but not of $\sqrt{3}$. Some other ratios that he advocated can be taken as rough approximations for $\sqrt{2}$ or $\sqrt{3}$. Diego Feinstein thus suggested interpreting the ratios 7/4 and 7/5, which Alberti had advocated as preferable room height/width ratios, as approximations for $\sqrt{2}/1$ and for $\sqrt{3}/1$.[26] Similarly, when Alberti gave 10/7 as the ratio between abacus width and column diameter of the Corinthian order, this was probably an approximation for $\sqrt{2}/1$, which was stipulated by Vitruvius. [27]

Golden Section

There is another group of room length/width ratios in Palladio's work which seem to invite the suggestion that Palladio's proportional decisions may have been motivated by a specific proportional system. A number of plans in the *Four Books* contain the ratio 1.58/1, and the same ratio can be also found in Palladio's executed buildings (see the final section of Appendix A). One may be tempted to see an approximation of the Golden Section in this ratio.

The Golden Section is the ratio $(1+\sqrt{5})/2$ or 1.61803.... This is also an incommensurable ratio and can be expressed as the ratio between the diagonal and the side of the pentagon or between two lines, such that the longer relates to the shorter as the sum of the both lines to the longer. The ratio can be approximated using the so-called Fibonacci numbers. These are the numbers 1, 1, 2, 3, 5, 8, 13.... Every number on this list is the sum of the previous two. The ratio between the bigger and the smaller of any two neighboring numbers gives an approximation for the Golden Section and the bigger the numbers, the more accurate the approximation.

In *Palladio's Erstling*, his book about the Villa Godi, Paul Hofer noted that the entrance room of this villa has a length/width ratio that is an extraordinarily precise approximation of the Golden Section. According to Hofer's own measurements, this ratio is l/w = 1.6185 (see Table 2, Appendix A). Hofer's survey indicates that the side rooms were built with less precision. Most of their walls are not parallel, and some are not even straight, a striking contrast to the precise execution of the central two rooms.

Golden Section theories were fashionable during the early decades of the twentieth century, but this interpretation of proportional relationships is now largely discredited. For Renaissance architecture, this interpretation is particularly unlikely since few Renaissance sources discuss the Golden Section. The mathematical concept was mentioned by Euclid and therefore not unknown in the Renaissance, but only Luca Pacioli advocated it in any depth.[28] In fact, it is highly likely that Daniele Barbaro (and probably Palladio as well) paid little attention to Golden Section. In his treatise on per-

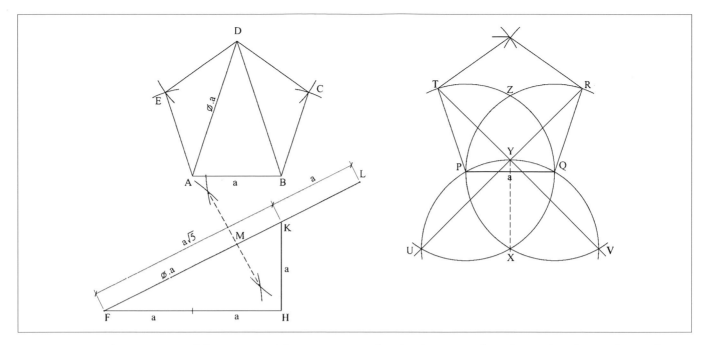

1-42 Geometrical construction of the pentagon. The pentagon ABCDE has been constructed using the Golden Section: a is the length of the side AB, and diagonals AD and BD are $a(1+\sqrt{5})/2$ long. FKH is a triangle whose sides are a and $2a$, KF is a $a\sqrt{5}$, KL is a and M divides FL into two equal parts, each $a(1+\sqrt{5})/2$ long. Consequently, DA=DB=FM=ML. Barbaro's method (the pentagon PQRST) starts from the side PQ (a) by drawing circles with radius a and centers in P and Q. The two circles intersect at points X and Z. X is then taken for the center of another circle, whose radius is also a and which intersects with the other two in points U and V. A vertical line from X intersects with this third circle in Y. The corners of pentagon T and R are where the lines UY and VY cut the first two circles. Barbaro's method is a very close approximation. In a regular pentagon the diagonal-to-side ratio is the Golden Section, i.e., $(1+\sqrt{5})/2=1.61803...$ The same ratio in the approximate method described by Barbaro is $1.61915...$ *Tim Ross*

spective, Barbaro supplied a method for the geometrical construction of a regular pentagon for a given side, but the method he described is approximative and unreasonably complex. He seems to have been unaware of the easier and exact construction method based on the Golden Section.[29] One of the two manuscript versions of his treatise has the same approximative construction obviously drawn by Barbaro himself[30] (1-42). He may have known Pacioli's book, and, according to the partial inventory of his books in the Vatican, he owned at least one manuscript of Euclid's *Elements*.[31] But clearly the Golden Section is not what interested him in Euclid. Barbaro's treatise on perspective came out well after the commentary on Vitruvius; had the Golden Section played an important role in Palladio's design work, it probably would have been discussed during Palladio and Barbaro's collaboration on the commentary, in which case Barbaro would have known about the easier and more accurate method of the construction of the pentagon.

Delian Cubes

Ratios close to 1.61/1 or 1.58/1 may be considered in conjunction with those close to 1.26/1. These appear both in the *Four Books* and in Palladio's executed buildings (see the last section of Appendix A). In the case of the Villa Rotonda, the Villa Forni Cerato, and the Villa Caldogno, both ratios appear in the same building. The ratio 1.26/1 is a good approximation for $\sqrt[3]{2}/1$, which is the ratio of the edges of two cubes, one of which has twice the volume of the other, while 1.58/1 is a good approximation for $\sqrt[3]{2^2}/1$, which is the ratio of the surface areas of two cubes, one of which has twice the volume of the other. The role of cube-derived ratios in Renaissance architecture has been extensively discussed by George Hersey in *Pythagorean Palaces*. Alberti used the cube in order to define irrational ratios. He also referred indirectly to a paragraph in which Vitruvius reported the Pythagorean view that the number of verses in a volume of precepts should be 216, a number derived from an analogy with a cube. Verses organized this way are supposed to be easier to remember.[32]

In this context, the ratios 1.58/1 and 1.26/1 bring to mind the ancient mathematical problem of the doubling of the volume of a cube. According to legend, Apollo required the Delians to double the volume of a cube-shaped altar in order to be delivered from plague. The Delian problem, together with those of squaring a circle and trisecting an angle, is one of the three great mathematical problems of antiquity. Like the other two, it cannot be solved in a finite number of steps using only a ruler and compass.

To solve the Delian problem, one must first resolve the problem of *two* mean proportionals. The problem of *one* mean proportional requires finding the geometric mean of two sizes or two numbers. For instance, if we have two numbers, a and b, their mean proportional is a number c, such that:

$$a : c = c : b$$

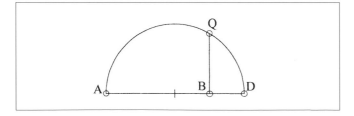

1-43 Geometrical construction of the geometrical mean of lengths AB and BD. Draw BD in extension of AB, find the center of the line AD, and draw a circle around this line. The vertical line from B to its section with this semicircle (BQ) is the geometric mean between AB and BD. *Tim Ross*

or, $c = \sqrt{(ab)}$. The geometric formulation of the same problem requires finding, for two lines of given lengths, the third one, whose length is the geometrical mean of the two (1-43). The geometric theorem that resolved this problem can be found in Euclid.[33] The method was well known to architects during the Renaissance, and Palladio actually defined the geometric mean by this method in the *Four Books*.[34]

The Delian problem requires resolving the problem of *two* mean proportionals. This problem requires finding two numbers (c and d) between two given numbers (a and b) so that:

$$a : c = c : d = d : b$$
(a and b are given, and c and d are to be found)

Formulated geometrically, the problem requires two lines whose lengths are c and d to be found; their lengths must satisfy the equation stated above. But if we take b to be equal with $2a$ and a to be the edge of the given cube, then c will be the edge of the cube with twice the given volume—i.e., the solution to the Delian problem.[35]

For a long time during antiquity, the Delian problem was conceived as separate from the problem of two mean proportionals. The history of mathematics usually credits Hippocrates of Chios with discovering the relationship between these two problems.[36] At the time, this discovery simply revealed that two obscure and unsolvable geometrical problems were closely related. Greek mathematicians invented a number of mechanical devices to approximate their solution by trial and error. The problem of two mean proportionals had a practical application in Greek and Roman artillery,[37] and was mentioned by Vitruvius.[38] Vitruvius actually mentioned only two solutions to the problem, those by Eratosthenes and Archytas; Barbaro, who commented on this passage extensively, supplied descriptions of these two solutions and, additionally, two other methods: one invented by Nicomedes and one ascribed to Plato[39] (1-44). There is no need to describe all these methods here, but the instrument called *mesolabium*, invented for this purpose by Eratosthenes, was well known in the Renaissance and described by Barbaro in the commentary.[40] Among the various solutions invented by Greek mathematicians, the mesolabium is the easiest

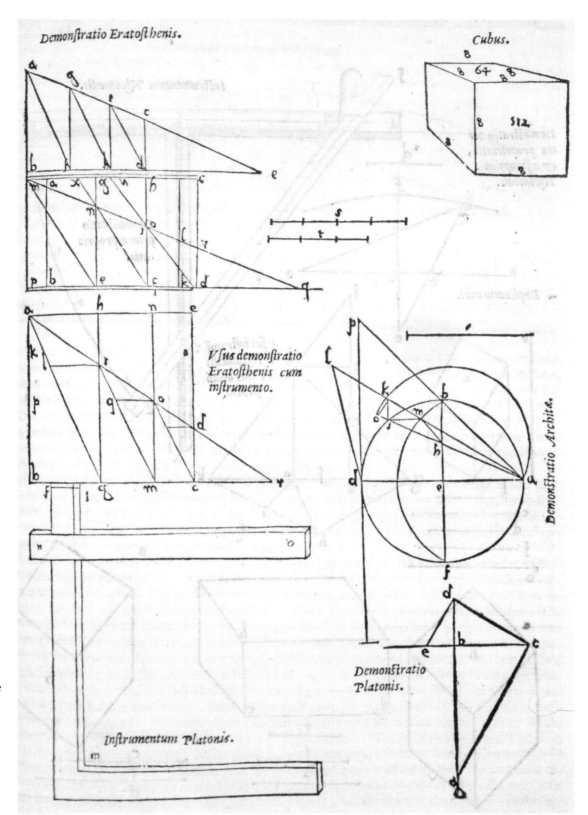

Demonstratio Eratosthenis.

Cubus.

8 8 64 8 8

8 512 8 8

s

t

Usus demonstratio
Eratosthenis cum
instrumento.

Demonstratio Architæ.

Demonstratio
Platonis.

Instrumentum Platonis.

1-44 Barbaro's
presentation of the
methods to solve
the Delian prob-
lem, including the
mesolabium, in
the commentary
on Vitruvius. *CCA,
cage, NA44. V848
(W8778) c.2. p. 279*

to use. An additional advantage was that it could produce not only two mean proportionals, but as many as were needed (1-45).

The Delian problem does provide a possible explanation for Palladio's choice of ratios close to 1.58 and 1.26. Palladio could have known about it through his collaboration with Barbaro, although it should be noted that these ratios appear in Palladio's work before this collaboration started. Nevertheless, the evidence that he really derived ratios close to 1.58/1 and 1.26/1 in such a

manner is scarce; some important authors such as Alberti and Vitruvius did talk about cubes, but they did not advocate the use of ratios derived from doubling the cube. Ultimately, it remains unclear why Palladio would consider using ratios derived from Delian cubes in his buildings, and there is no known Renaissance precedent for this kind of proportional procedure.

In any case, more than half of the room length/width ratios that Palladio used were derived from his list of preferred ratios. The list is to be taken seriously, but Palladio did not dogmatically insist on its application. Palladio's design process was influenced by many other considerations, especially the use of the orders, and ensuring the presence of certain ratios in the plan was only one of his concerns. At the same time, it is clear that Palladio did not limit himself to his list of preferred ratios, and it is plausible that he used other proportional systems, most likely triangulation, and conceivably ratios derived from the Delian problem.

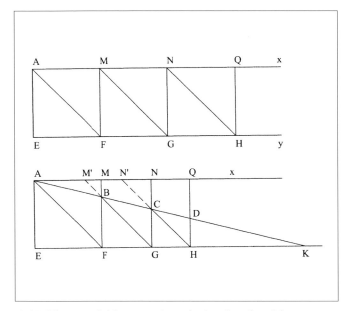

1-45 The mesolabium consists of triangles placed between axes x and y. The first drawing presents their initial position. Once triangles are moved along the axes, they produce new triangles M'NG and N'QH. NQH is thus moved to the position N'QH, so that QH passes through D; and MNG is found in the position M'NG so that points B and C (where MF, M'G, NG, and N'H intersect) are in a straight line with AD. If K is the point of intersection of the line AD and the axis y, then EK : KF = AK : KB = FK : KG

and   EK : KF = AE : BF
also   FK : KG = BF : CG
so: AE : BF = BF : CG
and   BF : CG = CG : DH

Therefore, AE, BF, CG, and DH are in geometric progression (i.e., BF and CG are the two mean proportionals of AE and DH). *Tim Ross*

PROPORTIONING INDIVIDUAL SPACES: ROOM HEIGHTS

Because of the lack of modern surveys, Palladio's methods for determining the heights of rooms can only be discussed on the basis of his statements in the *Four Books*. Bertotti Scamozzi's redesign of the unfinished parts of Palladio's buildings makes his surveys particularly unreliable when it comes to heights. It is uncertain to what extent he may have adjusted the heights of the executed sections of a building to conform to those of his own design.

The *Four Books* specify that the height of a room with a flat ceiling should equal the width of the room; if the room is vaulted, its height should be the arithmetic, geometric, or harmonic mean of the room's length and width. If the room is square, then the height should be 4/3 of the width, and if the ceiling is flat, then the height should equal its width (see Appendix B).

These formulas apply to rows of rooms adjacent to the sala or around the courtyard in the case of a palazzo. In only nine cases in the treatise did Palladio provide information about the height of a sala.[41] When it comes to rooms adjacent to a sala, there are fourteen buildings out of the forty-four in the *Four Books* in which it can be said with certainty that the room height was calculated as the arithmetic, geometric, or harmonic mean of the length and width, either because Palladio explicitly said so or because the height he stated corresponds to one of the means. The arithmetic mean was used seven times; the geometric mean was used three times, and the harmonic mean was used four times.[42] In those cases where exact heights are specified, there are three exceptions to the rule given in the *Four Books*.[43]

Proportional Relationships Between Rooms: CCH Rule

Were the proportions of individual rooms correlated in some way? Did Palladio have a method of relating the proportions of one room to another? The only guidance he provides is the statement that since all rooms on the same floor are the same height (unless they have mezzanines above) and since the height is calculated as the mean of the length and the width, the dimensions of rooms on the same floor must be carefully coordinated with each other.[44] The condition presents no difficulty for rooms with flat ceilings that are the same width, and where consequently the height equals the width, a typical situation with rooms in a wing of a palazzo.

Fulfilling this requirement becomes an interesting mathematical problem for rooms with varied dimensions. In that case, the height of one room, calculated as the arithmetic mean of length and width, must equal the height of another, calculated as the geometric mean of that room's length and width. This principle could be described as the Condition on the Concordance of Heights, or the CCH rule. The mathematical formulation of this principle is provided in Appendix B.

The lateral row of rooms of Palazzo Chiericati illustrates Palladio's application of the CCH rule (1-46 and 1-47). The large rooms on the side of the central hall are 30 by 18 feet and Palladio says that their height was calculated as the arithmetic mean: $(30+18)/2=24$ feet. The next room is square (18 by 18 feet) and vaulted; according to the rule, the height of such rooms equals 4/3 of

their width: $4/3 \times 18=24$ feet. By adjusting dimensions and using different kinds of means, it is possible to achieve the same height for all the rooms in a row.

Appendix B shows that the CCH rule works only if the room's height/width ratios are 4/3 or 5/4. If the CCH rule is to be applied to rooms with one dimension in common, only one combination of length/width ratios is possible for a row of three rooms (2/1, 5/3, and 1/1) and there are four possible combinations for rows of only two rooms (2/1 and 5/3; 2/1 and 1/1; 5/3 and 1/1; 3/2 and 5/3).

The lack of data in the plans of the *Four Books* makes it impossible to say how often Palladio used the CCH rule. Its precise use can be clearly detected in only two plans in the *Four Books*, Palazzo Chiericati and Villa Pisani (Montagnana); in Villa Mocenigo the rule seems to have been applied approximately.

Among Palladio's executed buildings, the CCH rule is applied in the Villa Cornaro (see plan in 3-31). The large rooms left and right of the main entrance have a length/width ratio of 1.7 (probably an approximation for $\sqrt{3}/1$), and their height is calculated as the geometrical mean of length and width.[45] The square rooms adjacent to the large rooms share the same height and width as these large rooms. The height/width ratio is 1.3, an approximation for 4/3, the ratio stipulated by Palladio as the height/width ratio of square rooms.[46]

We have seen that three out of four of Palladio's preferred ratios between 2/1 and 1/1 were the arithmetic, geometric, and harmonic means of ratios 1/1 and 2/1. At the same time these means were also used to calculate height. Therefore, three out of four preferred length/width ratios are also the preferred height/width ratios for a room with a length/width ratio 2/1. The height/width ratio of one room may easily turn out to be the length/width ratio of another. This could be described as the inverted CCH rule.[47]

There are examples of the use of such an inverted CCH rule in the *Four Books*. In the case of the Villa Rotonda, the length/width ratio of the larger rooms is $\sqrt{3}/1$. The height of these rooms was calculated as the arithmetic mean of the length and the width, and their height/width ratio is 1.367. The length/width ratio of the adjacent rooms is approximately the same (1-48).

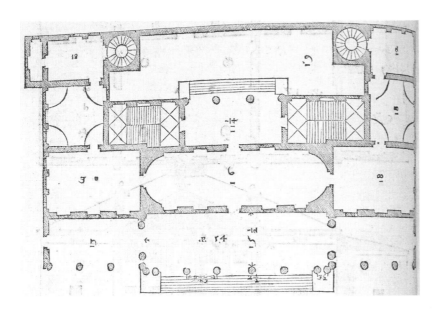

1-46 Plan of the Palazzo Chiericati
from the *Four Books*. *CCA, NA44.P164
(W161), c.2, p. 6*

1-47 Internal composition of spaces in
the Palazzo Chiericati (Vicenza). *CISA,
R0000446*

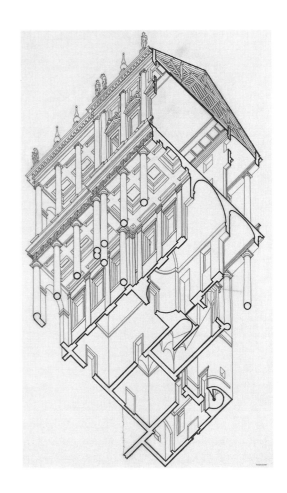

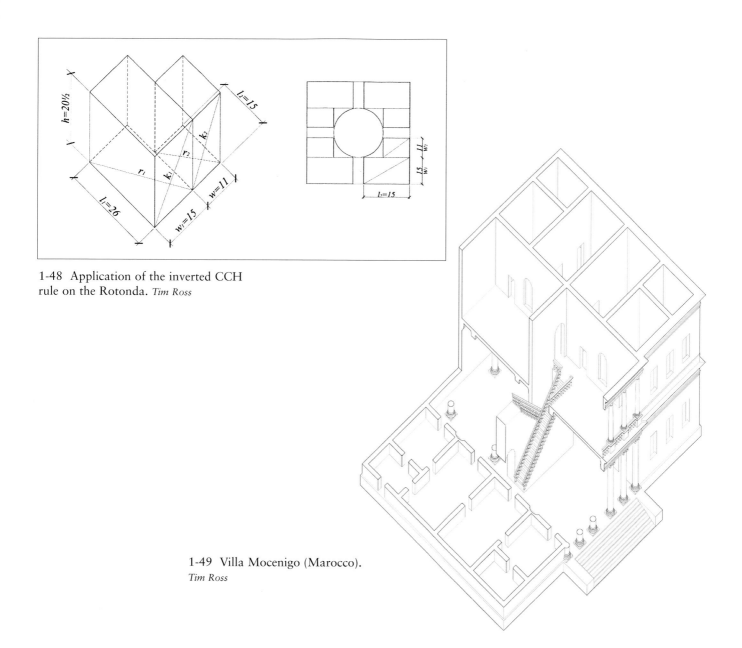

1-48 Application of the inverted CCH rule on the Rotonda. *Tim Ross*

1-49 Villa Mocenigo (Marocco). *Tim Ross*

Another example is the Palazzo della Torre. The height/width ratio of room is 1.264, while the length/width ratio of the room next to it is 1.267.

STAIRCASES

Information about Palladio's approach to the design of staircases can be gathered from his executed buildings, from the staircases drawn on the plans in the *Four Books*, and from Chapter 28 of the first book of the treatise, which is dedicated to their design. Internal staircases rarely played an important role in Palladio's designs; he seems to have shared Alberti's view that the staircase is a nuisance that compromises the ideal spatial organization of the building.[48] Chapter 28 opens with a warning about the difficulty of locating the stair so that it does not interfere with the building but still retains its functionality.[49] In his extensive study of Palladio's principles of staircase design, Friedrich Mielke noted that for

1-50 Drawing of the stair-
case in Chambord from the
Four Books. *CCA, NA44.P164
(W161), c.2, p. 65*

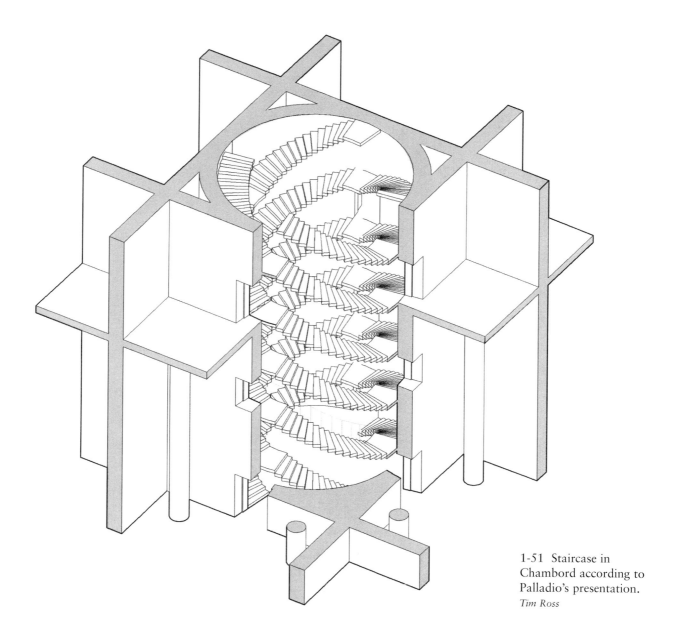

1-51 Staircase in Chambord according to Palladio's presentation.
Tim Ross

Palladio, staircases were always a technical device that was "unfortunately necessary" and subject to other considerations of the design process.[50] Palladio avoided allowing staircases to have great impact on the design and was inclined to enclose them in separate rooms, which became part of the building's internal matrix. Occasionally staircases did become central features of the design, as at the Villa Mocenigo (1-49). The villa is accessed through a large, deep loggia that culminates in two monumental staircases running in opposite directions up to the doors to the main hall. Palladio, with some pride, says of these staircases that they are "very practical, and beautiful, and adequately lit."[51] A similar situation occurs in the Palazzo Antonini, where the double staircase contributes to the monumentality of the access to the sala (see 1-5).

The staircase chapter in the *Four Books* lists a number of design principles, largely derived from Alberti as

Mielke has noted.[52] Staircases should provide good light and have three openings: the entrance to the staircase space at the lower level, the exit at the upper level, and the window for light. Palladio also pointed out that in antiquity staircases had an odd number of steps so that climbing is finished with the same leg on which it started.

In specifying the dimensions of steps, Palladio differs from Alberti and Vitruvius. Both Vitruvius and Alberti gave nine inches as the maximum riser height, with a minimum of two inches. Palladio corrected this to a maximum of six and a minimum of four inches. In his view, the depth of the tread should be between twelve and eighteen inches, and the depth should be twice the height of the riser. A run of stairs should not be more than eleven or thirteen steps. The width of the staircase should never be less than four feet. Mielke compared these requirements with five extant staircases that almost certainly were executed under Palladio's supervision: Palazzo Chiericati, Villa Pisani (Montagnana), Villa Cornaro, Villa da Porto, and Villa Barbaro. The requirement that staircases should not be less than four feet wide is fulfilled in all five cases—as well as the one regarding the height of individual steps. In all cases, the number of steps is either eleven or thirteen. However, in two out of five staircases, the steps are shorter than one foot, and only one staircase fulfils the condition that the length-to-width ratio should be 2/1.

Palladio's chapter also provides a typology of stairs. Stairs can be either straight or spiral. Straight stairs can either have two extended flights or be square and turn around in four flights. Spiral staircases can be either oval or circular and their center can be void or filled in— "column in the middle," as Palladio described it. At the end of the chapter, Palladio presents the very complex circular staircase at the palace of François I at Chambord (1-50 and 1-51). In Palladio's interpretation, the staircase is located around a large circular void and consists of four separate flights that connect individual apartments "so that those who live in one do not use the staircase of the other; and since it is void in the middle everyone can see everyone else going up and down with the minimum of interference."[53] Palladio would have known about this staircase only by hearsay and, as Mielke remarked, his

description is inaccurate.[54] Nevertheless, this "belissima inventione," as Palladio calls it, was often reprinted in Baroque architectural writings.[55]

In spite of this emphasis on circular staircases, Palladio's own staircases, as presented in the second book, are usually straight. According to Mielke's count, there are 178 internal staircases, of which 140 are straight, 13 circular/spiral, and 25 oval/spiral.[56]

During the sixteenth century, monumental spiral staircases became symbols of wealth and power in Italy and Germany.[57] Palladio mentioned Bramante's spiral staircase in the Vatican, but he probably did not see Vignola's work in Caprarola[58] (1-52). Unlike the works of Vignola and Bramante, Palladio's most successful executed spiral staircase, in the Convento della Carità, had no columns supporting stairs in the middle; rather, the central void was completely empty. Instead of heavy balusters, the staircase had only a light iron handrail (see page 38). Palladio noted with pride that this staircase "turned out marvelously."[59] The heavy stones, which appear to need no support, impressed Goethe, who wrote that one would not get tired of walking up and down this staircase.[60]

This staircase influenced Inigo Jones's Tulip Staircase in the Queen's House, and there is a similar staircase in Scamozzi's Villa Duodo, although it is not clear whether it is part of the original design or a later addition (1-53). Elena Bassi, who traced the history of this type of staircase, mentions its influence on a number of Baroque staircases, such as the work of Baldassare Longhena and Giuseppe Sardi in Ospedale dei Derelitti in Venice, Longhena's work in the Scuola di San Giorgio dei Greci, a staircase by Andrea Tiralli in San Giovanni in Laterano in Rome, and Giorgio Massari's staircase in the Dominican convent in Zattere (Venice).[61]

The alternative type, used by Vignola and Bramante, where a system of columns in the center supports the steps, is found in the project for an unidentified client on page 72 of the second book of Palladio's treatise (1-54). Unlike Bramante's and Vignola's works, however, this staircase is elliptical, a precursor of the great Baroque staircases of the Palazzo Barberini and the Palazzo Quirinale in Rome, among many examples[62] (1-55 and 1-56).

1-52
Staircase in
Villa
Caprarola,
by Giacomo
Barozzi da
Vignola.
CISA, F001275

1-53 Staircase
in Villa Duodo
(Monselice).

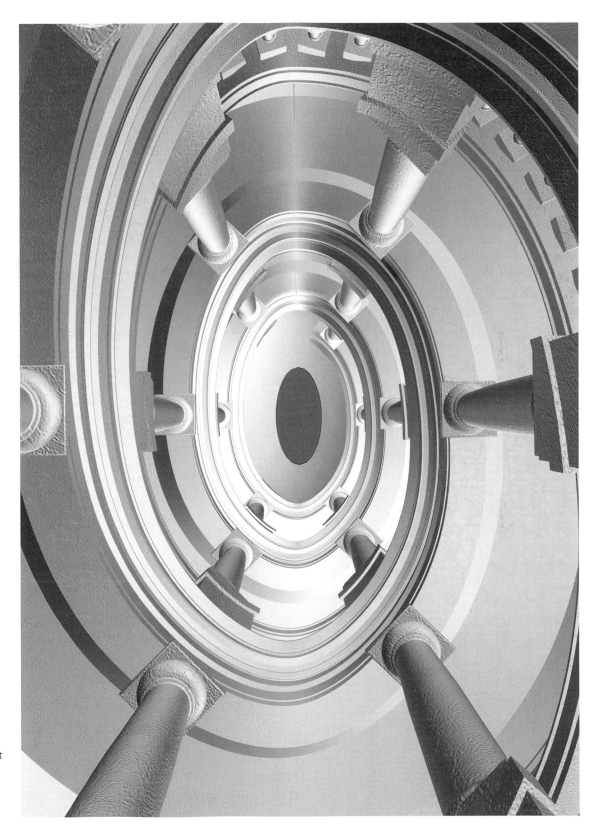

1-54 Palladio's elliptical spiral staircase from the project for an unidentified client on page 72 of Book Two of the *Four Books*.
Bojan Vučenović

1-55 Spiral staircase in the Palazzo Barberini (Rome).

1-56 Spiral stair-
case in the Palazzo
Barberini (Rome).

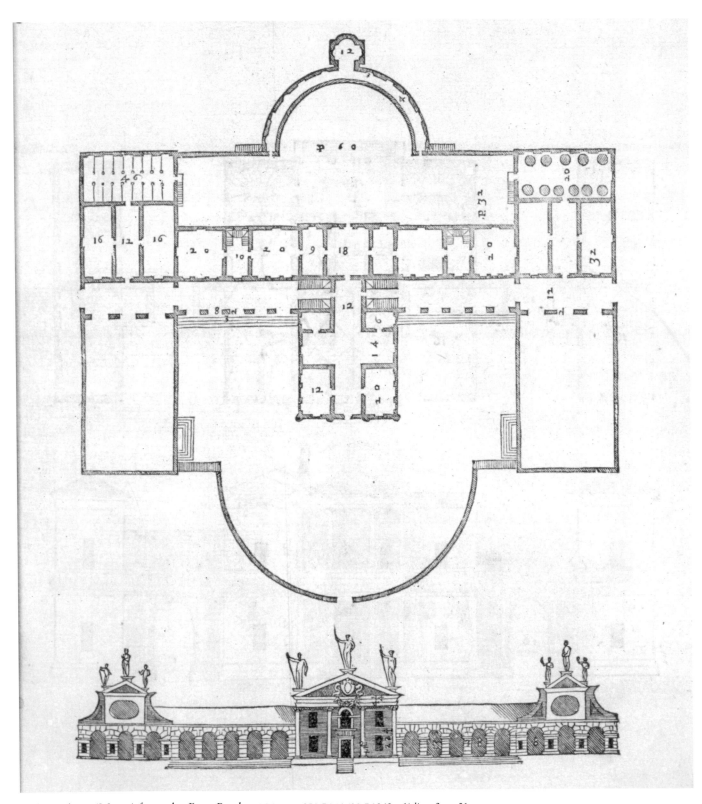

Villa Barbaro (Maser) from the *Four Books*. CCA, *cage NA P164 (88-B1843 c.1) livre 2, p. 51*

CHAPTER II

PROPORTIONS AND HARMONIES

RUDOLF WITTKOWER's *Architectural Principles in the Age of Humanism* is arguably the most influential twentieth-century book on Renaissance architectural theory.[1] Wittkower devoted a substantial section of the book to Palladio's work, and, for decades, his study has provided the standard interpretation of Palladio's use of proportions. Wittkower's work was based on the reconstruction of the Renaissance belief that God used harmonic, musical proportions in the creation of the world, which implied that architects should use these proportions as well. The assumption was that Renaissance architects—most notably Alberti and Palladio—preferred to use certain ratios because of their role in musical theory. The procedure for using musical ratios in proportioning room plans was indeed carefully described in Alberti's *Art of Building*. In the case of Palladio, Wittkower supported his thesis by relying on the room length/width ratios of the plans in the *Four Books*.

Wittkower's interpretation derived from a physical law whose discovery was traditionally ascribed to Pythagoras and which was widely known in the Renaissance: the musical interval produced by two strings when triggered (assuming that these strings are of the same thickness, material, etc.) depends on the ratio of the lengths of the strings. For instance, if the ratio is 2/1 it will give an octave, if it is 3/2 it will give a fifth, 4/3 a fourth, and so on. Wittkower's proportional analysis of Palladio's villas endeavored to show that Palladio selected room length/width ratios because of their possi-

ble interpretation as musical intervals. The term "musical" here must be understood in the context of the Renaissance belief that certain numerical proportions, which define musical intervals, are fundamental in the constitution of the world and that audible music is just a manifestation of the non-audible music of the world. The use of certain proportions in both audible music and architecture reflects the higher order that governs the world. As Wittkower put it, "The architect who relies on these harmonies is not translating musical ratios into architecture, but is making use of a universal harmony apparent in music."[2] Historians of aesthetics have referred to this view as the "Great Theory." While Wittkower was not alone in studying the idea of a musically-based architectural theory of proportions, his was a work of incomparable scholarship that focused attention of scholars on the role of such beliefs in Renaissance architectural writings.[3]

GREAT THEORY

The oldest written document discussing the Great Theory is probably Plato's *Timaeus*, though there must have existed a considerable, possibly only oral, tradition before this dialogue. Its content (Socrates listening to Timaeus of Locri) points to Plato's contacts with Pythagoreans in Sicily. The dialogue was well known during the Middle Ages—probably better than any other of Plato's dialogues. It contains a number of major ideas that became the basis of the Great Theory, the most important of which was the description of the physical law that musical intervals can be defined by simple ratios between whole numbers. Plato tried to define a musical scale by starting from the numbers 1, 2, 3, and their squares (1, 4, 9) and cubes (1, 8, 27). His interpretation of Pythagorean musical theory correlated these musical ratios with the ratios that determine the movements of the planets, and in the *Republic* he wrote explicitly about the music of the heavenly Spheres.[4]

Another text from antiquity that enjoyed great popularity throughout the Middle Ages was Macrobius's commentary on Cicero's *Dream of Scipio*. The *Dream of Scipio* is actually the last part of Cicero's *Republic*. Cicero's treatise was only partly preserved, but the *Dream of Scipio* survived in transcripts included in Macrobius's commentary, which had wide circulation in the Middle Ages. In the dream, Scipio Africanus Minor, a young Roman soldier, meets his ancestor, Scipio Africanus Maior, who shows him the functioning of the Universe, how celestial Spheres produce music, and explains that the entire world is actually a temple of God. In the commentary, Macrobius summarizes the numerological teachings about individual numbers, particularly stressing the importance of the numbers 7 (the number of errant Spheres) and 8 (the number of revolving Spheres). Book Two of his commentary is particularly important for understanding of the music of the Spheres. Macrobius explains that since the Sphere of immovable stars rotates with the greatest speed around the Earth, it produces the highest tone and that of three musical genera—methods of dividing musical intervals—it is the diatonic that actually corresponds to the music of the Spheres.[5]

The author who provided the most comprehensive synthesis of the Great Theory during antiquity was Ptolemy. His *Almagest* was the authoritative treatise on astronomy for many centuries, while *Tetrabiblos* discussed what is known as astrology today—the effect of movements of planets on regions and nations as well as their impact on individuals. *De Musica* presents Ptolemy's explanation of the music of the heavenly Spheres. This treatise consists of three books, of which the first two deal with music in the modern sense, i.e., audible music. Book Three, however, is a synthesis of astronomy, astrology, and music. Ptolemy explains that intervals express certain original and primary relations and that all who care for beauty will admire the inner strength and harmony of these relationships. This admiration comes from the sense of the Divine; the force of harmony is neither object nor purpose, but a cause which gives a regular and natural form to matter. All that is subject to natural laws participates in reason; especially those movements that give form, such as the movements of the stars and the human soul. The forces of the human soul are three: the ability to think, to feel, and to live; to these correspond (in the same order) the following musical intervals: octave, fifth, and fourth. Equally, different musical *genera* correspond to the forces of the soul: the *enharmonic* genus corresponds to the ability to understand physical and moral phenomena; the *diatonic* to theological and political reasoning, the *chromatic* to mathematical and economic reasoning. More generally, modulations and transpositions in tonal systems correspond to changes in the human soul. Because of this, Ptolemy says, Pythagoras advocated listening to music upon awakening: this should help the soul overcome the shock it undergoes when waking up.

Similarly, according to Ptolemy, there are parallels between the Great Perfect System, a method of organizing musical scales, and the Zodiac—since both are circular, the ratios of the angles between the different positions of the planets are definable as musical ratios. The movement of the heavenly Spheres from east to west thus corresponds to a continuous movement through the system of musical tones. If the circle of the Zodiac is divided into 360 degrees, then different positions on it can be assigned to the tones of the Great Perfect System; Ptolemy took great care to determine which pitch is at 180 degrees, which at 90 degrees, and which at 60 degrees, and so on. Finally, in the last chapter, Ptolemy explained that the ratios of the distances between the heavenly Spheres and Earth correspond to musical ratios; in contemporary notation individual Spheres would correspond to the following tones: Saturn A, Jupiter E, Mars D, Sun B, Venus A, and Moon E.[6]

The Great Theory was by no means forgotten during the Middle Ages. The works of Boethius, Cassiodorus, and Macrobius were widely read, and the Renaissance rediscovery of Greek scholarship added considerable sophistication to these theories. Renaissance musical treatises typically contained extensive sections about *musica mundana* and *harmonia mundi*. A good example is the work of Franchino Gaffurio, a preeminent figure in late fifteenth-century Italian musical theory, whose writings offer extensive summaries of views of various authors on audible and non-audible music. In *Humanism in Renaissance Musical Thought*, Claude Palisca commented that "Gaffurio's timely lesson is that harmony is universal, and audible music only one of its manifestations."[7] Book Three of Gaffurio's *De Harmonia* deals with the three types of means (arithmetic, harmonic, and geometric), and discusses the way they correspond to public affairs (arithmetic to those regulated by magistrates, harmonic to those governed by the best men, and geometric to those governed by all people). His account of non-audible music in Book Four explained that musical modes and ratios between string-lengths relate to muses and constellations and that muses are presided over by Apollo, who is the god of harmony. The Spheres, which carry the planets, correspond to individual muses (the Moon to Clio, Mercury to Calliope, etc.) and to individual tones. Like Ptolemy, Gaffurio defined the distances between the Spheres as tones and semitones. Some of the heavenly bodies have masculine sounds, others feminine; heavenly sounds are perceived by means of virtue alone. Finally, all arts depend on proportions. Gaffurio reiterated Ptolemy's analysis of the relationship between musical ratios and the human soul, discussed how these ratios affect the human body, and how they appear in natural phenomena.[8]

For the discussion of Wittkower's analysis of Palladio's proportional theory, the works of Gioseffe Zarlino, another major Renaissance musical theorist, are particularly important. A contemporary of Palladio and Barbaro, Zarlino was a native of Chioggia but spent most of his life in Venice. His contacts with Barbaro are particularly likely. Both lived in Venice at the same time and both held ecclesiastical positions. Zarlino is recognized today as probably the greatest musical theorist of his time, while Barbaro had strong interests in music. Wittkower pointed to a reference to Barbaro in Zarlino's *Sopplementi Musicali*,[9] but since this book came out eighteen years after Barbaro died, it cannot be taken as evidence of personal contact. Much more indicative is their collaboration with Antonio Gogava on the 1562 Latin translation of Aristoxenus and Ptolemy's *De musica*; in the Preface, Gogava mentions that he consulted Daniele Barbaro for the translation of Ptolemy and that Zarlino asked him to translate Aristoxenus as well. Both Barbaro and Zarlino were in contact with Federico Badoer, who founded Accademia della Fama in 1557. Zarlino was one of its members, and, as Manfredo Tafuri noted in *Venice and the Renaissance*, Barbaro was a good friend of Badoer, although there is no record that he was a member of the academy.[10]

Zarlino's writings contained extensive discussion of, and relied heavily on, the belief in the Great Theory. In his *Istitutioni Harmoniche* (1558), Zarlino divided music into *musica humana* and *musica mundana*. *Musica mundana* pertains to the harmony of the heavenly Spheres: it is observed in distances and movements as well as aspects and the nature of the planets. Zarlino ascribed to Pythagoras the view that such a huge mechanism could not move without producing some noise, and referred to similar sections in Plato and in the *Dream of Scipio*. The Spheres that carry planets and stars are themselves intelligent beings who adjust their movements to harmony; the distances between the Earth and the planets stand in musical ratios, while the positions of the planets explain their astrological virtues. The world is thus the organ of God. "The great architect God" created the world according to number and measure, and organized everything according to the four qualities and working with the four elements. Zarlino also discussed the issue of whether lower Spheres produce lower or higher tones, and explained the distances between Spheres as musical ratios.

Musica humana pertains to the relationship between the soul and the body. Zarlino says that, according to Ptolemy, the intellectual part of the human soul relates to the octave, the four senses of the human body correspond to the musical fifth (which has four tones); the fourth in music (which includes three tones) is related to the growth of the body, its maturity and decline. The *musica humana* is thus *concordia harmonica* between human spiritual and corporeal nature.

Zarlino relied on a numerological explanation of the importance of the number 6 to justify his expanded definition of consonances. Traditionally, ratios between the numbers 1, 2, 3, and 4 were thought to generate consonances. But Zarlino felt the need to expand the list to the first six numbers in order to treat the third (5/4) and the semiditone (6/5) as consonances. He also listed the sixth (5/3) among the consonances, because it is made up of a fourth and a semiditone. His justification for the extension of the number of consonances is pure numerology. Six signs of the Zodiac are always above the horizon, there are six errant planets (Saturn, Jupiter, Mars, Venus, Mercury, and the Moon) and six substantial qualities of the elements: rarity, acuity, movement, obtuseness, density, and stillness; there are six necessary conditions for a body to exist (size, color, interval, shape, motion, and state), six species of movement (generation, corruption, increase, decrease, alteration, and change of place); six is the first perfect number, and so on.[11]

Great Theory in Renaissance Architectural Writings

The idea that musical proportions, with which God organized the universe, should also be used by architects appears from time to time in Renaissance architectural writings. Alberti wrote in the *Art of Building* that "The same numbers that cause sounds to have that *concinnitas*, pleasing to the ears, can also fill the eyes and mind with wondrous delight."[12] Alberti also advocated the use of incommensurable ratios, which he defined on a cube; but the majority of his discussion of room proportions pertains to the ratios derived from musical theory. He listed consonances such as the octave, fifth, and fourth, repeated the traditional view that such intervals were generated as the ratios between numbers 1, 2, 3, and 4, and recommended that architects use such numbers in laying out the plans of buildings.

The belief that the harmony of the world should directly influence architectural design is explicitly stated in a memorandum regarding the building program for the Church of San Francesco della Vigna written by Francesco Giorgi in 1535 and signed by Titian, Sebastiano Serlio, and the humanist Fortunio Spira. The memorandum, which Wittkower included in his *Architectural Principles*, derived the dimensions and proportions of the building directly from a set of musical and numerological considerations.[13] It is quite possible that Palladio was aware of this memorandum since he was commissioned to design the facade of the same church thirty years later.

The same idea—that the ratios that result in musical beauty result in architectural beauty as well—appears three times in Barbaro's commentary on Vitruvius. Barbaro directly stated that what is harmony for the ear is beauty for the eye.[14] He expressed the view that those proportions that delight the eyes delight the ears as well and that proportions between spaces and tones are equivalent.[15]

Barbaro also stated that stars send "their divine virtues" down on Earth or that the celestial bodies have the power to act and influence the events on Earth.[16] However, this is not a reference to what we call astrology today. The influences Barbaro referred to are those that establish the temporal order on the Earth, such as the changes of seasons, days, and nights. In architecture, Barbaro said, there is no place for the kind of interest which tries to predict the outcome of future events by consideration of the position of stars. Rather, the architect must be acquainted with *non fucata astrologia*, which determines the time to work on a building in order to avoid unsuitable weather, too hot or too cold.[17] Astrology for Barbaro thus embraces both what we call astrology and what we call astronomy today; only the latter, the *non fucata*, has importance for architects. Barbaro insisted that the architect's interest in astrology should exclude judicious astrology, which studies the position of stars at the moment of birth.[18] Although many individuals try to achieve the latter kind of knowledge, the discipline is as dubious as it is useless.[19] Manfredo Tafuri has pointed out the absence of any kind of esotericism in Barbaro's commentary on Vitruvius.[20] In the first edition of the commentary, Barbaro mentioned that he hated superstition as much as heresy.[21] The comment is omitted in both

Italian and Latin versions of the second edition, but, coming from Barbaro, it is a very strong statement. Not only was Barbaro a high-ranking priest, but he also actively collaborated with the Roman inquisition in the prosecution of those accused of heresy on Venetian territory, an activity that far exceeded his ecclesiastical duties.[22]

Barbaro's statements are very similar to the only mention of this kind of theory in Palladio's writings. Palladio did not discuss the relationship between architectural proportions and music in the *Four Books*, but he did posit a direct analogy between music and architecture in his memorandum for the Cathedral of Brescia. Palladio says that in the same way that proportions of voices are harmonies to the ears, so those of visual dimensions result in harmony for the eyes; the reason for this is not known "except to those who study and know the reasons of things."[23] The statement shows that Palladio shared this kind of belief, but later in the memorandum he made no effort to deduce design principles from it. Nor does his statement suggest that Palladio regarded himself as one of those who knew "the reasons of things." Palladio's attitude recalls that of Vignola, who justified his systematic reliance on whole number ratios by the fact that musical theorists in their works prove that such ratios produce harmonies. Vignola was equally hesitant to claim such knowledge for himself.[24] Palladio's memorandum thus sounds more like a reference to an explanation of why certain proportional relationships cause delight than a programmatic statement of an approach to design. This is an important distinction: the beauty of music can be explained in terms of numerical ratios, but this does not mean that composers systematically use mathematical calculations in their work. Similarly, the beauty of formal relationships may be conceived as explicable by the presence of numerical and musical relationships, but this does not necessarily mean that architects use such proportions intentionally in their design work. Least of all should we expect Palladio or Vignola to have been acquainted with the large corpus of astrological and numerological writings of their contemporaries. Rather, we should expect them to have followed their visual and formal judgments. It is reasonable to expect that

insofar as their contemporaries found architectural works aesthetically successful, they would have explained this with reference to the Great Theory. However, while the narrative about the harmony of the world may have been attached to successful works of architecture at the time, it still does not follow that architects derived their design principles from it.

WITTKOWER'S ANALYSIS OF PALLADIO'S LENGTH/WIDTH RATIOS

Wittkower's analysis of the plans presented in the second of the *Four Books* suggested the interpretation of room length/width ratios as equivalent to musical intervals. Wittkower assumed that Palladio, following the precepts described by Alberti, intentionally used certain room length/width ratios because they corresponded to musical intervals. These ratios could have been derived from the intervals of the Pythagorean or Just tuning systems, both of which were in use during the Renaissance. In the Pythagorean system whole tones (but not semitones) are equal (9/8).[25] The ratios of the Pythagorean scale are:[26]

CC	CD	CE	CF	CG	CA	CB	CC_1
1/1	9/8	81/64	4/3	3/2	27/16	16/9	2/1

In Just tuning, whole-tone intervals are not equal and their corresponding ratios are either 9/8 or 10/9; the difference of 81/80, called also the syntonic comma, is minimal but audible. The semitones are not equal either, which also means that a sharp tone is not equal to the flat higher tone, i.e., C sharp is not the same as D flat. Just tuning ratios are:

CC	CD	CE	CF	CG	CA	CB	CC_1
1/1	9/8	5/4	4/3	3/2	5/3	15/8	2/1

One important aspect of the conversion of musical intervals into numerical ratios is that the addition of intervals takes the mathematical form of the multiplication of their ratios:

C - E	+ E - A	= C - A
major third	+ perfect fourth =	major sixth
5/4	x 4/3	= 5/3

Conversely, the deduction of intervals will have the form of division with the corresponding ratio.

Wittkower based his analysis on the study of eight of forty-four plans in the *Four Books*. While the analysis made a great impression on his contemporaries, ultimately the problem remained that it was derived from a limited number of plans.

In 1982, Deborah Howard and Malcolm Longair provided an extensive statistical study that explored the applicability of Wittkower's interpretation to all of the plans in the second book of the *Four Books*. Howard and Longair developed two theoretical models to test the analysis. The more direct method was to establish the number of ratios with harmonic interpretation in the total number of room length/width ratios in the plans. The starting point of this approach was a list of all rooms whose dimensions Palladio has specified, a list similar to Table 1 in Appendix A. There are 153 ratios of which 89 correspond to the ratios of Palladio's list of preferred ratios. The number of ratios that have harmonic explanation is only slightly higher. It is between 98 and 103, depending on what is considered an acceptable approximation for the major second (a full tone interval, which can be 10/9 or 9/8, depending on the tuning system).

Howard and Longair developed a second model based on a list of numbers that they called harmonic numbers: all numbers from 1 to 100 that can be made by multiplying 2, 3, and 5. Whichever two numbers from this list are chosen, their ratio will be the numerical expression of a musical interval. Even a ratio such as 25/24 is a kind of semitone.[27] The idea was to establish the presence of these harmonic numbers (taken as dimensions of rooms in Vicentine feet) in the plans in the *Four Books*.

All ratios between harmonic numbers stand for musical ratios, but some of the musical ratios on which Wittkower relied are not multiples of 2, 3, and 5. For instance, a room with the ratio 28/14 would have a ratio that corresponds to an octave but neither 28 nor 14 can be produced by the multiplication of 2, 3, and 5 only. In other words, Howard and Longair's list of harmonic numbers does not define all harmonic ratios that can be found in Palladio's plans. Nevertheless, the number of rooms that would be excluded is minimal, and this problem can be disregarded.

Another problem—but, at the same time, an advantage—of the approach based on harmonic numbers is that, strictly speaking, only ratios and not individual numbers can be harmonic. A list of the dimensions on a plan which are also harmonic numbers will establish the presence of musical proportions between any two dimensions on the building but disregard the proportions between room lengths and widths. If one horizontal dimension in every room of a building is a harmonic number, these dimensions will all stand in some ratios that can be expressed as musical intervals. In this case, it is still possible that no individual room length/width ratios will correspond to musical intervals.

The model based on harmonic numbers addresses the possibility of interpreting the relationship between any two or more dimensions in a plan in musical terms. What may appear to be the weakness of the model is actually its strength. It answers the question of whether Palladio may have tried to adjust proportions between the dimensions of different rooms so that their ratios were harmonic. This means that the method based on harmonic numbers accounts for any case where two dimensions of a building stand in a harmonic ratio, not only the case of the dimensions of the same room. In the case of the Villa Barbaro, for instance, this model is better suited to Wittkower's interpretative approach (see page 82). In his analysis of this villa, Wittkower noted that the rooms were organized in groups of three so that their widths (related as 16/12/16, 20/10/20, 9/18/9) correspond to harmonic ratios 4/3/4, 2/1/2, and 1/2/1. Wittkower's interpretation in this case targeted ratios between the widths of different rooms and not individual room length/width ratios.

Howard and Longair found that of 365 numbers appearing in the plans of the *Four Books*, 239 are harmonic and 126 are not, which means that harmonic numbers make 65.5 percent of all dimensions that appear in plans (almost 70 percent if we look only at the main blocks of buildings); if these numbers were chosen randomly, only 45 percent would be harmonic.[28] However, this statistic does not confirm Wittkower's thesis, since it does not prove that Palladio chose certain numerical ratios because of their musical interpretation. All ratios from the list of Palladio's preferred length/width ratios except $\sqrt{2}/1$ have a musical interpretation within the Pythagorean or Just tuning system. This list could have been developed empirically (as Palladio says himself) or by calculating means between ratios 1/1 and 2/1 (as March suggested). To prove Wittkower's thesis, it would be necessary to show that among the ratios Palladio used, there are many that could be explained as musical ratios but are not among his preferred ratios. However, we have seen that in the list of all length/width ratios from the *Four Books*, 89 ratios out of 153 correspond to the ratios from Palladio's list of preferred ratios, while 98 can have musical interpretation—this difference is not sufficient to suggest that harmonic interpretation can substantially change the understanding of Palladio's proportional theory. Similarly, the list of harmonic numbers is, ultimately, only the list of all numbers between 1 and 100 that are the products of 2, 3, and 5. There is no proof that Palladio would have understood such a list as musical. Conversely, Palladio could have intentionally used harmonic numbers to ensure that he was using his preferred ratios, all of which (except $\sqrt{2}/1$) contain the numbers 2, 3, and 5. As Howard and Longair noted, "It seems entirely feasible that Palladio could have developed a system of proportion based upon harmonic numbers simply because more often than not he would be able to use room dimensions corresponding to his preferred ratios."[29] Howard and Longair made two additional points in favor of the view that Palladio relied on his list rather than on harmonic proportions in determining room length/width ratios. Had he relied on harmonic proportions, then ratios 6/5 or 5/4 (which correspond to musical intervals) should appear as frequently as 4/3 or 5/3. But there are only two examples of 6/5 and five examples of 5/3, compared with eight of 4/3 and seventeen of 3/2. Similarly, there should be ratios corresponding to intervals CD or CB, but there are no rooms with proportions of 9/8 or 15/8.

Wittkower's harmonic interpretation of length/width ratios does not explain Palladio's proportional procedures more effectively than the assumption that Palladio relied on the ratios from his preferred list. Palladio himself said that he used the ratios from his list, and he never mentioned musical considerations as his motive. He was content to say that he developed his list of preferred ratios empirically.

HARMONIC INTERPRETATION OF INCOMMENSURABLE RATIOS

Statistically speaking, the case for Wittkower's approach is unresolved. From the purely interpretative point of view, for Wittkower's thesis to be correct, it would be necessary to establish that the preferred ratios were selected because of their musical interpretation. As mentioned, all except one ($\sqrt{2}/1$) have a musical interpretation in the context of the Just and Pythagorean tuning systems. If it were possible to show that $\sqrt{2}/1$ was a musical interval, then one could argue that all preferred ratios have a musical interpretation and could have been chosen for that reason. When commenting on the problematic status of $\sqrt{2}/1$ in the *Four Books*, Wittkower remarked that when Alberti and Serlio gave lists of preferred room length/width ratios, they "both mention the incommensurability of the diagonal of the square, while Palladio, with his usual restraint, does not make the point."[30] Wittkower thought that $\sqrt{2}/1$ came directly from Vitruvius, where its occurrence could be "the residue of the Greek architectural theory of proportion, all but forgotten in Roman times."

In fact, it is not impossible to provide a musical interpretation of $\sqrt{2}/1$. While in both Pythagorean and Just tuning, semitones are not equal, the idea of equal temperament, which is used in modern keyboard instruments, is to make them equal. The result of equal temperament is that a sharp tone becomes equal to the flat higher one. For instance, C sharp becomes identical to D flat. This implies dividing the whole-tone interval into two equal parts and assuming that there are twelve equal semitones in a scale. If semitones are to be equal and make an octave when added to each other, the ratio corresponding to an equal temperament semitone must be a number which, when multiplied twelve times by itself, gives 2. The ratio of an octave is 2/1 and, as explained, the addition of intervals corresponds to the multiplication of their ratios. In modern mathematical notation, this interval is expressed as $\sqrt[12]{2}/1$.

A complete major equally tempered scale starting from C has the following intervals:

CD	CE	CF	CG	CA	CB	CC_1
$(\sqrt[12]{2})^2/1$	$(\sqrt[12]{2})^4/1$	$(\sqrt[12]{2})^5/1$	$(\sqrt[12]{2})^7/1$	$(\sqrt[12]{2})^9/1$	$(\sqrt[12]{2})^{11}/1$	$(\sqrt[12]{2})^{12}/1$

A tritone CF# is $(\sqrt[12]{2})^6/1 = \sqrt{2}/1$, i.e., the square diagonal-to-side ratio. Our modern mathematical notation simplifies operations involving irrational numbers, but during the Renaissance, there was no such notation available. The expression of ratios of equal temperament mathematically was a significant problem, and irrational ratios of equal temperament, awkward-looking even in modern notation, were a considerable challenge for Renaissance instrument builders. By the middle of the sixteenth century, equal temperament was accepted in tuning lutes, viols, and fretted instruments, but not in the construction of keyboard instruments.[31] However, instruments using equal temperament had to be tuned by ear. Exact mathematical calculation for equal temperament string lengths became possible only after logarithms were invented in 1614, and it seems that they were not used by the manufacturers of musical instruments until the end of the seventeenth century.[32] The ratio corresponding to the augmented fourth (CF sharp) is the easiest one to express in geometrical terms, since $\sqrt{2}$ is the diagonal-to-side ratio of a square.

It would be possible also to claim that $\sqrt{2}/1$ was not the only ratio of equal temperament Palladio used. The two ratios related to the Delian problem ($\sqrt[3]{2}/1$ and $\sqrt[3]{2^2}/1$) correspond to the ratios of equal temperament: $\sqrt[3]{2}/1$ is CE, and $\sqrt[3]{2^2}/1$ is CG sharp. Thus, there is an important connection between equal temperament and the problems of one and two mean proportionals.

Historically, the first musical theorist to advocate equal temperament was Aristoxenus of Tarentum, a pupil of Aristotle and the authority Vitruvius chose for the discussion of music in Book Five of *De architectura*. Aristoxenus explicitly formulated the idea of dividing the whole-tone interval into two equal parts. This would entail finding the geometrical mean between the lengths of two strings that produce a whole tone. But if the whole-tone interval is taken to correspond to the ratio of 9/8, since the second root of this ratio is irrational, the exact value of a semitone cannot be expressed as a ratio between two whole numbers. Because of this argument, Aristoxenus's idea was dismissed by most ancient authors, including Ptolemy, Theon of Smyrna, and even Euclid himself, assuming he was truly the author of the *Sectio Canonis*.[33] Among Renaissance musical theorists who dismissed it for the same reason were Gaffurio and Vicentino,[34] and we shall see that Barbaro agreed with them. Had Palladio supported the idea of equal temperament, he would have done so against the mainstream of musical theory of his time.[35]

At the same time, the geometrical solution to the problem of dividing a single tone was well known, since it was identical to the problem of finding one-mean proportional between the strings, which defines the whole tone interval. As mentioned earlier, the solution of this problem was presented in Euclid's *Elements* (see page 68). It became known to musical theorists after the publication of Campanus's translation in 1492.[36] In 1496, Lefevre d'Etaples suggested using this theorem from Euclid in order to discover the mean between two string lengths; he was followed by Schreiber of Erfurt in 1518, and Ludovico Fogliano suggested using the same method to divide the syntonic comma.[37] The dismissal of the possibility of dividing a whole tone into two equal halves in spite of the knowledge of the geometrical method for achieving it cannot be explained without taking into account that in the Pythagorean tradition audible music was only a manifestation of the numeric relationships that pervaded the universe. Even if a musical problem could be solved geometrically, the solution would not be accepted unless it could be expressed as a ratio of whole numbers.

The method of finding one geometrical mean (i.e., one mean proportional) allows any musical interval to be divided into two equal parts. In order to divide an octave into twelve equal semitones, one must first divide it into three equal intervals (CE, EG#, and G#C). Further division can be completed using the geometrical method of solving one mean proportional, but for this first step, we need to solve the problem of two mean proportionals. Zarlino proposed the use of the mesolabium in order to resolve equal temperament in

1558, and he was the first to grasp the relationship between the Delian problem and the geometrical solution of equal temperament.[38] This was two years after Barbaro described the mesolabium in his commentary on Vitruvius, but Zarlino mentions Giorgio Valla and not Barbaro as his source.[39]

The fact that Zarlino was the first Renaissance author to treat equal temperament as a problem related to Delian cubes makes it particularly unlikely that Palladio could have seen musical intervals in ratios such as $\sqrt{2}/1$, $\sqrt[3]{2}/1$ and $\sqrt[3]{2^2}/1$. The ratios of the Delian cube appear in his very early buildings, such as Villa Caldogno and Villa Forni. Ascribing musical intentions to Palladio in these cases would credit him with a major discovery in musical theory and suggest that he had understood the relationship between the Delian problem and equal temperament ten or fifteen years before Zarlino.

DANIELE BARBARO AND EQUAL TEMPERAMENT

Daniele Barbaro argued the theoretical impossibility of equal temperament in his commentary on Vitruvius because it implied relying on incommensurable ratios. In the commentary on Book Five, he criticized Vitruvius's reliance on Aristoxenus, in part because of the latter's advocacy of equal temperament.[40] Barbaro emphasized the impossibility of equal temperament by explaining that an octave corresponds to the ratio of 2/1, and since 2 is not a square of any whole number, it cannot be divided into two equal musical intervals.[41] In other words, he did not think that $\sqrt{2}/1$ stood for a musical interval.

Palladio would have taken Barbaro's opinion about music seriously, and he must have known about his opposition to the idea of equal temperament. There is no documentation of Palladio's views about equal temperament (or any kind of musical theory, for that matter), but he would have learned from Barbaro that the entire musical theory of his time and of the ancients was opposed to the idea. These are very strong reasons against the theory that Palladio thought about $\sqrt{2}/1$ as a ratio of equal temperament.

There is another compelling reason to believe that Barbaro—and Palladio with him—failed to grasp the relationship between $\sqrt{2}/1$ and equal temperament. In the commentary on Book Nine, when Barbaro discussed Vitruvius's explanation of the incommensurability of the square diagonal-to-side ratio, he came up with a startling statement:

> It is possible to find the square diagonal using numbers, but it is necessary to use fractions . . . Calculate the sum of the squares of the lengths of the two sides of the square and then calculate the square root of this sum. This will give the length of the diagonal. Let *abcd* be a square, each side of which is 5 feet. Multiply *ab* by itself, i.e., five times five makes twenty-five— and do the same with *bc*, which will also make 25. Added to the previous 25 it will give the sum 50. The square root of 50 is $7^1/_{14}$, and this will be the length of the diagonal.[42]

It is astonishing that Barbaro could have made this mistake. If d is the length of the diagonal of a square, and a is the side, then, indeed according to Pythagorean theorem:

$$d^2 = a^2 + a^2$$

or:

$$d = \sqrt{(a^2 + a^2)}$$

But Barbaro failed to see that from this it follows that:

$$d = \sqrt{2a^2} = a\sqrt{2}$$

This clearly shows that the ratio between the diagonal and the side is $\sqrt{2}$ and, therefore, the calculation he proposed can only yield an approximation. It appears that Barbaro was genuinely unaware of the mathematical (geometrical) implications of his critique of equal temperament. He failed to recognize that the ratio that divides an octave into two equal parts and the ratio between the diagonal and the side of a square were the same ratio.

It is hard to imagine that Barbaro and Palladio could have completed the commentary on Vitruvius without discussing the status of $\sqrt{2}/1$. Defined as the square diagonal-to-side ratio, it appears in Vitruvius's Book Six (a preferred atrium length/width ratio); expressed as $\sqrt{2}/1$, it appears in Vitruvius's Book Nine as an example of an incommensurable ratio. Barbaro explained the impossibility of equal temperament precisely by taking $\sqrt{2}/1$ as the example. If the use of musical ratios was a central principle of Palladio's architecture, and if it included the use of ratios derived from equal temperament, it makes little sense to argue that the possibility of a musical interpretation of $\sqrt{2}/1$ was a minor issue that Palladio and Barbaro failed to discuss. Had Palladio considered the square diagonal-to-side ratio as a musical ratio of equal temperament, Barbaro would have realized its connection with equal temperament and would have revised the text where the commensurability of $\sqrt{2}/1$ is incorrectly affirmed. Had this discussion taken place after 1556, at least the error would not have been repeated in the 1567 editions.[43] In other words, $\sqrt{2}/1$ was certainly not included in Palladio's list of preferred ratios because of its musical connotations.

CHROMATICISM

Wittkower's account of Renaissance musical theory failed to take into consideration the important debate on chromaticism to which Barbaro paid great attention in the commentary on Vitruvius. Barbaro's extensive commentary on the chapter on music in Vitruvius's Book Five is a small treatise in its own right—at least it seems to have been treated as such by his contemporaries and was occasionally transcribed as an independent manuscript.[44] This is the musical theory Palladio was surely acquainted with. If he had any musical interests, it is hard to imagine that he would not have read the section on music in the commentary on which he collaborated. At the same time, an important aspect of Barbaro's account of musical theory is his staunch support for musical chromaticism.

Musical chromaticism provides a particularly wide range of ratios between 1/1 and 1.2/1; i.e., it uses a great diversity of quarter-tone, semitone, and whole-tone ratios. At the same time, among the room length/width ratios in the plans in the *Four Books* (see Appendix C) there is a substantial number of ratios between 1/1 and

1.2/1 which could not have been explained by the kind of musical theory Wittkower proposed. There are sixteen rooms with ratios which are smaller than 1.2/1. Three of these ratios correspond to the smaller whole-tone ratio of the Just tuning (10/9 or 1.11111); the bigger whole-tone ratio of Just tuning (9/8), which is also the whole-tone ratio of Pythagorean tuning, does not appear among these ratios at all. As for the remaining thirteen ratios, it would be hard to claim that they may have a musical interpretation according to the kind of musical theory Wittkower presented. If these ratios could be explained by musical chromaticism, this would substantially increase the number of ratios in Palladio's plans that harmonic theory could explain. If not, it would mean that Palladio used a large number of room length/width ratios in the range for which chromatic theory provided a number of close alternatives, and while he knew about the theory, he never bothered to apply it or to adjust the ratios he used to chromaticism.

The musical system Vitruvius discussed (which was common both in antiquity and during the Renaissance) is the so-called Greater Perfect System, which worked with chains of tetrachords. Tetrachords span the interval of a perfect fourth, and are subdivided by two tones into three smaller intervals. There are three ways (also called genera) this division can be done: diatonic, chromatic, and enharmonic. A perfect fourth normally consists of two whole tones and a semitone; depending on the genus, it can be divided in the following ways:

Diatonic:	semitone	tone	tone
Chromatic:	semitone	semitone	trisemitone (tone-and-a-half)
Enharmonic:	diesis	diesis	ditone

A *diesis* is a quarter of a tone; a *ditone* is a double whole tone. The diatonic resembles our contemporary scales, since scales with intervals like *diesis* or tone-and-a-half are not in use today.

In the commentary on Vitruvius Barbaro explained that the diatonic is "severe, firm, and constant" and it "shows masculine habits and behavior," whereas the chromatic is "soft and sad." He warned that the *scala* in which the instrument is going to be tuned has to be chosen according to the appropriateness of the genus, and criticized those who think that everything can be achieved by only using the diatonic genus.[45] In saying this, Barbaro joined in a major polemic of sixteenth-century musical theory. So far as we can reconstruct, Renaissance musical practice was predominantly diatonic, with occasional use of other genera.[46] The debate about the use of chromatic and enharmonic *genera* escalated in the middle of the sixteenth century. Two major books that discussed it—Vicentino's *L'antica musica* and Zarlino's *Istitutioni*—were published, respectively, in 1555 and 1558.

The revival of interest in the genera of the ancients was largely the work of Nicola Vicentino. Born in Vicenza in 1511, he studied under Willaert in Venice (Willaert was also Zarlino's teacher) before leaving for Rome in 1549. He returned to Vicenza in 1563 as chapel master in the cathedral and died two years later in Milan, in the service of Cardinal Borromeo.[47] Contacts with Palladio are likely, but not documented. During the 1550s, Vicentino was in the service of Hipolito d'Este, Cardinal of Ferrara, to whom Barbaro dedicated his commentary on Vitruvius. In 1554, Barbaro, who was probably in Rome with Palladio, met the Cardinal and saw the plans for the Villa d'Este at Tivoli.[48] Vicentino's book, *L'antica musica ridotta alla moderna pratica*, advocated the revival of musical chromaticism. This was not an easy project, considering the additional training and effort this kind of music required from singers. Macrobius wrote that in late antiquity the chromatic and enharmonic genera were completely out of use, the former because it "induces voluptuousness" and the latter because of its extreme difficulty.[49] A few centuries before Macrobius, Ptolemy remarked that the diatonic was generally preferred.[50]

During the 1560s, Vicentino organized public concerts of enharmonic and chromatic music. He had a number of disciples, but soon after his death, the whole experiment was forgotten. In her study about chromaticism in Renaissance musical theory, Karol Berger cites Vincenzo Galilei (the father of Galileo), who related that after Vicentino's death everyone lost interest in chromaticism. Galilei attended a number of performances and reported that the music required an exceptional effort from the singers, who had always to be carefully accompanied by a suitable instrument. Galilei's impression was that all attempts to revive the enharmonic and chromatic genera in modern times were unsuccessful.

Nevertheless, chromaticism supplies a large number of ratios that correspond to different versions of a diesis, semitone, and whole tone. It thus provides a substantial number of ratios which can serve as potential interpretations of Palladio's ratios smaller than 1.2/1. The result is, on the whole, discouraging: if we do not count ratios corresponding to 10/9 (which, as mentioned, could have a harmonic interpretation independent of chromaticism), only three ratios from Palladio's room length/ width ratios may have some kind of harmonic interpretation within the chromaticist system (see Appendix C). Some of the room ratios may seem to approximate, for up to two decimal points, the ratios of the chromaticist system. In fact, if we look at the first two decimal points only, then only ratios starting with 1.13/1, 1.15/1 and 1.17/1 will *not* have a chromaticist interpretation. However, the point is not so much that a higher degree of precision should be required in order to claim that the ratios of the chromaticist system were used, but that the intervals of the chromaticist system are all simple ratios between whole numbers, easy to apply in the architectural design process, and that there is simply no need to approximate them. Palladio could easily have applied the *exact* ratios of the chromaticist system by minimal adjustments of room lengths and widths had he wanted to.

While Palladio must have known about the chromaticism debate through his collaboration with Barbaro, and while he used a significant number of room length/width ratios which could have easily been adjusted to chromaticism, he never bothered to do this.

ORNAMENTS AND HARMONIES

Wittkower's harmonic interpretation, right or wrong, does not expand the understanding of Palladio's design procedures. It explains few more room length/width ratios than those included on the preferred list, and it does not provide the interpretation of the irrational ratios such as √2/1 or √3/1. It is certainly possible that

Palladio may have, on occasion, been requested by an individual patron to apply certain ratios because of their role in musical theory, but there are no documents confirming this and it is far from certain that his design decisions were systematically motivated by musical concerns. Nevertheless, although Wittkower's thesis fails to provide any relevant insights into Palladio's design procedures, it is still a very important reconstruction of a narrative that was occasionally attached to architectural works in the Renaissance. While it is uncertain that Palladio derived his design procedures from such a narrative, this is certainly the way the aesthetic properties of his buildings would have been explained by the contemporary intelligentsia.

It is, in fact, easy to see why a musical paradigm could not have been one of the determining principles of Palladio's designs. The architectural design process is not reducible simply to the determination of room length/width ratios. It would have been very difficult for Palladio to derive his designs solely from calculations based on the belief in harmonic ratios—just as it was impossible to apply the preferred ratios consistently. In his mature works, the use of the orders was decisive for the totality of Palladio's spatial compositions. Renaissance architectural treatises contain extensive discussions of proportions, but most of this material (sometimes all of it) pertains to the proportioning of the classical orders. The theory of the classical orders is the proportional theory that interested Renaissance architects the most.

The immense popularity of Wittkower's thesis over the past fifty years was actually based on an approach that would be unacceptable to Palladio. Orders and ornaments were important for Palladio and for Renaissance architects in general. Wittkower argued that the principles of Renaissance architecture were limited to rules for establishing proportions between bare walls, and there was a strong correlation between Wittkower's interpretation of Renaissance architecture and the design approach advocated by the Modernist movement. By arguing that the orders were irrelevant in Renaissance design, Wittkower provided important theoretical support for the Modernist movement. Wittkower's interpretation declared that the formal and visual differences between Renaissance and Modernist architecture (e.g., the use of ornamentation) were irrelevant at the very moment when Modernist architects sought to legitimize the suppression of ornament. In the background of both the rise of Modernism and the great attention Wittkower's book received stood the commercial interests of the architectural profession in the late 1940s and early 1950s. In the years after World War II, when architectural offices were overwhelmed with commissions, the switch to Modernist design principles, which eliminated the labor of drafting ornamented facades, was economically by far the most viable option. Wittkower's book, with its claim that what matters is the narrative about proportions, and not what the building looks like, provided a theoretical justification for this move.[51] This is particularly evident from the great attention paid to Colin Rowe's article "The Mathematics of the Ideal Villa," which came out in the late 1940s. The article claimed to have established proportional similarities between Le Corbusier's villa at Garches and Palladio's Villa Foscari. However, an illustration from the article shows how different the two buildings are, whatever the "fundamental relationship" Rowe claimed to have discovered (2-1). Indeed, the similarities he identified are meager and pertain only to the proportions of the matrix of the structural elements. The proportions within structural matrix are the same in one direction and similar (but not the same) in another. It is obvious that the similarity of the proportions of the structural grid cannot outweigh the visual and formal differences between these buildings, such as ornamentation of facades or the composition of internal spaces. Rowe's attempt to compare different elements of these two buildings ultimately reads as a list of differences between them. But, in spite of all this, the article has been cited repeatedly as a study showing similarities, or even providing "a careful geometrical proof" of those similarities.[52] That the article was read as describing similarities shows not only the need of the Modernist movement to legitimize itself in the late 1940s and early 1950s but also the readiness to suppress the awareness of the obvious formal and visual differences in order to promote a specific ideological position, which, in its turn, provided justification for the radical commercialization of the profession.

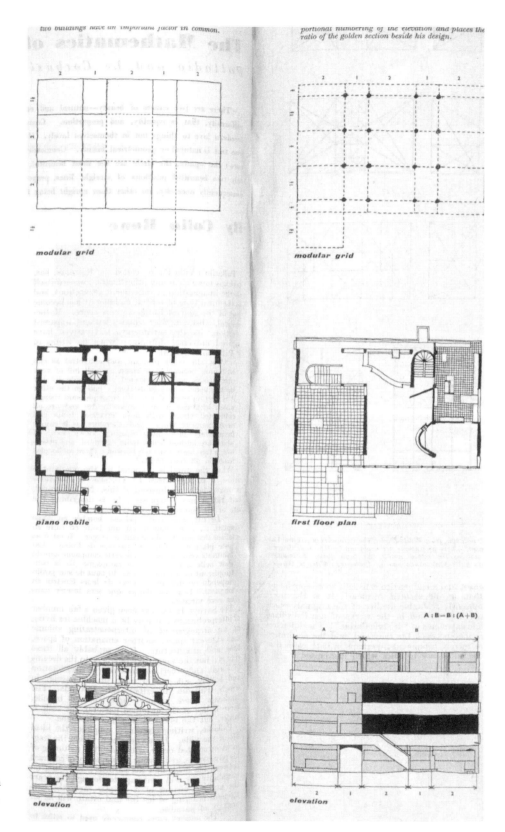

2-1 Colin Rowe's comparative analysis of Villa Foscari and Le Corbusier's villa in Garches. *CCA, WA 766, vol. 101, pp. 102–103*

Portico colonnade
on the Rotonda.

CHAPTER III

CLASSICAL ORDERS

THE THEORY OF THE CLASSICAL ORDERS is the basis of Renaissance architectural theory. All Renaissance architectural treatises explain how to make the Tuscan, Doric, Ionic, Corinthian, or Composite orders. The orders played a central role in Palladio's most important works, especially after 1550; their systematic use actually heralded what is known today as Palladio's mature style. At the same time, his use of the orders diverged from common Renaissance practice. In Palladio's work, the orders determined the overall planning of a building, not just the design of the facade.

The central document for the study of Palladio's theory of the classical orders is chapters 12 through 20 of the first of the *Four Books*. The very formulation of the canon of the five orders—the idea that there are five of them and that they form a coherent system—was the work of Palladio's generation of architects and theorists, and this concept has had a huge impact on subsequent generations of architects. It is not surprising that Palladio's and Vignola's formulations of the canon are the most influential architectural texts inherited from the Renaissance; they were the result of at least a century of effort by Renaissance architects to understand and learn, from Roman ruins and from Vitruvius's descriptions, the correct way to work with the ornaments the ancient Romans and Greeks used in their buildings.[1] Generations of architects before Palladio and Vignola had labored to achieve this understanding. The illustrations of early printed books on architecture, such as Fra

Giocondo's edition of Vitruvius, clearly show the challenges Renaissance architects faced (3-1). By the time Palladio and Vignola entered the profession, the architectural community had accumulated a substantial body of knowledge from measuring and surveying Roman ruins. Early in their careers, Palladio and Vignola spent much time studying Roman remains. The tradition of systematic scholarly work on Vitruvius was also well established. Daniele Barbaro's commentary was the culmination of at least a century of work by Renaissance scholars to understand the only architectural treatise preserved from classical antiquity. The reconstruction of Roman methods of using the classical orders, as described by Vitruvius in Books Three and Four, represented a substantial part of Barbaro's effort.[2] The historical significance of Barbaro's explanation of the theory of the five orders, as well as many other complex segments of *De architectura*, cannot be overemphasized. His analysis provided answers for many problems that had made the reading of Vitruvius so difficult for generations of architects. Modern scholars have noted that Barbaro's translation was the first based on a full understanding of the Latin text.[3] His account of the five orders constitutes a treatise in its own right; within the commentary, it is organized into a separate block of text.[4] Scholarship after Barbaro has provided an abundance of new archaeological data, but very few new interpretations beyond Barbaro's account of what Vitruvius said about the use of the orders.

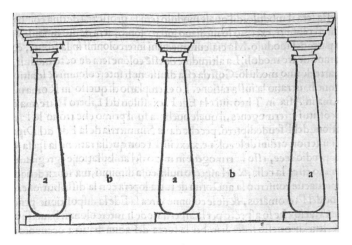

3-1 Doric order in Fra Giocondo's *Vitruvius*. *CCA, cage M NA44. V848 (W3246), p. 26*

Unlike their predecessors, both Vignola and Palladio formulated their theories after the publication of Barbaro's commentary with full confidence in the accuracy of his explanation of Vitruvius. They could both afford to step boldly away from the Vitruvian tradition, complete the canon where Vitruvius had left it incomplete, and make the changes and adjustments that they thought necessary.

THE CONCEPT OF *ORDINE* IN PALLADIO AND VIGNOLA

Vitruvius did not talk about the five orders. He used the terms *mores* and *genera* in discussing what we call orders today and the word *ordinatio* to describe the balanced adjustment of details.[5] It is commonly thought that it was Raphael who first applied the word *ordine* in the modern sense. The sixteenth-century commentators used many other terms—*generationi, opere, specie, genera* (Cesariano)[6] and *maniere, ragioni,* or *opere* (Barbaro).[7] Serlio referred to the Doric, Ionic, Corinthian, and Composite as *ordini*; for the Tuscan he generally used *opera*, although he called it *ordine* occasionally[8] (3-2). Vignola was the first to use the term *ordine* systematically for all five orders and that is the usage Palladio adopted.

However, there is a great disparity between the concept of the classical orders in Vignola's *Canon of the Five Orders* and the one Palladio formulated in the *Four Books*. The principal difference lies in the way the elements of the orders—especially columns, engaged columns, and pilasters—relate to the internal structure and planning of a building. For Vignola, the orders are applied to the facade after the basic dimensions have been determined. The first step is to divide the height of the building into a prescribed number of parts to determine the size of the module, which, in turn, determines the size and disposition of all other elements of the order. For example, to apply the Doric order, the height of the facade is divided into 20 parts, one of which will be the module. The height of the architrave will then be 1 module, the frieze $1\frac{1}{2}$ modules, the distance between columns $5\frac{1}{2}$ modules, and so on. If the Ionic order is used on the facade, the module is determined by dividing the total height of the building into $22\frac{1}{2}$ parts, Corinthian 25 parts, and so on. The implication is that the building's dimensions (and especially its height) are fixed before the orders are applied. The method invites the use of the colossal orders, where the columns rise the full height of the facade and do not express the division of the building into stories.

Vignola's approach is not without its problems. The use of a module to determine the column diameter and the size of intercolumniations assumes that the total length of the facade consists of a whole number of intercolumniation widths plus the corresponding number of column diameters. Vignola did not explain what happens when the length of the facade cannot be divided according to this formula. Presumably, this is where the architect's invention must come into play, by doubling corner columns, for example.

Palladio's concept of *ordine* is different from Vignola's. Palladio was certainly aware of the way Vignola (and Serlio before him) used the term *ordine*, but he also knew that the word was the Italian equivalent of *ordinatio*, which, according to Barbaro, pertained to the quantitative properties of architecture—"the disposition of even and odd, equal and unequal parts," as Barbaro put it.[9] Barbaro explained the concept with the example of a temple with four columns in

3-2 The system of
orders according to
Sebastiano Serlio. *CCA,
cage NA 44. S485 (w193),
livre 4, p. 127*

3-3 Leon Battista Alberti's San Andrea (Mantua).

the front: if the column diameter is taken as the module and if the central intercolumniation of such a temple is 3 modules, while the side intercolumniations are 2¹/₄ modules, then the total facade will make 11¹/₂ modules. This type of mathematical analysis of spatial properties was *ordine* for Barbaro, whereas he defined proportion as the ratio of the sizes of individual parts. On this basis, *ordine* encompassed the organization of parts by size throughout the entire building.

The term *ordine*, for Palladio, combined both Barbaro's and Vignola's interpretations. Like Vignola, Palladio referred to the Tuscan, Doric, Ionic, Corinthian, and Composite as *ordini*. However, he also adopted Barbaro's usage. He identified the Vitruvian systems of column dispositions with the orders, expanding this notion to cover the position of all structural elements within a building. Vitruvius listed five kinds of intercolumniation spacing: *araeostylos* (more than 3 column diameters), *diastylos* (3 diameters) *eustylos* (2¹/₄ diameters), *sistylos* (2 diameters) and *picnostilos* (1¹/₄ diameters). In the description of the orders in the *Four Books*, Palladio identified these five kinds of intercolumniations with the five orders: the Tuscan order, having wooden beams, can have intercolumniations wider than three column diameters; the Doric corresponds to diastylos, the Ionic to eustylos, the Corinthian to sistylos, and the Composite to picnostylos.[10] This identification of *ordine* in Barbaro's sense with the use advocated by Serlio and Vignola was Palladio's original theoretical move. Barbaro would probably have disagreed with this interpretation, or at least he would have pointed out that the use of the term *ordine* in the sense of Doric, Ionic, and

INTERCOLUMNATION TYPES	DISTANCE BETWEEN COLUMNS	APPROPRIATE COLUMN HEIGHTS (VITRUVIUS)	PALLADIO	APPROPRIATE ORDER IN PALLADIO'S VIEW	INTERCOLUMNATION FOR THESE ORDERS ACCORDING TO VIGNOLA
ARAESTYLOS	More than 3D	8D	7D	Tuscan	2.33D
DIASTYLOS	3D	8¹/₂D	7¹/₂-8D	Doric	2.75D
EUSTYLOS	2¹/₄D	8¹/₂D	9D	Ionic	2.25D
SISTYLOS	2D	9¹/₂D	9¹/₂D	Corinthian	2.33D
PICNOSTYLOS	1¹/₄D	10D	10D	Composite	2.33D

D is the lower-column diameter.

Corinthian contradicted Vitruvius's designation of column height/diameter ratios appropriate for individual intercolumniation types.[11] To formulate the concept of *ordine* as he proposed it, Palladio had to dismiss the column-height-to-lower-diameter ratios which Vitruvius had prescribed for individual intercolumniation types.[12] The table opposite shows the problem clearly.

Palladio's concept was a very radical theoretical move because it implied that the choice of the order not only determines the placement of ornament of the facade but also affects the composition of the entire building. Vignola reduced the use of the orders to the ornamentation of buildings, but for Palladio, they constituted the building's spatial system.

PALLADIO AND FACADE INTERCOLUMNIATIONS: A HISTORICAL SURVEY

The principal problem of Renaissance architecture before Palladio and Vignola was the lack of discipline in applying engaged columns and pilasters on the facade. For more than a century, architects had ignored Vitruvian precepts for intercolumniations and any other systematic reasoning about them. Vitruvius advised making intercolumniations less than three column diameters because stone entablatures broke easily if this length was exceeded. He advised using the *araeostylos* only in combination with wooden entablatures. Nevertheless, it is extremely unusual to find intercolumniations of three lower-column diameters or less on Renaissance works before Vignola and Palladio. Since they predominantly used engaged orders as ornamental representations of the columns and entablatures of Greek and Roman temples, Renaissance architects were little concerned with the structural implications of wide intercolumniations. Only the greatest among the early Renaissance architects realized that these excessively wide intercolumniations were visually disturbing. Alberti's San Andrea in Mantua, whose two side pilasters on the main facade have an intercolumniation of about 2.6 times the pilaster thickness, is a rare exception (3-3). Two other exceptions are by Bramante: both

3-4 Giuliano da Sangallo's Madonna delle Carceri (Prato).

the Tempietto and the upper-story colonnade of the cloister of Santa Maria della Pace have diameter/intercolumniation ratios of about 3/1. However, much more common was the practice, seen in Giuliano da Sangallo's Madonna delle Carceri, of simply placing pilasters in the corners of the building (3-4). In this case, it is clearly impossible that the ornaments represent a structurally credible composition of elements. The pilasters and entablatures frame the facade, but the span between

101

3-5 Giovanni Maria Falconetto's Porta Savonarola (Padua). *CISA, F0010094*

3-6 Giovanni Maria Falconetto's Porta San Giovanni (Padua). *CISA, F0010098*

3-7 Michele Sanmicheli's
Palazzo Canossa (Verona).
CISA, F0012542

3-8 Villa Trissino
(Cricoli). *CISA, F0006675*

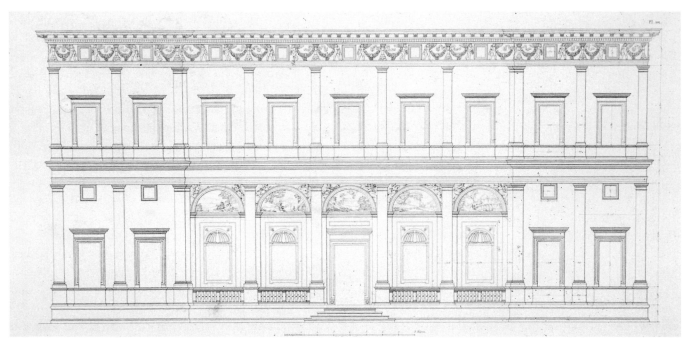

3-9 Drawing of the Farnesina in Rome by Letarouilly.
CCA, M NA44.L645.A63 1868a, vol.1, pl. 101

3-10 Giacomo Verda's Bishop's Palace (Vicenza).

columns is visually uncomfortable. The orders on most of the contemporary works the young Palladio could have seen near Vicenza had intercolumniations that far exceeded the Vitruvian recommendations. Giovanni Maria Falconetto's Porta Savonarola in Padua had an intercolumniation-to-diameter ratio of 4.9; Porta San Giovanni in the same city, 5.8; Michele Sanmicheli's Palazzo Canossa in Verona, 4.4; the Villa Trissino, on which the young Palladio worked, had ratios of 5.7 on the ground floor (Ionic order), and 7.9 on the facade of the upper floor (Corinthian order) (3-5–3-8). Even where freestanding columns with entablatures were used, for instance by Brunelleschi on the Pazzi Chapel, the ratio is 3.5; on Pirro Ligorio's Casino of Pius IV it is 3.7. The large empty surfaces on early Renaissance facades are disturbing because the orders often failed to establish a visual rhythm. Until the time of Palladio and Vignola, columns and pilasters were placed at the points of intersection of the internal walls with the facade, with further columns added to provide a regular rhythm, as at the Farnesina in Rome, for example (3-9). This facade is symmetrical because the plan of the building is symmetrical, an approach common in the classical tradition in later centuries as well. The facade composition would be achieved by placing engaged columns and pilasters where interior walls meet the facade. This method avoids more careful work on the composition of the elevation and results in facades similar to the nineteenth-century bishop's residence in Vicenza by Giacomo Verda (3-10). It is not surprising that early Renaissance architects, who often struggled with the orders, adopted this approach.

When Palladio and Vignola defined intercolumniations, their precepts were directed against this practice, though the solutions they proposed were different. Both were aware that their contemporaries had more than one reason for making intercolumniations wider than Vitruvius had prescribed. They knew that entablatures used as ornaments cannot break and they were aware of the tradition of using wide intercolumniations inherited from Brunelleschi and his Foundling Hospital in Florence (3-11). Renaissance architects were used to larger intercolumniations than their Roman predecessors because of the early Renaissance practice of combining columns and arches, and arches allowed bigger spans to be easily achieved. There also was the reasonable intuition that a pilaster or engaged column should be placed at the intersection of the facade with the interior walls, regardless of the distance between interior walls. Finally, there was the problem of incorporating windows. If Vitruvius's rules for intercolumniations are applied, the columns become so dense that there is no space for window openings.

Vignola's program provided solutions for all these issues. His application of the orders on the facade depends on the dimensions of the facade itself and does not correspond to the position of interior walls. Columns and their entablatures cover the full height of

3-11 Filippo Brunelleschi's Foundling Palace (Florence). *CISA, F0009676*

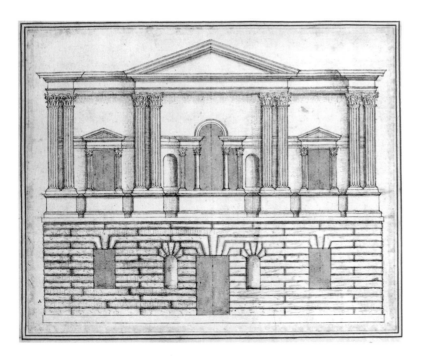

3-12 and 3-13 Facade
designs by Palladio from
the 1540s. *RIBA XVII/19*

3-14 Palladio's design drawing for Palazzo Iseppo Porto. *RIBA XVII/9r*

the facade, which implies the use of the colossal order. The colossal order also solves the window problem. Because of their height, these columns or pilasters will have sufficiently large intercolumniations to allow easy placement of windows. Vignola's departure from the idea that the facade should represent the interior of the building led to the subsequent development of the Baroque sensibility for facade composition and allowed much greater sophistication in the integration of the facade elements.

Palladio's approach to the intercolumniation problem was less radical than Vignola's, but it required much greater complexity in design. Palladio never abandoned the principle that the position of columns on the facade should express the disposition of interior bearing elements (walls and columns), but he sought to coordinate this internal disposition with his canonical intercolumniations. Table 1 in Appendix D shows the intercolumniation-to-column-diameter ratios, chronologically ordered, in Palladio's most important works. His earliest works clearly belong to the category of Renaissance buildings where the orders have been applied without concern for intercolumniation size. The intercolumniation-to-pilaster-width ratio is 5.8 on Palazzo Civena (1540), 6.6 on the Villa Gazzotti (1542), and 4.5 on the Palazzo Thiene (1542–46). Palladio's drawings from the same period also ignore the intercolumniation problem (3-12 and 3-13).

3-15 Palladio's detailed drawing of the facade of Palazzo Chiericati from the *Four Books*. *CCA, NA44.P164 (W161), c.2, p. 7*

3-16 Palladio's detailed drawing of the facade of the Palazzo Iseppo Porto. *CCA, NA44P164 (W161) c.2, p. 9*

Palazzo Iseppo Porto (1549) also belongs to this group, partly because of the form in which the intercolumniations were built and partly because these intercolumniations appear as 3.3 lower-column diameters in a preparatory drawing (3-14). During the 1540s, villas without classical orders predominate in Palladio's oeuvre: Godi (1537); Forni (1541–42); Saraceno (1545); Caldogno (1545); and Poiana (1548–49). It is tempting to interpret this as a lack of confidence in the use of the classical orders; this was, indeed, the period when Palladio spent much time studying the orders in Rome.

In 1550, a major change occurred in Palladio's treatment of intercolumniations and of the orders, first visible in the Palazzo Chiericati. The reasons for this sudden change are difficult to explain. The work on the Basilica in the late 1540s involved large arcaded openings that would not have inspired the use of smaller intercolumniations. Similarly, Palladio's collaboration with Barbaro on Vitruvius could not have been a factor since it did not begin until after the designs for the Palazzo Chiericati were completed.[13]

Whatever the reason, the Palazzo Chiericati is Palladio's first work where intercolumniations have dimensions of less than three lower-column diameters, and it is fair to say that from this point on, he avoided wider intercolumniations.[14] This discipline brought his facade designs to a level of visual refinement with which no contemporary works could compete. Twenty years later, during the preparation of the *Four Books* for publication, Palladio subtly acknowledged that his treatment of intercolumniations had changed with his work on the Palazzo Chiericati. The drawing of Chiericati clearly shows both the dimensions of columns and intercolumniations (3-15), while those of palazzi Iseppo Porto and Thiene, which both belong to the earlier period, omit this information. The illustration of Iseppo Porto (3-16) specifies the column height as 18 feet and the diameter as 2 feet. Since these are Ionic columns, the proper intercolumniation would be that of the *eustylos*, in this case 4½ feet. However, the window within this intercolumniation is itself 4 feet wide; only three inches on each side would leave no space for the ornamental surround. Similarly, in the case of the drawing of the Palazzo Thiene (3-17), Palladio actually chose to present

the corner intercolumniation, which is obviously much bigger than three column diameters. In these drawings, he conveniently refrained from stating numerically the information that did not conform to the rule stated in the first book of the treatise.

Once Palladio formed his views on intercolumniations, he applied them consistently. Just as it is impossible to find intercolumniations of less than three column diameters in his buildings before 1551, it is similarly difficult to find wider intercolumniations in the post-Chiericati works. The survey of intercolumniations in Appendix D is nevertheless not precise enough to allow us to determine the accuracy of Palladio's use of Vitruvian rules regarding intercolumniations. All that can be said is that he did not exceed three lower-column diameters and that intercolumniation-to-diameter ratios close to eustylos (2.25D) appear often. But the principle that intercolumniations should not exceed three lower-column diameters was obviously not intended for arcaded intercolumniations—the Basilica, Convento della Carità, or Loggia del Capitaniato—nor central intercolumniations enlarged in order to accommodate the main entrance. Similarly, the upper stories of his buildings typically had intercolumniations greater than three diameters: he used thinner columns which had to align with those on the ground floor, which resulted in wider intercolumniations.

In general, the exceptions to the rule occur on only a few buildings, each of which has a special status in Palladio's work and whose attribution is not absolute. In the case of the Palazzo Schio, for example, Palladio seems to have redesigned the facade of an existing building, and he placed engaged columns on the axes of interior walls (3-18). In other words, when he had to choose between applying precepts for intercolumniations and the accurate expression of internal walls on the facade, he chose the latter. Unlike Vignola, he was unwilling to abandon the representation of the internal structure on the facade. Villa Barbaro seems to be another exception, but it is generally recognized that the design was greatly influenced by Daniele Barbaro. The villa seems to have incorporated the remains of an older building, which also may have affected the position of the interior walls and consequently the placement of columns on the

3-17 Palladio's detailed drawing of the facade of the Palazzo Thiene. *CCA, NA44.P164 (W161), c.2, p. 14*

3-18 Palazzo Schio.

accordance with which the clients had started building and, as in the case of the palazzi Iseppo-Porto and Thiene, in this detailed drawing the intercolumniation size is missing. The facade as ultimately built does not even have all the intercolumniations equal.[17] On the whole, the only exception from the rule that intercolumniations should not exceed three lower-column diameters, and a difficult one to explain, is the Villa Sarego in Santa Sofia.

Palladio's mature works from the 1550s have intercolumniations of less than three column diameters. The only executed palazzo from this decade is Antonini (1556)—but by its structure and design this building rather resembles Palladio's major villas from the same years: Cornaro (1553) and Pisani (Montagnana) (1552) (see I-18 and I-19). Together with villas Badoer (1556), Chiericati (1554), and Foscari (1559–60), these works established the canonical form of the Palladian villa facade, which ultimately became emblematic of Palladio's entire output (see I-20–I-22).

Palladio's villa designs of the 1560s continued in this vein with the intercolumniations of Emo (1564) and Rotonda (1567) conforming to the paradigm of the early 1550s (see I-27 and I-28). In the latter half of the decade, Palladio received commissions for a series of palazzi in Vicenza. The remarkable aspect of these buildings—and of the Loggia del Capitaniato from about the same period—is the use of the colossal order (see I-30). Except in the case of the Villa Barbaro, Palladio's application of the colossal order follows the publication of Vignola's treatise.[18] The colossal orders on the Palazzo Valmarana (1565) and the Palazzo Porto Breganza (1570s) provided an elegant resolution of the potential conflict between the width of window openings and the canonical intercolumniation size (3-19 and 3-20).

THE IMPLICATIONS OF THE CANONICAL USE OF INTERCOLUMNIATIONS

Unlike Vignola, Palladio never rejected the idea that engaged columns and pilasters on the facade should reflect the internal disposition of structural elements.

facade.[15] We shall see that the anomalous intercolumniations in this case are actually the consequence of the atypical placement of corner columns. With respect to Palazzo Pretorio in Cividale, scholars generally agree that it was not completed according to the model Palladio provided.[16] Large intercolumniations also appear on the Palazzo Barbarano, but Palladio distanced himself from this project by presenting an alternative version of the facade with the colossal order in the *Four Books*. He also included the design of the facade, in

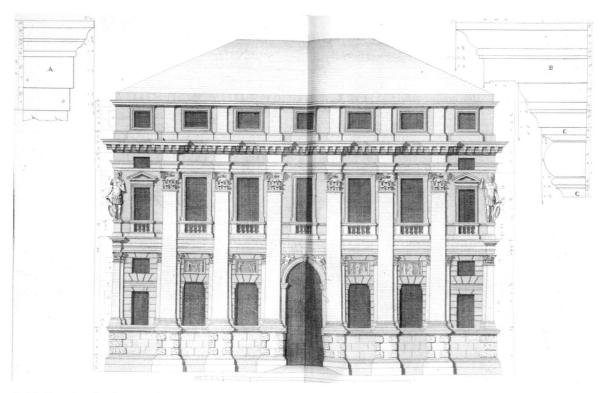

3-19 Facade of Palazzo Valmarana according to Ottavio Bertotti Scamozzi. *CCA, M7616:1, 1786 Tavola XXI*

3-20 Facade of Palazzo Porto Breganza according to Ottavio Bertotti Scamozzi. *CCA, M7616:1, 1786 Tavola XXI*

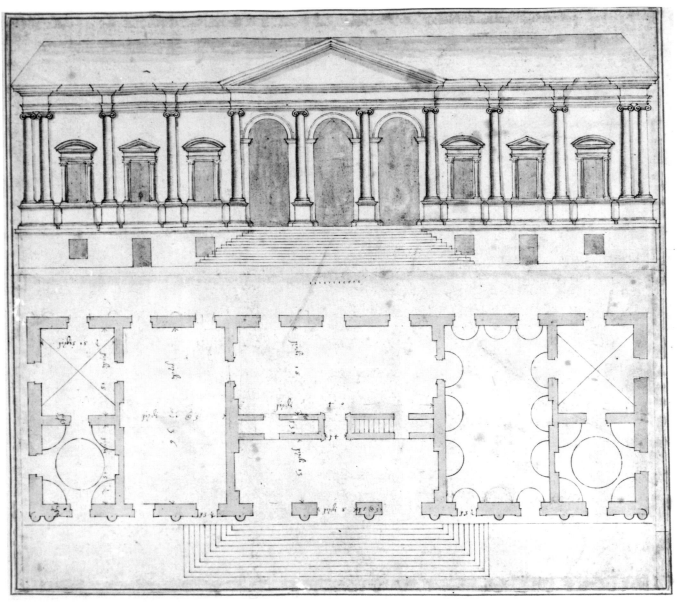

3-21 Palladio's preparatory drawing for Villa Gazzotti. *RIBA XVII, 27*

A preparatory drawing for the Villa Gazzotti from the early 1540s shows that he confronted the problem at the beginning of his career (3-21). At that time, he was not concerned about the width of intercolumniations and directed his efforts towards ensuring that all intercolumniations were equal. In this drawing, it appears that Palladio was willing to sacrifice the principle of representing the position of interior walls with columns on the facade. The third and the fifth semi-columns from right and left are clearly off-axis with the walls behind. Such axial shifts were, in fact, a standard design procedure that Palladio used throughout his career. Engaged columns and pilasters, when they stand at the point where interior walls intersect the facade, are slightly shifted so that they are not exactly on axis with the walls. In the case of corner columns, which indicate

3-22 Corner detail of Palazzo Chiericati.

the intersection of the front and side elevations, Palladio typically left a segment of the wall exposed between the corner of the building and the column (3-22). Similar axial shifts occur when columns are placed at the end of side porticos. At the Villa Cornaro, the axis of the column is shifted towards the center of the building creating a 22-centimeter lateral distance between the edge of the wall and the column[19] (3-23).

Lateral distance (edge-to-edge) is about 17 centimeters on the Palazzo Chiericati; the surveys published by Erik Forssman suggest that it is 7.5 centimeters on the Villa Foscari (between the side column of the portico and the internal wall aligned with it). Uncharacteristic placement of corner columns occurs on a number of buildings where Palladio is believed not to have had full control over the project: palazzi Thiene and Barbarano

3-23 Placement of the corner column in relation to the side wall of Villa Cornaro's portico.

as well as the villas Barbaro, Chiericati (Vancimuglio) (3-24–3-27), and the Rotonda (see page 96).[20] In the case of the Villa Barbaro, the columns completely encircle the corner rather than leaving it exposed according to Palladio's standard procedure. Bertotti Scamozzi's survey suggests that the proportions of the entablature on this villa are similar to those prescribed in the *Four Books*.[21] That suggests that Palladio determined the

dimensions of the elements, but then, in his absence, or following Barbaro's direction, the columns were placed in a way contrary to Palladio's usual practice. The atypical placement of columns in this villa also explains the enlarged intercolumniations, mentioned earlier. In the case of Villa Chiericati in Vancimuglio, the corner column of the portico has been positioned according to Palladio's standard procedure, but it is separated from

3-24 Corner detail of
the Palazzo Thiene.

3-25 Corner detail
of the Palazzo
Barbarano.

3-26 Corner detail of the Villa Barbaro. *CISA, F0001463*

3-27 Placement of the corner column in relation to the side wall of Villa Chiericati's portico (Vancimuglio).

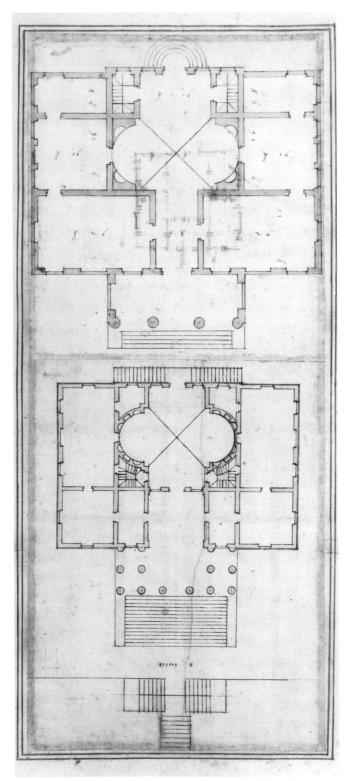

3-28 Palladio's preliminary drawing for Villa Chiericati (Vancimuglio). *RIBA XVI/20-A*

the lateral walls of the loggia. In this case too, Palladio's participation in the execution of the villa has been doubted by some scholars,[22] and his original drawing shows that he intended to apply his standard solution[23] (3-28). The corner column is pulled away from the wall of the loggia at the Rotonda too (see page 96). Martin Kubelik, Christian Goedicke, and Klaus Slusallek have demonstrated that the current columns of the Rotonda were re-erected in the eighteenth century by Francesco Muttoni.[24] Thermoluminescence dating shows that the bricks in the external skin of the columns were fired within twenty years of Palladio's death, while the infill dates from the eighteenth century. It is probable that the porticos of the Rotonda were completed by Vincenzo Scamozzi and then subsequently rebuilt in the eighteenth century by Muttoni, using some of the existing material. The drawing of the Rotonda in the *Four Books* shows these columns engaged with the side walls of the portico, following Palladio's standard procedure (see 4-1).

The idea of correlating the orders on the facade with the plan meant that the rules for the composition of the orders substantially dictated the layout of the interior spaces. From the early 1550s, Palladio's approach to design implied a very high level of coordination between the composition of the facade and the internal disposition of the parts of the building. A major internal wall orthogonal on the facade is indicated by a semi-column, column, or pilaster and (unless a colossal order has been used) the floor-to-floor height is expressed by the position of the entablature. While the dimensions of rooms are defined according to Palladio's rules for room length/width/height ratios, the height of the room must relate to the position of the entablature on the facade. The distance between the two walls of the room that intersect the facade must equal the sum of column diameters and intercolumniations. In other words, the lower diameter of the column used on the facade determines the height of the column, the height of the entablature, and the size of the intercolumniation. But columns also have to be positioned according to the rhythm of the internal walls, and their position consequently affects the internal composition of spaces. At the same time, the interior division of space follows

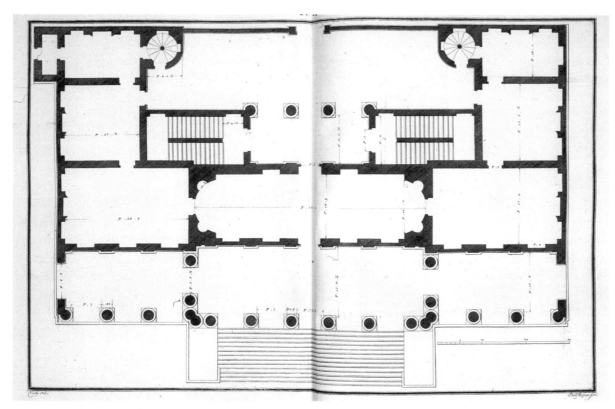

3-29 Plan of Palazzo Chiericati according to Ottavio Bertotti-Scamozzi. *CCA, M7616:1, 1786, Tavola X*

3-30 Facade of Palazzo Chiericati according to Ottavio Bertotti Scamozzi's survey. *CCA, M7616:1, 1786, Tavola XI*

121

its own proportional rules. The distance between two internal walls affects the room's length/width ratio and consequently the height of the ceiling, while the position of the ceiling determines the position of the entablature, which, in turn, depends on the height and diameter of the column. Palladio's design method, if strictly applied, requires complex coordination between the dimensions of interior spaces and the elements of the classical orders on the facade.

The classic example of such coordination seems to be the Palazzo Chiericati, whose design can be studied on the basis of the plan in the *Four Books*, Bertotti Scamozzi's survey and a modern survey available in the Centro Internazionale di Studi d'Architettura in Vicenza[25] (see 3-29, 3-30, and 1-46). The intercolumniations on the facade are less than three lower-column diameters, whereas the lateral rows of rooms conform to the CCH rule. There are four columns in front of the large side rooms; the position of the third column from the corner coincides with the position of the wall of the back room (taking into account the usual axial shift). In other words, the lengths of both front and back rooms have been determined as the sums of intercolumniations and column diameters. At the same time, room proportions were calculated according to Palladio's proportional rules.[26] The height of rooms, calculated to enable the CCH rule (and with the ceiling thickness added to it), must equal the sum of the column height plus the entablature.

The use of complex mathematics of this kind is apparent in a number of Palladio's villas from 1550 onward. Earlier buildings do not use the corresponding system of intercolumniations, while later palazzi were designed with colossal orders, which eliminated the requirement that the height of the columns plus the entablatures express the heights of internal spaces. The use of the colossal orders not only resolved the problems with windows but also simplified the mathematics of internal planning.

The villas of Palladio's "mature style" provide numerous examples of his efforts to coordinate external ornamentation and internal planning. At the Villa Cornaro, the position of the side walls of both front and back loggias corresponds to the walls of the sala—in other words, the size of the sala is determined by the rhythm of the intercolumniations (3-31 and 3-32). The final columns of the portico colonnade are axially shifted, while the penultimate columns are aligned with the four columns of the sala. In the *Four Books*, Palladio says that the distance between the columns of the sala equals their height.[27] This means that the disposition of external columns is not only subject to the usual rules about intercolumniations, but also depends on the disposition of internal columns and their height, which, in turn, depends on the height of the sala and consequently on the heights of other rooms on the same floor. We have seen earlier that these heights derive from the proportions of rooms mutually adjusted according to the CCH rule. At the Villa Pisani (Montagnana), the columns of the front and rear facades are aligned with interior walls; the central columns have been shifted to align with the engaged columns of the sala (3-33 and 3-34). Exterior and interior columns are aligned at the Palazzo Antonini, but there, exceptionally, the walls of the corridors are not expressed in the system of the orders on the facade (3-35 and 3-36). In the Villa Chiericati the central columns of the portico are aligned with the walls of the large rooms next to the facade, while the side of the portico shares the same axis as the wall of the rooms in the back (3-37 and 3-38). The corner columns of the portico of the Villa Foscari are directly aligned with the wall behind, and we have seen that the lateral shift is only 7.5 centimeters; these columns determine the total width of the sala.[28] The sala is cruciform, and its narrower width is determined by the walls that are orthogonal to the facade and aligned with the penultimate columns of the portico. The lateral shift is particularly large—almost 50 centimeters—but it is still less than the full column diameter of 69 centimeters[29] (3-39 and 3-40). The plan of the Villa Badoer indicates no attempt to align columns with the walls of the interior; in the case of the Rotonda such alignment exists along one axis but not another.

In all these cases—except for the Villa Badoer—the position of the interior walls had to conform to the use of the orders on the facade. At the same time, the *Four Books* indicates that some of these buildings, notably the Palazzo Chiericati and the Villa Pisani in

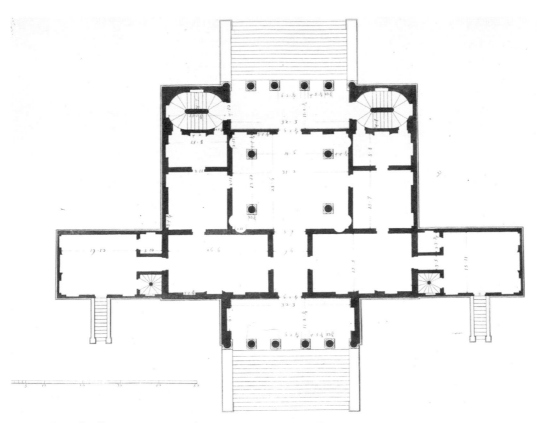

3-31 Plan of Villa Cornaro according to Ottavio Bertotti Scamozzi. *CCA, M7616:3, 1786, Tavola XXIX*

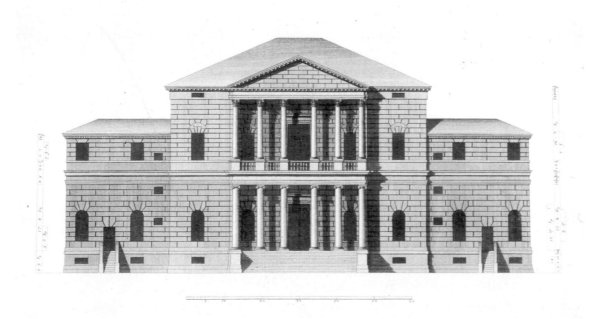

3-32 Facade of Villa Cornaro according to Ottavio Bertotti Scamozzi. *CCA, M7616:3, 1786, Tavola XXX*

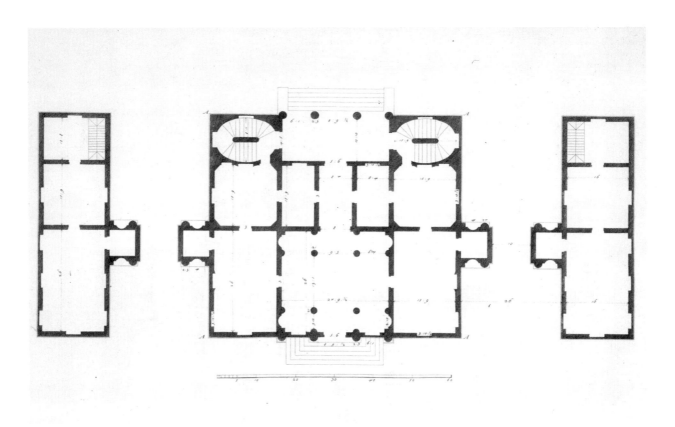

3-33 Plan of Villa Pisani (Montagnana) according to Ottavio Bertotti Scamozzi. *CCA, M7616:2, 1786, Tavola IX*

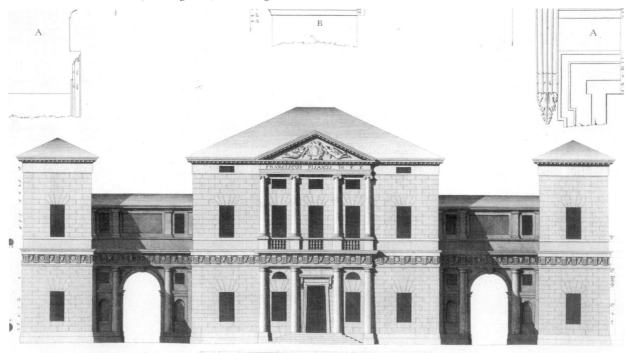

3-34 Elevation of Villa Pisani (Montagnana) according to Ottavio Bertotti Scamozzi. *CCA, M7616:2, 1786, Tavola X*

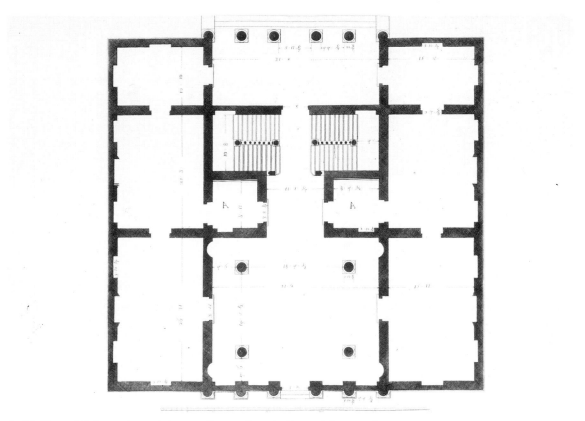

3-35 Plan of Palazzo Antonini according to Ottavio Bertotti Scamozzi. *CCA, M7616:3, tav. XII*

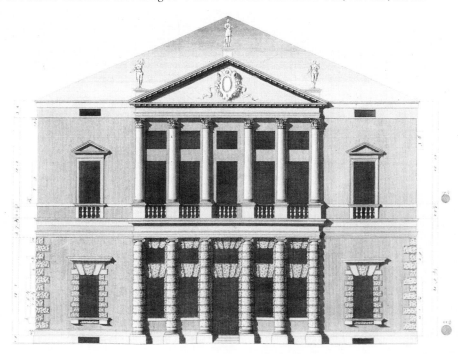

3-36 Facade of Palazzo Antonini according to Ottavio Bertotti Scamozzi. *CCA, M7616:3, tav. XIII*

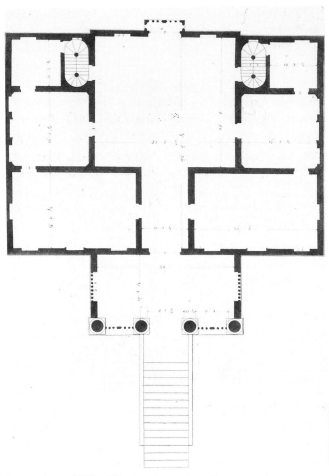

3-37 Plan of Villa Chiericati, Vancimuglio, according to
Ottavio Bertotti Scamozzi. *CCA, M7616:3, tav. XLVII*

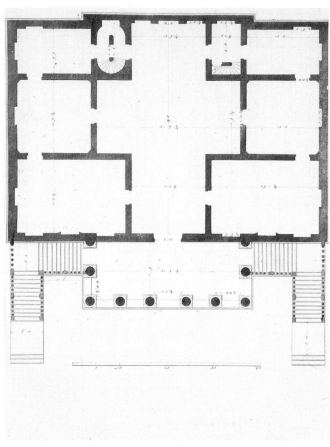

3-39 Plan of Villa Foscari according to Ottavio Bertotti
Scamozzi. *CCA, M7616:3, 1786, Tavola I*

3-38 Facade of Villa Chiericati, Vancimuglio, according to
Ottavio Bertotti Scamozzi. *CCA, M7616:3, TAV. XLVIII*

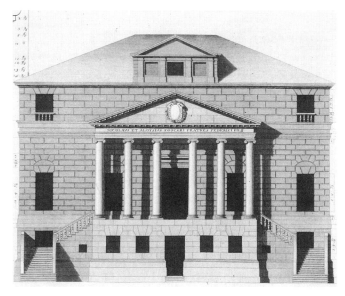

3-40 Facade of Villa Foscari according to Ottavio Bertotti
Scamozzi. *CCA, M7616:3, 1786, Tavola II*

Montagnana, were designed using proportional principles, such as the CCH rule. Without accurate and detailed surveys, it is impossible to say how Palladio integrated such complex mathematics, but it is clear that the way in which he used the orders affected not only the facade but also the overall design of the building.

PALLADIO'S FORMULATION OF THE CANON OF THE FIVE ORDERS

The first of the *Four Books* contains not one but two formulations of the canon of the five orders, one in the text and the other in the illustrations. It is possible that this distinction reflects different stages of the preparation of the treatise.[30]

A comparison of the ratios Palladio specified for the elements of the orders with those stipulated by his predecessors can show that Alberti and Serlio predominantly repeated Vitruvius's proportions of the elements of the orders, and Vignola's *Canon of the Five Orders* of 1563 was the first serious attempt to break away from the Vitruvian tradition.[31] Palladio's text follows Barbaro's suggestions in the commentary on Vitruvius, but the ratios Palladio stipulated in his illustrations indicate a conscious effort to formulate a system independent of Vitruvius's precepts. Palladio's ratios often correct Vitruvius's for minimal amounts, such as 1/180 of the lower-column diameter. Occasionally, ratios specified by Palladio are identical with those of Vignola.

The differences between Barbaro's and Palladio's textual formulation of the canon of the five orders pertain predominantly to the Corinthian and Composite orders; Palladio formulated the former under Vignola's strong influence, while Barbaro did not deal with the latter. Apart from this, the differences between the formulation of the canon in Palladio's text and Barbaro's commentary either pertain to details[32] or were clearly the result of a slip of the pen.[33]

Barbaro's influence is also evident in many of the details of Palladio's text. Palladio, for instance, avoided Vitruvian terms that Barbaro had not defined consistently, such as *apophysis*[34] or *hypotrachelium*.[35]

Similarly, Palladio did not address the issue of the corner metope of the Doric frieze. The problem is well known from Greco-Roman architectural history: the Greeks regularly placed triglyphs in the corners of the Doric frieze, and, as a consequence, they were forced to reduce the corner intercolumniation or to expand the metope next to the corner triglyph (3-41). Vitruvius suggested placing what he called "semi-metopes" instead of triglyphs in the corners.[36] A calculation shows that this "semi-metope" is actually a third of a metope, rather than a half. In his commentary, Barbaro noted that it was less than half.[37] The manuscript of his commentary, preserved in the library of San Marco in Venice, includes Barbaro's calculations of the Doric frieze length according to Vitruvius, which show that he was bewildered by the situation. In his treatment of the Doric order in the *Four Books*, Palladio did not mention the problem, although he was certainly aware of it.[38] In the drawings of the Palazzo Chiericati and the Basilica, corner semi-metopes are shown as one-third metopes; but on the executed buildings they are a quarter of the metope.[39] Similarly, in Palladio's illustration of the Doric corner detail for Barbaro's commentary and in the presentation of the Doric entablature detail in the *Four Books*, semi-metopes are less than one third of the normal width.[40]

PALLADIO'S CORINTHIAN: THE MORPHOLOGY

Palladio's approach to the five orders is best illustrated by the way he defined the proportions of the Corinthian entablature. The Corinthian entablature was the most important element of the system of the five orders that was still undefined by Palladio's time. Vitruvius provided no guidance, and Palladio formulated it on his own, relying on the work of his predecessors, especially Vignola, and the remains of Roman ruins.[41] Since his surveys of Roman Corinthian entablatures are preserved—nineteen are published in the fourth book of his treatise—it is easy to determine the influences on his canonical version of this element. Study of his methodology also yields important

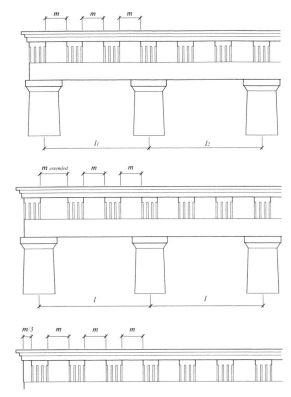

3-41 The corner problem of the Doric frieze. *Tim Ross*

insights into his overall approach to the combination of formal elements and his attitude towards the use of ancient precedents.

The Renaissance inherited the problem of the Corinthian entablature from Greco-Roman antiquity, when the idea of a specifically Corinthian entablature seems to have been non-existent.[42] Alberti explained that the Corinthian entablature differs from others by "mutules bare and cut into like waves."[43] The very common Roman solution, which combined dentils and modillions, was frequently used in the early Renaissance, although not necessarily in combination with the Corinthian order. In Florence, it can be found on the top cornice of palazzi Strozzi and Medici, neither of which has columns applied to the facade (3-42 and 3-43). In a very non-standard form, this combination appears on the facade of Santa Maria Novella in Florence[44] (3-44). It was also used by Donatello and Michelozzo for the pulpit of the Cathedral of Prato[45] (3-45). In Venice, it appears on Mauro Cadussi's works, such as Palazzo Zorzi a S. Severo and Palazzo Loredan in Vendramin Calergi.[46] At the same time, Renaissance theorists did not approve of this configuration because they identified the ancient Roman combination of modillions and dentils with that of mutules and dentils. According to Vitruvius, it was incorrect to place mutules, which represent primary rafters, above dentils, which represent secondary rafters.[47] This critique was endlessly repeated by Renaissance authors, including Serlio.[48] Inconsistent terminology, typical of the Renaissance, further contributed to the confusion. Francesco di Giorgio Martini, for instance, made drawings in which mutules in the Doric entablature are indicated as "mutoli," but he remarked that they were also called "modiglioni" by his contemporaries.[49] Barbaro used the terms "modioni" and "mutuli" interchangeably in reference to the projections of rafters under the soffit.[50] Vignola apparently was the first to suggest that modillions have nothing to do with primary rafters and that they represent small cantilevers supporting the corona.[51] In his presentation of the Doric entablature, Vignola drew an element that resembles the brackets Palladio used on his Ionic entablatures. When referring to this element, Palladio used Vignola's spelling ("modiglioni," as opposed to Barbaro's "modioni"), which may also be taken to indicate Vignola's influence.

The morphological similarity between Palladio's and Vignola's canonical Corinthian entablatures is remarkable, especially since the morphology of Corinthian entablature was not standardized at the time (3-46 and 3-47). The Corinthian entablatures Palladio and Vignola might have studied in Roman ruins also show great diversity. It seems almost impossible to deny Vignola's direct influence on Palladio in this case. A comparison of the morphology of the two entablatures, leaving aside decorative elements such as the lion heads or the curve of the frieze, shows that the differences are limited to a small number of minute details. No major parts of the

3-42 Cornice of Palazzo Strozzi, Florence.

3-44 Cornice of Santa Maria Novella (Florence).

3-43 Cornice of Palazzo Medici (Florence).

3-45 Pulpit on the external wall of the cathedral in Prato.

3-46 Canonical
Corinthian entablature
according to the *Four
Books*. *CCA, cage NA44
P164 (88. B1843 C1) livre 1,
p. 43*

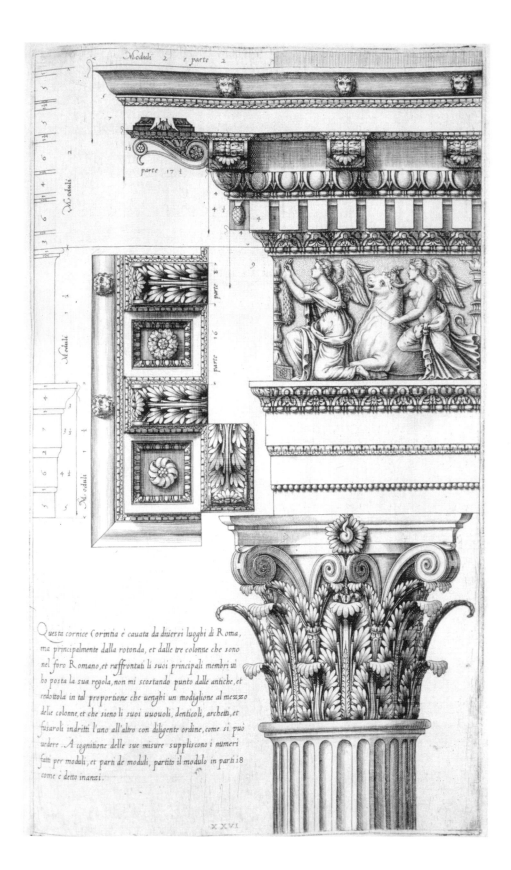

parte 17 ⅓

parte 8 ⅓

parte 16

Moduli

Moduli 1 ⅓

Moduli

Questa cornice Corintia è cauata da diuersi luoghi di Roma,
ma principalmente dalla rotonda, et dalle tre colonne che sono
nel foro Romano, et raffrontati li suoi principali membri ui
ho posta la sua regola, non mi scostando punto dalle antiche, et
redottola in tal proportione che uenghi un modiglione al mezzo
delle colonne, et che sieno li suoi uuuoli, denticoli, archetti, et
fusaroli indritti l'uno all'altro con diligente ordine, come si può
uedere. A cognitione delle sue misure suppliscono i numeri
fatti per moduli, et parti de moduli, partito il modulo in parti 18
come è detto inanzi.

3-47 Canonical
Corinthian entablature
according to Vignola.
*CCA, cage M NA44.V686
(W3245) pl. 26*

XXVI

131

3-48 Entablature of the temple of Castor and Pollux (Rome).

entablature were affected by Palladio's reworking of Vignola's morphology. It is also highly unlikely that this entablature could have been derived from a Roman model that both Palladio and Vignola coincidentally selected for a prototype. Vignola said that he had arrived at the shape of the cornice by combining the cornices from the Pantheon and "the three columns on the Roman Forum"—probably the remains of the Temples of Castor and Pollux or Vespasian and Titus (3-48 and 3-49). It is improbable that Palladio simply happened to do the same thing the same way. In addition, it is not only the morphology of Palladio's Corinthian entablature that repeats

Vignola's; even the composition of the drawing is extremely similar.

A comparison of the proportions of the parts of the Corinthian entablature according to Palladio and Vignola can show that Palladio's ratios require greater precision in the execution of details than Vignola's, but the ratios stipulated for individual elements are very similar.[52] The only exception is the height of Palladio's frieze, which is only half of that stipulated by Vignola. The total thickness of the entablature, architrave, frieze, and cornice differ significantly, however. Palladio adapted Vignola's morphology but proposed radically different proportions for its elements.

3-49 Entablature of the temple of Vespasian and Titus (Rome).

The table below summarizes the difference between proportions proposed by Vignola and Palladio.

	CORINTHIAN		IONIC	
	VIGNOLA	PALLADIO	VIGNOLA	PALLADIO
TOTAL ENTABLATURE	2.542D	1.881D	2.243D	1.82D
ARCHITRAVE	0.75D	0.638D	0.625D	0.608D
FRIEZE	0.75D	0.475D	0.75D	0.45D
CORNICE	1.042D	0.768D	0.868D	0.762D
	D is the lower-column diameter			

The difference between total entablature height according to Palladio and Vignola is more than 35 percent. A comparison of Palladio's and Vignola's canonical Ionic entablatures throws some light on the way these entablatures were derived. According to Vitruvius, the Ionic frieze, if ornamented, should be 5/4 of the architrave height, and 3/4 if the frieze is unornamented.[53] For the Ionic frieze, Palladio followed the latter prescription, Vignola the former. Vignola used the proportion of his Ionic frieze for both his Corinthian frieze and architrave, and his Corinthian architrave and cornice are 6/5 of their Ionic equivalents. In contrast, Palladio's proportions for the Corinthian architrave, frieze, and cornice are only

3-50 Capital of
the Temple of
Sibyl in Tivoli;
drawing by
Normand and
Mauch. *CCA, 5184,
pl. 43*

134

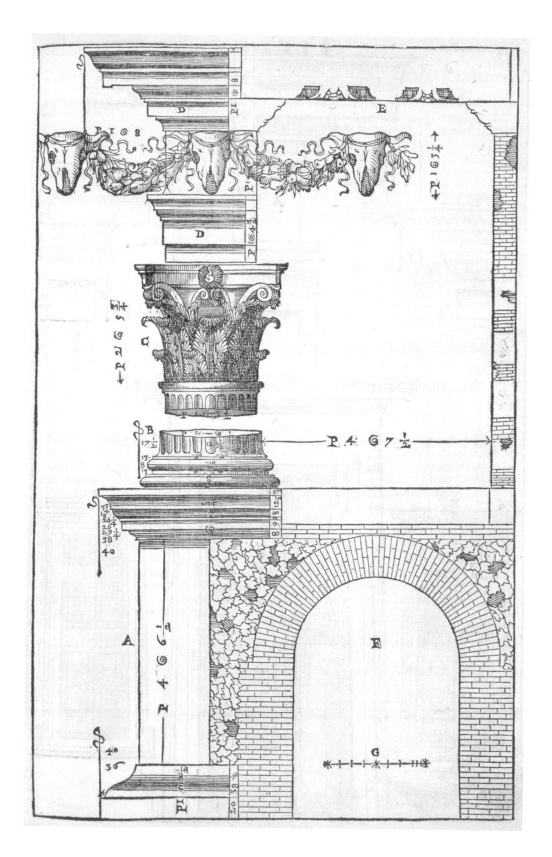

3-51 Capital of the Temple
of Sibyl, according to the
*Four Books. CCA, cage
NA44.P164 (ID88-B1843) c.1
p. 93*

slightly larger than his Ionic, with the result that Vignola's frieze is 57 percent and his cornice 35 percent taller than Palladio's.

PALLADIO'S ARCHAEOLOGICAL SURVEYS AND THE CANONICAL CORINTHIAN ENTABLATURE

The question of the way in which Palladio's archaeological surveys affected his formulation of the canonical Corinthian order is a complicated one. In the *Four Books*, Palladio often presented idealized versions of his own designs, and, in a study of his archaeological works, Bruce Boucher pointed out that the tendency to idealize can also be found in his unpublished archaeological drawings.[54] In some cases, such as that of the mausoleum of Romulus on the Via Appia, Palladio's surveys were extremely accurate, but occasionally he would project his own preconceptions as he did in his surveys of the Roman theater in Verona. Boucher cited the survey of the Temple in Assisi as an example of "creative rearranging," directed towards "imagining what the Roman architect had done, or perhaps what he ought to have wanted to do."[55] Boucher's findings in Palladio's unpublished archaeological surveys raise the question of whether those in the *Four Books* may also have undergone "creative rearranging," perhaps to show, for instance, that his formulation of the Corinthian order conformed to Roman Corinthian entablatures. An example of such a procedure can be seen in the fact that Palladio presented all the Corinthian temples with his own (i.e., Vignola's) standard version of the Corinthian capital—even when this drastically differed from reality, as at the Temple of Sibyl in Tivoli[56] (3-50 and 3-51). This could clearly be taken as an example of "creative rearranging." Palladio systematically indicated capital heights in his drawings. When these data are compared to modern surveys collected by Mark Wilson Jones, it transpires that in some cases Palladio's measurements are very accurate—the Temple of Antoninus and Faustina, the Temple of Castor and Pollux, the portico of the Pantheon—while in others the inaccuracies range from 9 centimeters on the columns of the piazza of the

forum of Nerva, to more than 20 centimeters on the circular temple near the Tiber.[57]

It is difficult to judge the accuracy of the surveys in the *Four Books*. This is potentially a very fruitful field for future Palladian scholarship. At this moment, it cannot be thoroughly discussed because there are no modern archaeological surveys of Roman buildings with which to compare Palladio's published measurements. The situation is further complicated by the uncertainty about the standard of measurement he used—a problem that has been discussed in the Introduction. In spite of all these difficulties, a careful comparative analysis of the data supplied in Palladio's surveys, as well a comparison of the published surveys with Palladio's canonical Corinthian entablature, can reveal a great deal and, in fact, resolve many issues. The nineteen Roman Corinthian entablatures whose surveys Palladio presented in the *Four Books* are morphologically diverse and only those that share an appropriate morphology can be compared to Palladio's canonical Corinthian entablature (3-52). It makes little sense to make proportional comparisons of elements of different shape. While the cornices exhibit great diversity, there are nine that are sufficiently similar to allow a proportional comparison.[58] Of these nine, two have not survived, so Palladio's surveys cannot be compared with modern ones.[59] Of the remaining seven, sufficiently detailed nineteenth- and twentieth-century surveys are publicly available for five entablatures,[60] and a comparison can show that Palladio's surveys are very accurate in the disposition and shape of the elements, and reasonably accurate for proportions.[61] Generally, the sizes Palladio stated are more accurate when it comes to larger elements. When Palladio formulated the proportions of his canonical Roman Corinthian entablature, he had at his disposal a substantial number of reasonably accurate surveys of Roman entablatures, and he knew that he could rely on them.

There are two ways in which Palladio's canonical Corinthian entablature can be compared to his archaeological surveys. One can compare only major elements (total entablatures, architraves, friezes, and cornices) or base the comparison on smaller elements.

Of the nineteen surveys of Roman entablatures in

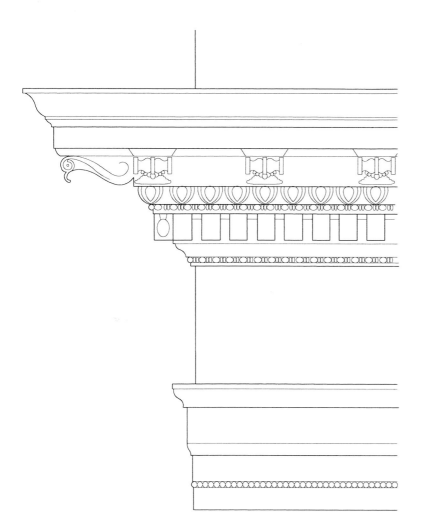

3-52 In order to be comparable to Palladio's, the standard Corinthian entablature should have both dentils and modillions. Between the dentils and modillions there should be an ovolo (exceptionally a cyma) and a fillet, astragal, or a combination of these. Below the dentils (between the dentils and the frieze) there is a cyma or an ovolo, accompanied by a fillet or an astragal next to the frieze. Above the modillions is the corona. At the top of the cornice there is always a cyma recta with a fillet; between this cyma and the fascia of the corona is usually another layer consisting of a smaller cyma or, more rarely, an ovolo. *Tim Ross*

the fourth book, fifteen contain enough data to be compared with the canonical Corinthian entablature.[62] But if we compare major elements (architraves, friezes, cornices, total entablature thickness), only three entablatures have proportions similar to those stipulated by Palladio: the entablatures from the Basilica of Maxentius, the Hadrianeum, and the Temple of Minerva in Assisi. According to the surveys published in the fourth book, the Temple of Minerva in Assisi is closest to Palladio's canon, but the accuracy of the survey has long been challenged. Goethe noted that it was inaccurate, and early in the nineteenth century

Giovanni Antolini published a comparison of Palladio's surveys with his own, demonstrating Palladio's inaccuracy.[63] It seems likely that in this case Palladio indeed adjusted archaeological data to suit his canon. In any case, only the sizes of the entablatures of the Basilica of Maxentius and the Hadrianeum somehow relate to the proportions of Palladio's canonical Corinthian entablature.

Vignola defined the height of the canonical entablature as 2.54D, and four temples, according to Palladio's surveys, have similar entablature dimensions.[64] However, eight temples in Palladio's surveys have entablature thicknesses close to 2.2D, midway between his and Vignola's canonical Corinthian. This is a bigger group by far than that of the entablatures whose proportions correspond to either Palladio's or Vignola's canon. While formulating the proportions of his canonical Corinthian entablature, Palladio must have noticed that Vignola's was taller than the common Roman practice, but he opted for a substantially lower entablature than the majority of the entablatures to be found in Rome. At the same time, he adopted Vignola's morphology.

In specifying the proportions of minor elements, Palladio seems to have been much more inclined to follow what his surveys suggested was the common Roman practice. Nevertheless, his proportions were not derived from a single entablature. There is no entablature in Book Four which has more than 50 percent of its elements similar in proportion to Palladio's canonical Corinthian entablature. It follows that, in Palladio's surveys of Corinthian entablatures (except for the survey of the Temple in Assisi), there was no attempt to manipulate the surveys to show that Palladio's canon was particularly faithful to Roman practice. Palladio appears to have combined and adjusted the proportions of elements from various entablatures, according to what he saw as the best composition. Only occasionally, in the case of certain elements, did he completely disregard ancient examples. For instance, his choice of the thickness of the corona and interfascial elements in the architrave has almost no precedent in his surveys.

FORMAL JUDGMENT

Was Palladio's formulation of the canon of the five orders motivated by harmonic proportions? Could the proportions of the orders he stipulated have been derived from the harmonic system, as Wittkower described? If the answer could be positive, then Wittkower's approach would be vindicated, although it would have to be reformulated in a much more complex fashion. The question can be easily resolved by looking at the proportions Palladio stipulated for his canonical Corinthian entablature. Table 2 in Appendix D presents

a systematic comparison of the sizes of all the elements of his Corinthian entablature, with each other and with the lower-column diameter. Ratios that can be interpreted as musical intervals are very rare. The Corinthian entablature is the largest single element of the classical orders whose proportions Palladio revised, and he did not use harmonic proportions to formulate this element of the canon. Working with a computer, it is easy to compare proportions of all elements of the entablature, but in Palladio's time, adjusting these proportions to fit a harmonic scheme would have been a monumental task. Even then, if dentils, for instance, were proportionally adjusted to the proportion of the frieze, this would not ensure that they would be equally well adjusted to other visible parts of a building, such as doors and windows. Ultimately, the architect had to rely on his formal judgment. The sheer quantity of proportional considerations to be taken into account makes it incredible that any single proportional system could have been consistently applied. A Renaissance architect could have opted to use a specific proportional system (for instance for room length/width ratios), but this would have always been contingent on other proportional decisions required of the project.

For the same reason, it is impossible to explain the way Palladio derived the proportions of his canonical Corinthian entablature on the basis of meanings or narratives he may have attached to individual elements. What set of narratives could explain, for each individual element of the Corinthian entablature, Palladio's choice of the proportions from one Roman temple over another? Ultimately, architects have to make formal decisions that cannot be entirely based on meanings attached to the parts of the buildings they design. Formal is never fully reducible to verbal. Palladio's approach to the formulation of the proportions of the canonical Corinthian entablature must have relied on the systematic application of formal judgments, not only in the proportions of the entablature itself, but also in the formulation of the morphology and especially proportions of the canon of the five orders. No set of narratives or general rules about proportions can provide guidelines for such a great number of formal decisions.

Introducing his canon, Palladio explained that he

intended to present the proportions of the orders "not so much in line with what Vitruvius teaches but according to what I have observed in ancient buildings."[65] He combined and adjusted the proportions surveyed on different Roman remains to achieve the best possible combination. The proportions he stipulated for the largest elements of entablature (architraves, friezes, and cornices) are the result of an empirical process, probably sums of the proportions of individual elements. Palladio could have believed, as he stated in the memorandum on the Cathedral in Brescia, that the architect's competent judgments will result in a harmonious building and that the aesthetic properties of such a building can be explained in terms of musical proportions and harmonies. However, it would have been beyond his capacity to apply a specific system to the totality of proportional decisions.

In fact, during the Renaissance, the concept of purely formal aesthetic judgment was well established in the Aristotelian explanation of the functioning of the human mind.[66] In *The Judgement of Sense*, David Summers presented the history of the idea of formal aesthetic judgment and how it was conceived in the Aristotelian tradition through the Middle Ages and in the Renaissance. The concept of internal senses—a set of lower, material, capacities of the soul—explained the human preference for certain formal relationships. This need not have been the only explanation of such preferences. In his *Commentaries on Porphyry*, Daniele Barbaro explained the same capacity for formal aesthetic judgments as the function of the higher stratum of the soul, the intellect.[67]

Palladio could have relied on his formal aesthetic preference without any awareness that the Aristotelian explanation existed. Alberti defined beauty as the relationship between parts and commented that there is nothing more odious or offensive than angles, lines, and surfaces that are composed carelessly.[68] Alberti says that the form and figure of buildings have qualities that excite the mind; this perfection is recognized if present and desired if missing. The eyes need beauty and are unhappy if it is absent. The implication is that human beings can make purely formal judgments and be moved by them. Vignola explained his approach to the formu-

lation of the canon of the five orders along very similar lines, noting that he adopted proportions from the version of the order which was most widely appreciated by the common judgment (e.g., in the case of the Doric order, it was the one on the Theater of Marcellus).[69] Following such judgments, for instance, he combined elements from several temples to formulate his canonical Corinthian entablature. It is impossible to say whether Palladio was aware of the Aristotelian explanation of his procedures, which was so prevalent at the time, but it is clear that he had to rely on formal aesthetic judgments in his work.

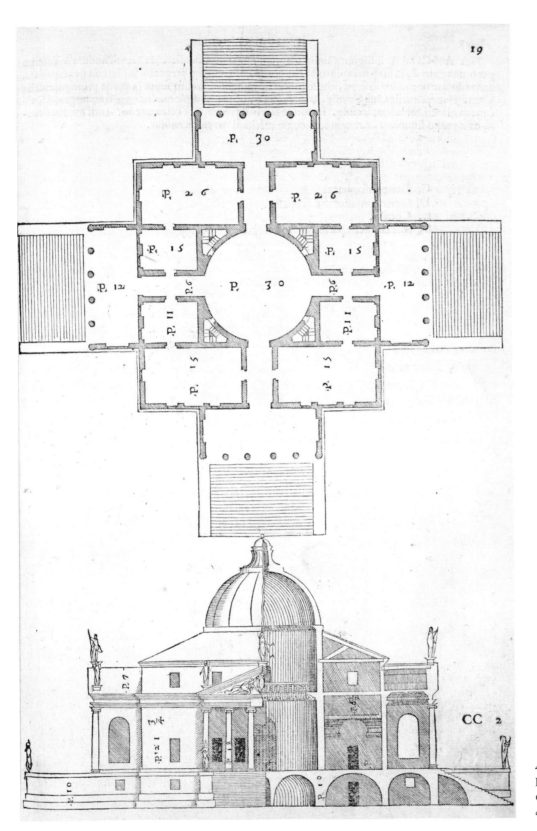

4-1 Presentation of the
Rotonda in the *Four Books*.
*CCA, cage, NA44 P164 (88-B1843
c. 1) livre 2, p. 19*

CHAPTER IV

PALLADIO'S PLATONISM

PALLADIO'S MOST FAMOUS BUILDING, the Villa Rotonda, is a work whose many aspects present substantial difficulties for scholars. Palladio's text in the *Four Books* praised the site and landscape that surrounds it[1] (4-2). Generations of visitors—including such dignitaries as Goethe and Hofmannsthal—have contributed a wealth of literature praising the villa's surroundings.[2] Nevertheless, Palladio's drawing in the *Four Books* presents the building as an object that could be placed anywhere, with no regard for the site (4-1). Its shapes and symmetries are absolute and do not emerge from any aspect of the surroundings. Palladio's description praises the natural landscape around the villa, but, in his drawing, the building is derived from a set of abstract axes, ideal and perfect. The drawing presents an architectural idea whose form may accidentally relate to or conflict with some aspect of the site, but the design is certainly not derived from its specific properties. In reality, the villa is not even placed on the hilltop; it sits on a platform built on the hill. The history of this platform has largely remained a mystery to Palladian scholarship, and, whatever Goethe or Hofmannsthal may have said

4-2 Villa Rotonda.

about the beauty of the surroundings, the site was artificially altered to accommodate the building.

The understanding of the Rotonda's design is further complicated by the fact that its placement on the platform is in direct contradiction to its planning. While the four equal porticos imply equal access from all sides, the villa stands in a corner of the platform with two of its entrances abutting the edge of the retaining wall. Entering the villa through these two monumental porticos is uncomfortable, and it would be dangerous if there were no fence to prevent the visitor from falling over the edge of the platform (4-3). The two rear porticos could not have been intended as entrances. Their paradoxical status is further emphasized by the secondary staircases under the porticos that open through the platform's walls[3] (4-4).

4-3 The staircase in the monumental entrance to the Rotonda (behind the wall on the right) ends at the edge of the platform.

IDEAL AND MATERIAL

The Rotonda's placement at the edge of the platform is one of many examples of the problematic relationship between the abstract and material, ideal and built in Palladio's work. The problem occurs in every architect's practice; the trials of bringing an architect's idea to completion are legion. It is also an issue that pervades the interpretations of the *Four Books* because of the discrepancies between the published plans and the executed buildings. The explanation of these differences is one of the oldest problems of Palladian scholarship, to which various scholars have suggested alternative solutions. In a number of articles published during the 1960s, Gian Giorgio Zorzi argued that because of the inaccuracies in the plans of the *Four Books*, it is the executed buildings that correctly convey Palladio's intentions. In his view, the illustrations of the *Four Books* are either the work of unknown xylographers employed by the publisher, Domenico de Franceschi, or represent Palladio's later style, rather than his original ideas at the time the buildings were executed.[4]

However, the point is not so much the inaccuracy of the drawings as that the tendency to idealize is such a systematic feature of the drawings. A good example is the highly regular plan of the Basilica and reality of the medieval structure to which the facade was added (4-5 and 4-6). It is commonplace in Palladian scholarship that the illustrations of the treatise are actually much closer to Palladio's early style. Contrary to Zorzi, who was inclined to dismiss Palladio's drawings from the *Four Books* as unreliable, Franco Barbieri suggested a different way of looking at them by pointing out that these illustrations often represent architectural ideas that could not have been built within the physical constraints in which the actual buildings were placed.[5] Barbieri pointed to such examples as the Villa Godi, which could not have been executed on its site according to the plan published in the *Four Books*—or, as Barbieri observed, "If someone were so insane as to face the huge expenses necessary to level the ground, the result would be the destruction of one of the most attractive landscapes in the Veneto."[6] Similarly, the Palazzo Valmarana, as presented in the treatise, is so large that it would have taken

4-4 The underground staircase behind the door in the retaining wall leads to the passageway underneath the monumental portico.

over public land (4-7). In addition, the rooms next to the facade are shown as rectangular, which was obviously impossible on the irregular site (4-8 and 4-9). Barbieri concluded that in spite of the pragmatic and site-related narratives in Palladio's descriptions, the published plans present ideal (or fantastic) reworkings of the original projects. The villas in these plans are imposed in "a space without limits and outside time; rivers and hills, gardens and fields, they all disappear, and what remains is the clarity of the paradigm in the multitude of its variations."[7] The city of Vicenza—the wider context in which these buildings were placed—as conceived in the treatise is a "passive receptacle" capable of receiving whatever monument is imposed on it.

However, it is not only in the *Four Books* that Palladio's designs have an ideal, immaterial character. The same often applies to his built work as well; here too, Palladio's efforts often seem to be directed at representing an ideal prototype. In his biography of Palladio, Bruce Boucher described the architect's inclination to follow the internal logic of a design, which would lead him to attempt to correct the existing situation rather than to work with it.[8] Because of this tendency, discussion of Palladio's "ideal" architecture and implicitly about the Platonism of his theoretical views pervades Palladian scholarship—notably in the writings of Rudolf Wittkower, Bernhard Rupprecht, Bruce Boucher, Rosario Assunto, and Marcello Fagiolo.[9] Some have directly

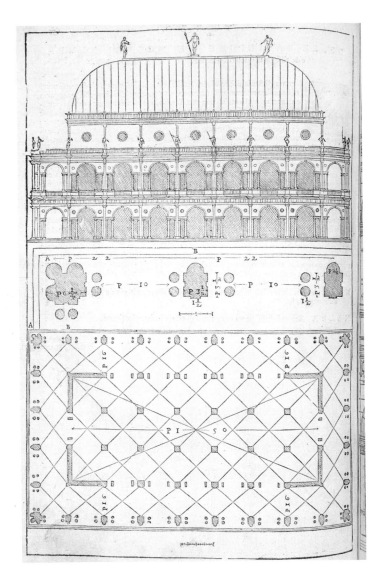

4-5 Palladio's presentation of the Basilica in the *Four Books*. CCA, *cage, NA44 P164 (88-B1843 c.1) livre 3 p. 42*

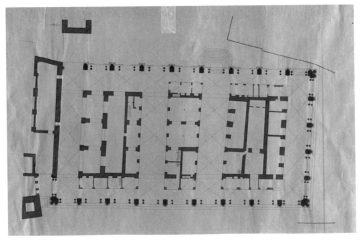

4-6 Modern survey of the ground plan of the Basilica. *CISA, R0000027, survey by D'Agaro and Terlà.*

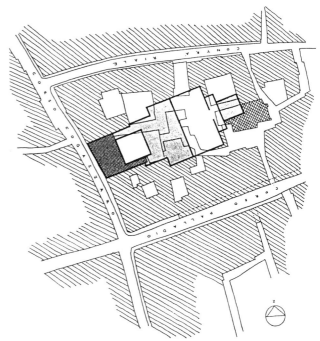

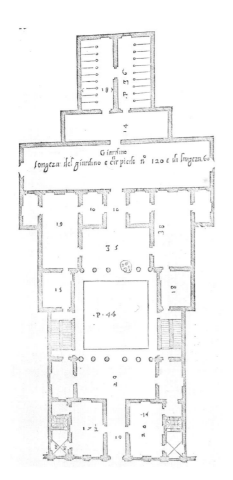

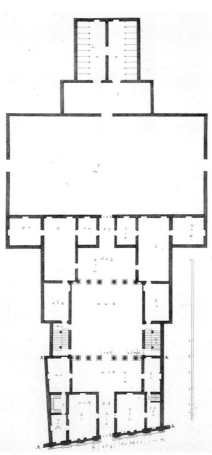

4-7 Outline of the Palazzo Valmarana from the *Four Books* superimposed on its actual urban site, according to Carboneri, "Spazi e planimetrie," illustration XVIII, p. 183 The section which has been built is shaded darker. *CISA.*

4-8 (far left) Plan of Palazzo Valmarana from the *Four Books*. *CCA, NA44.P164 (W161), c.2, p. 16*

4-9 (left) Plan of Palazzo Valmarana by Ottavio Bertotti-Scamozzi. *CCA, M7616:1, 1786, Tavola 20*

talked about Neoplatonism; others have described design procedures that rely (or may rely) on Platonist theoretical assumptions. The connection between "ideal architecture" and Platonist theoretical views, between "architectural idea" and "architectural form" is easy enough to make. In order to reconstruct Palladio's design theory, it is important to analyze the presence of such tendencies in his design procedures.

THE AESTHETIC OBJECT OF ARCHITECTURE

The problem we face here is one of the oldest in the history of aesthetics: what is the object of our aesthetic judgments? What is the object (e.g., a house) to which we ascribe aesthetic properties, such as beauty or ugliness? Is it the built, executed building? We often judge the beauty of a building on the basis of its plans, so this answer seems unlikely. Besides, we never perceive three-dimensional objects, such as buildings, from all sides at the same time. Only gradually, by seeing the building from different sides and by studying its plans, do we acquire the knowledge about the building's three-dimensional properties. The object of our judgment thus has to be our knowledge about a possible building and *not* an executed building. This knowledge constitutes something that could be called the *mental model* of the building, which allows us to imagine and draw the building from different sides. (Such a mental model is not a single mental image, i.e., a building imagined from one side or another, but rather *knowledge* about the building's formal properties, which enables us to imagine the building's shape from different sides.) If this is so, then the executed building, like a set of drawings or a wooden model, is merely a medium the architect uses to communicate to us the idea of a building he or she has conceived.

However, the architectural idea need not be something in the architect's mind. Mental models, plans, and executed buildings all express the same content, they are all manifestations in different media of the same architectural idea. One could further argue that architectural ideas have independent existence and that they are merely *reflected* in the executed buildings or plans of an individual architect. This would mean that they are similar to mathematical objects: the idea of a circle is conceived to be reflected in circles drawn on a piece of paper, in the wheels of a car, or in human thoughts. Mathematical objects such as numbers and geometrical figures are regarded as Platonic forms *par excellence*, and they are necessarily conceived to exist independently from human thoughts or from their material manifestations. We can imagine that the material world could perish; we can not imagine that 2 plus 3 could not make 5. Mathematical theorems would be true even if there were no humans to discover them. It is easy to extend the view that mathematical theorems are true independently of whether humans know about them, and to claim that the same applies to the beauty of works of art. The view that works of art are mere reflections of Platonic forms and that individual artists do not create but discover them has been around for at least two millennia. Its history has been described in Erwin Panofsky's seminal study about Platonism in the history of art theory.[10]

We may thus choose between two possible views. We can claim that the aesthetic object of architecture is a mental entity, the architect's idea, conveyed to the minds of other humans through buildings, drawing, or models. Its aesthetic value is constituted through our mental reaction to it (e.g., pleasure or displeasure)—and, supposedly, we agree about our aesthetic judgments because we share similar mental apparatus. The alternative would be to postulate immaterial and eternal Platonic forms of architecture, reflected imperfectly in our thoughts, drawings, and buildings. In this case we agree about the beauty of buildings because we recognize in them their eternal prototypes—but they would be beautiful even if there were no humans to appreciate them.

Our question here is, what was Palladio's view—or more exactly, can his works be consistently interpreted from one of these two positions? We have seen that different scholars have mentioned platonizing tendencies in Palladio's work—but how thorough is this Platonism? How did it affect his design, and did it ever constitute a consistently thought-out theoretical position?

One should specify here what such consideration entails. On the one hand, Palladio did not express his theoretical views in the *Four Books* by relying on Platonist arguments, and it makes little sense to talk about Palladio's Platonism as an explicitly formulated theory. On the other, we are here concerned with the internal consistency of his views in order to see how they motivate his approach to design. Many problems in architectural design theory are counterparts of wider philosophical problems: it is impossible to deal with problems such as optical corrections or the use of perspective in architectural presentation without discussing the functioning of human cognition; one cannot discuss the problems of signification and meaning in architecture without discussing the way the human mind subsumes under concepts; it is impossible to have a view on the appreciation of architecture without taking into account the relevant problems in aesthetics and/or psychology. These problems cannot be avoided in architectural design practice, and if a design theory is to have internal consistency, it must rely on a consistent set of philosophical assumptions. It is therefore important to explore the consistency of Palladio's design theory and see whether the intuitions of twentieth-century scholars are accurate and whether Palladio's theoretical framework relied on assumptions such as the existence of eternal and immaterial Platonic forms. This need not mean that Palladio had ever read Plato or Renaissance Neoplatonists (after all, one can read Plato without becoming a Platonist); but rather that Palladio's design principles consistently relied on premises and postulates which would qualify as Platonist. We shall see later that underlying the Platonism of Palladio's system could have been a highly simplified (and predigested) doctrine to which Palladio was likely to have been exposed during the years he spent with Trissino.

FORM AND VISION

When it comes to architectural theory, Renaissance or modern, the discussion of the problem of the aesthetic object of architecture is far from mere theoretical quibbling: implicit or explicit answers to this dilemma can affect important aspects of design. In fact, often an individual architect's design decisions are by themselves implicit answers to this question.

Renaissance theorists—at least those with formal philosophical education, such as Leon Battista Alberti or Daniele Barbaro—would understand the problem as a version of the well-known medieval debate about universals. They would also know about it as one of the differences between Aristotelian and Platonic philosophy: contrary to Plato, Aristotle denied that entities such as geometrical figures or numbers can exist separately from the material world, or that there are such things as eternal and imperishable Platonic forms.

If the aesthetic object of architecture is the mental model, the idea of the building in the mind of the observer, then the architect must use optical corrections and adjust the proportions to perceptual conditions in order to ensure that the executed building produces the desired architectural idea in the observer's mind. Alternatively, one could believe that executed buildings are mere reflections of eternal architectural ideas, and that buildings can be beautiful even if nobody sees them, the way a mathematical theorem can be true even if it is unknown to humans. In that case, optical corrections would be pointless. Even worse, they would obstruct the architect's efforts to achieve an accurate reflection of eternal forms of architecture in building.

The idea that the eyes cheat us and that architectural works need to amend for this was already present in Vitruvius. Vitruvius particularly emphasized the necessity of optical corrections for the Ionic entablature, whose size had to be adjusted, in his view, to the perceptual conditions and the height of columns. He also argued that corner columns of a temple should be thicker (because otherwise they appear thinner) and he justified the use of entasis on perceptual grounds.[11] The need for optical corrections was accepted in Renaissance architectural theory, although it is difficult to say how seriously it was considered in the process of design. The idea was discussed positively by Alberti.[12] Vignola warned that while the ratios he stipulated were given with no concern for the perceptual conditions, such considerations certainly needed to be taken into account.[13] His canon thus stipulated the proportions that should be perceived as the result of optical corrections. Barbaro's commentary on Vitruvius was similar, referring to the description of optical corrections on the Ionic entablature as "beautiful reasoning about perspective." He regarded optical corrections as aspects of *eurythmia*, which in its turn is "the most dignified part of architecture."[14] While Vitruvius said that he had provided the explanation of how to make entasis at the end of the book (one of the lost drawings), in Barbaro's view this was much more an issue of moderation and skill than of art and rule, in spite of the fact that Serlio and others claimed to have found some methods to accomplish it.[15] Similarly, while Barbaro thought that perspective was not of great use for architects as a presentation method, he emphasized the importance of perspective for optical corrections and the design of theaters.[16] A similar emphasis is made in his treatise on perspective.[17]

The emphasis on optical corrections implies that the mind receives data from the senses and is further able to extract information about the spatial relationships of perceived objects. In other words, the mind is able to reconstitute real dimensions from what it perceives; the object of aesthetic judgment is our knowledge about the building's spatial properties after the mental model has been formed. But in order to be able to reconstitute the proportions that the architect intended, the senses must perceive correctly. If perceptual conditions will distort perception, the architect must compensate for this. An interesting example of this reasoning occurs in Giovan Paolo Lomazzo's *Treatise on the Art of Painting, Sculpture, and Architecture*. Lomazzo warned against dismissing optical corrections on the basis of the argument that visually perceived images are directed not to the eye but to the mind and memory.[18] To say that optical corrections are unnecessary because the mind is able to reconstitute the accurate spatial relationships from the perspectival images the eyes perceive is not correct. On the contrary, says Lomazzo, the mind and memory can only be reached through the eyes. Aristotle pointed out that nothing can be in the mind until it has passed through the senses. It is important to ensure that images are first perceived in such a way that enables the mind to extract the proportions intended by the architect.

The underlying assumption is that buildings possess certain aesthetic properties (e.g., beauty) because our mind reacts in a certain way (e.g., derives pleasure) from contemplating their shape. Optical corrections ensure that the process of perception provides the mind with the appropriate proportions and spatial relationships. However, if buildings are considered reflections of eternal architectural forms and if they are beautiful in the same way mathematical theorems are true, then the way they are perceived is irrelevant. In the *Sophist*, Plato dismissed optical corrections and criticized those sculptors who gave to their sculptures "not the real proportions but those that will appear beautiful."[19] If an object, sculpture or building, is to reflect accurately the true proportions of its ideal prototype, then there is no place for optical corrections; adjusting proportions in order to make them perceived as desired means departing from their accurate application.

Palladio's treatment—or better, lack of treatment—of optical corrections in the *Four Books* appears to follow Plato's line of thought. Palladio did not take into account the argument that proportions need to be adjusted in order to be perceived in a certain way. In the case of the Ionic entablature, whose proportions were routinely treated as subject to optical corrections by the entire Vitruvian tradition, Palladio simply prescribed a set of ratios related to the lower-column diameter and independent of perceptual conditions. Similarly, while his rule for entasis did depend on the column's height, unlike Vitruvius, he did not refer to the functioning of human vision when explaining it. Palladio was concerned with formal judgments of the totality of the spatial relationships on a building, and not with the way the building is perceived from one point in space. It is thus more appropriate to discuss the role of formal, rather than visual, judgments in Palladio's design theory. Design decisions based on formal judgments are visual insofar as they are based on properties that can be visually imagined; the shape of the building needs to be contemplated visually (e.g., using visual imagery); but formal decisions and judgments are not visual in the sense that they are derived directly from individual acts of perception.

The reluctance to acknowledge the role of human perception in the design or aesthetic judgment of architecture can be seen in a very unusual aspect of Palladio's design theory: his excessive precision in the formulation of the ratios of the elements of the five orders. The precision with which he defined the proportions of the elements of the orders exceeds anything that can be executed or even perceived. His proportions of the orders were largely derived from minute corrections to the ratios stipulated by Vitruvius and Barbaro. For the Doric entablature, Vitruvius and Barbaro gave 0.0714D (1/14 of the lower-column diameter) as the thickness of the *taenia*. Palladio corrected the amount to 0.075D (or 3/40 of the lower-column diameter). The *guttae* in the same entablature are D/18 according to Barbaro; Palladio makes them 11D/180—i.e., he corrects Barbaro by 1/180 part of the lower-column diameter. The thickness of the Ionic abacus Palladio stipulated differs from the rest of the Renaissance tradition by 1/720 part of the lower-column diameter. In his formulation of the canon of the five orders, Palladio systematically corrected the ratios stated by the majority of other Renaissance authors by amounts that could not have been perceived and often required a precision that could not have been achieved in stone cutting. If an Ionic abacus made according to Palladio's precepts was going to differ by 5 millimeters from its equivalent made according to the precept stated by Vitruvius, Serlio, and Barbaro, the column would have to be almost 29 meters tall (!) and at that height certainly the difference would be imperceptible. Or, if the column were smaller, the difference of 1/720 part of the lower-column diameter would be so small that it would be hard to make an abacus with the required precision. As a stonemason, Palladio knew this only too well. The only conclusion to be drawn is that the formulation of the canon of the five orders in the *Four Books* pertains to an ideal system of the orders, independent of anything that can actually be made in stone or perceived when built.

SEEING THE IDEAL

An architect who rejects optical corrections is also likely to be unwilling to use those architectural presentation techniques which show the way that things look and not the way they are. Strictly speaking, this need not amount to an argument against perspective—when we perceive a building in a perspectival drawing we can still reconstruct in our mind the accurate proportions and angles of its parts. However, perspectival drawings cannot compete with plans, sections, and elevations in providing accurate data efficiently—a situation which seems to have led to a general agreement among Renaissance authors that perspective is unsuitable for architectural delineation. This did not mean the rejection of perspective. All major Renaissance architectural theorists except Palladio wrote extensively on perspective. Alberti was the first to describe it in his treatise on painting; Serlio dedicated one book of his treatise to perspective; Vignola's treatise on perspective was published posthumously; Barbaro's came out a year before his death; and Scamozzi wrote a treatise on perspective in six books which was never published and whose manuscript is lost. Nevertheless, Renaissance authors were uneasy about perspective as a method of architectural delineation. Alberti wrote that the architect should make drawings that accurately represent relationships between dimensions and angles and avoid perspective and shadows so that his work will be judged "not by deceptive appearances but according to certain calculated principles."[20] In a similar vein, a letter to Pope Leo X from Raphael's circle spoke about perspective as *apparenza*; its lines are those that appear and not those that are.[21] It would follow that the proper modes of architectural presentation are those derived from what are known today as orthogonal projections, i.e., elevation, section, and ground plan. The letter to Leo X suggests a lack of awareness that the exact proportions, angles, and dimensions can be geometrically restituted from a perspectival image; the idea of such a procedure developed only in later centuries.

Barbaro also dismissed perspective as a method of architectural presentation.[22] Vitruvius listed *ichnographia*, *orthographia*, and *scaenographia* as the three modes of architectural presentation; his explanations indicate that these terms meant plan, elevation, and one-point perspective.[23] This was the standard understanding of the fragment in the Renaissance, as demonstrated by the illustrations from Fra Giocondo's Vitruvius[24] (4-10). Barbaro, while translating *orthographia* as elevation and *ichnographia* as ground plan, proposed reading

4-10 Scaenographia in Fra Giocondo's *Vitruvius*.
CCA, cage M NA44. V848 (W3246) p. 4v

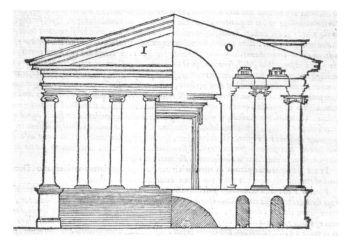

4-11 Presentation of elevation and section in Barbaro's commentary on Vitruvius. *CCA, cage NA44. V848 (W8778) c.2 p. 21*

4-12 Sebastiano Serlio's drawing of the Basilica of Maxentius. *CCA, NA44.S485 (W193) book 3, p. 59*

scaenographia as *sciographia*, and then translating it as section (*profilo*) and not as perspective. A drawing by Palladio, showing a section through a Greek temple designated as *profilo*, was included to make the interpretation clear[25] (4-11). In the Latin version of the commentary, Barbaro overtly intervened in Vitruvius's text, where he replaced *scaenographia* with *sciographia*.[26] He justified the revision by saying that perspective is less useful for architects than section.[27] Perspective, he said, is important in theater design and for optical corrections,[28] whereas section, elevation, and plan make it possible to see the disposition of objects and parts.[29] Barbaro thus did not argue against perspective, but he thought its value was limited for architectural communication.

Palladio seems to have agreed with his contemporaries. In the *Four Books*, he used perspectival drawings only for specific purposes, to show the layers of a wall, for example (4-13). But he made the rejection of perspective an important part of his program of describing three-dimensional formal properties of architectural objects. Instead of perspective, he developed a system that combined visual images in such a way as to present all three-dimensional aspects of a spatial detail in one drawing. In his study of Palladio's methods of architectural presentation, Bernhard Rupprecht pointed to Palladio's preference to work with orthogonal projections when presenting architectural ideas.[30] Similarly to Barbieri, Rupprecht argued that Palladio's goal was not to show the building de facto, but to illustrate an architectural idea. Consequently, in his view, Palladio's methods of illustration negate the sense of space based on experience and perception. In Palladio's illustrations, the relationship between the subject and architecture has been cancelled, and architecture has ceased to be something that surrounds the human subject. Rupprecht refrained from directly formulating the question about the kind of entity Palladio assumed these architectural ideas to be, but he clearly ascribed the Platonist stance to Palladio in discussing his attitude towards Roman ruins. Serlio's drawings of Roman ruins, Rupprecht argued, emphasized their historicity, their ruinous flair (4-12). In contrast, Palladio was concerned with the reconstruction of their ideal forms: "for him the archi-

Di pietre quadrate muri si veggono in Roma, oue era la piazza, & il Tempio di Augusto : ne' quali
schiauauano le pietre minori con alcuni corsi di pietre maggiori.

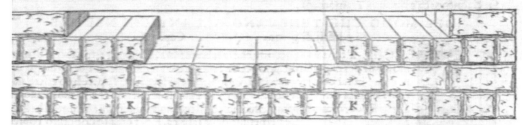

k, Corsi di pietre minori.
L, Corsi di pietre maggiori.

La maniera riempiuta, che si dice ancho à cassa, faceuano gli Antichi pigliando con tauole poste in
coltello tanto spacio, quanto voleuano che fusse grosso il muro, empiendolo di malta, e di pietre di
qualunque sorte mescolate insieme, e così andauano facendo di corso in corso. Si veggono muri di
questa sorte à Sirmion sopra il Lago di Garda.

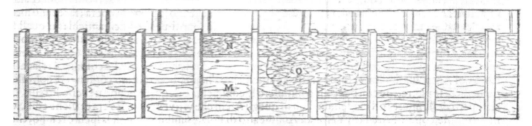

M, Tauole poste in coltello.
N, Parte di dentro del muro.
O, Faccia del muro tolte via le tauole.

Di questa maniera si possono ancho dire le mura di Napoli, cioè le Antiche : le quali hanno due
muri di sasso quadrato grossi quattro piedi, e distanti tra se piedi sei. Sono legati insieme questi muri da altri muri per trauerso, e le casse, che rimangono fra detti trauersi, & muri esteriori sono sei piedi per quadro, e sono empiute di sassi e di terra.

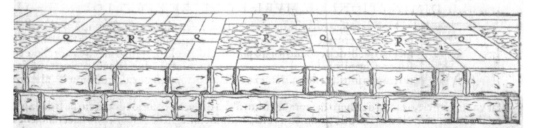

P, Muri di pietra esteriori.
Q, Muri di pietra posti per trauerso.
R, Casse piene di pietre, e di terra.

Queste in somma sono le maniere, delle quali si seruirono gli Antichi, & hora si veggono i vestigi :
dalle quali si comprende che ne i muri di qualunque sorte si siano, debbono farsi alcuni corsi, i quali siano come nerui, che tengano insieme legate l'altre parti ; ilche massimamente si osseruerà,
C   quando

4-13 Drawings from the
Four Books presenting
layers of walls—rare
examples of Palladio's use
of perspective. *CCA, cage
NA44 P164 (88-B1843 c.1),
livre 1, p. 13*

Quest'altra parte d'ordine Dorico, e cauata da diuersi fragmenti delle antiquità di Roma et fattone un composito tale che in opera l'ho prouato reuscire molto bene.

XIIII

4-14 Vignola's presentation of the Doric order in the *Canon of the Five Orders*. *CCA, cage, M NA44. V686 (W3245) pl. 14*

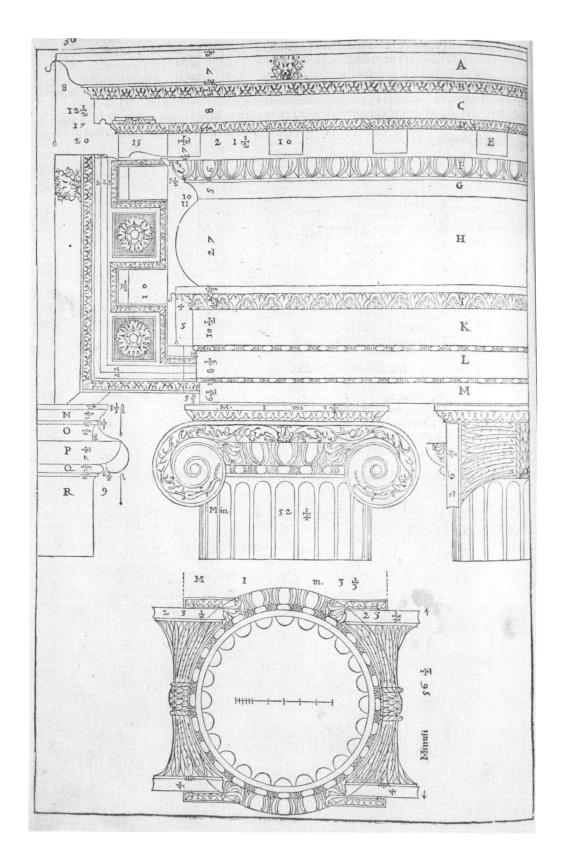

4-15 Palladio's presentation of the Ionic order in the *Four Books*. CCA, *cage, NA44 P164 (88-B1843 C.1) livre 1, p. 36*

tecture of antiquity is not historically remote; it is eternal, valid in all times and super-historical."[31]

This kind of (Platonist) position, in Rupprecht's view, explains Palladio's dismissal of perspective. Orthogonal projections transpose architecture in the "Absolute Realm," something perspective cannot do because it allows for the random choice of the viewing point. Palladio's drawing of the Rotonda in the *Four Books* is a good example of this approach: it combines in one drawing plan, section, and elevation, thus fully rendering the spatial system of the building (see 4-1). Palladio derived this method from Vignola, especially when it comes to presenting the elements of the five orders (4-14 and 4-15). The assumption is that the person looking at the drawing will recognize individual elements and then compose the "mental model" of the spatial object by combining them. Occasionally, Palladio pushed this method of delineation to the extreme, as in his drawing of the details of the Ionic order (4-16). The drawing requires careful reading to understand how its different parts fit together. Nevertheless, the information it provides is complete: on the basis of such a drawing, one can reconstruct the shape of the Ionic column from its base to the last element of the capital.

Rupprecht used the Greek term *diaphany* to describe Palladio's use of orthogonal projections in drawings in order to show simultaneous presence of all sides.[32] The Greek term means, among other things, "to shine through," and it could also be applied to an important aspect of Palladio's facade designs. Palladio combined visual images representing buildings not only in drawings, but on buildings as well. A number of scholars have drawn attention to Palladio's technique of using his built works in order to represent other buildings or ideas of buildings by incorporating a series of ideal facades interpenetrating each other. Cristoph Luitpold Frommel has pointed out that the use of *pietra finta* allowed Palladio to revive the architectural splendor of ancient Rome in a little city like Vicenza.[33] In some cases, the same prototype can be seen in a number of buildings. Decio Gioseffi has argued that such a relationship exists between the facade of the Palazzo Valmarana and the section (through the courtyard) of the Palazzo Iseppo Porto.[34] The Platonist implications of this process have

been particularly emphasized in a study by Marcello Fagiolo. Fagiolo used the term *metaprogettazione* for Palladio's tendency to project "spaces behind spaces" on the front facade. In his view, such "true architecture" reflects "the realm of virtue" in the facades; the procedure was intended to help the architect invoke timeless beauty and lead to the "speculation of eternal forms."[35] In this interpretation, Palladio's Vicentine palazzi superimpose an ideal city on the matrix of Vicenza.

The strategy of superimposing several facades on a single building is particularly evident in Palladio's church facades. In *Architectural Principles*, Rudolf Wittkower described how Palladio became the first to resolve the problem of using the classical orders in the design of a church facade.[36] Renaissance architects found it difficult to add a Roman temple facade to a Christian basilica, with its high central block and lower side aisles. Palladio provided the solution of superimposing ("metaprojecting," as Fagiolo would say) two temple fronts (4-17 and 4-18). The facade of San Francesco della Vigna and San Giorgio Maggiore represent two temple facades interpenetrating each other.[37] In the same way that different views, visual manifestations, plans, sections, and elevations of an Ionic column can be fragmented and combined into one drawing in order to represent the idea of an Ionic column, so different visual manifestations of the idea of a temple can be combined in a single building or building facade. Similarly, representations of more than one spatial system are combined in the facade of the Palazzo Valmarana (4-19). Representing multiple spatial systems superimposed over each other in a single building means representing a condition that cannot normally exist in three-dimensional space.

The complexities of this procedure can be very well illustrated by the Redentore (4-20 and 4-21). Already, Wittkower had remarked that the Redentore's facade represents a Roman temple *in antis*.[38] The corners of the central temple pictured on the facade have pilasters instead of engaged columns. In plan, the church is a triconch with a nave added to it; the nave has small chapels on each side. The pilasters of the facade are placed in the axis of the wall that separates the chapels from the nave and at the same time defines the width of

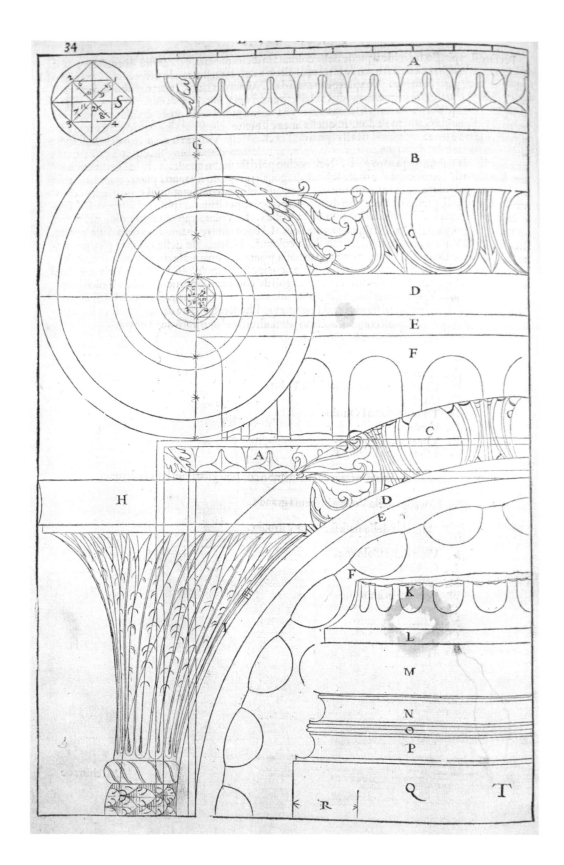

4-16 Detail of the Ionic order in the *Four Books*.
CCA, cage, NA44 P164 (88-B1843 C.1) livre 1, p. 34

DEO UTRIUSQUE TEMPLI ÆDIFICATORI AC REPARATORI

4-17 Facade of San Francesco della Vigna according to Ottavio Bertotti Scamozzi. *CCA, M7616:4, 1786 Tavola XVII*

4-18 Facade of San Giorgio
Maggiore according to
Ottavio Bertotti Scamozzi.
CCA, M7616:4, 1786 Tavola VIII

4-19 Facade of Palazzo
Valmarana from the *Four
Books.* CCA, cage, NA44 P164
(88-B1843 c.1) livre 2, p. 17

the square inscribed in the center of the triconch.

In a study of the inconsistencies in the design of the Redentore, Staale Sinding Larsen has emphasized that the facade, as it was built, would be better suited for a centrally planned church, consisting of a triconch with a short narthex without the nave and side chapels.[39] Larsen has shown that at the time the design of the church was discussed in the Venetian Senate, both Palladio and Marcantonio Barbaro advocated the idea of a centrally planned church. There is a direct connection between the fact that the Redentore was a votive church to Christ for relief from the 1575 plague and the fact that the church was conceived as a monument to the Resurrection of Christ. The most suitable form for such a monument would be a centrally planned, triconchal church, such as that of the Holy Sepulcher in Jerusalem. Larsen thinks that the idea was rejected because of the need to accommodate large audiences for official ceremonies. That consideration would have led to the introduction of the nave, while the central plan with triconch was retained for the sanctuary. It follows that the original, ideal version of the project envisioned by Palladio and Marcantonio Barbaro is represented by the ideal temple *in antis* in the main facade.

TECTONIC INTERPRETATION AND THE MORPHOLOGY OF THE ORDERS

Palladio's introduction of the Vitruvian principle that intercolumniations should not exceed three lower-column diameters can also be seen as a manifestation of the principle that what is built is a reflection of eternal architectural forms. Vitruvius explained that wider intercolumniations cannot support entablatures, but Renaissance architects, including Palladio, predominantly used the orders as ornament, applying pilasters and engaged columns to the facade. In that circumstance, Vitruvius's advice becomes irrelevant, and it is not surprising that Renaissance architects ignored it. But if the orders are used to represent another building, material or ideal, then they must convey the idea of a feasible structural system. Palladio's application of Vitruvian precepts for intercolumniations indeed implied that the orders

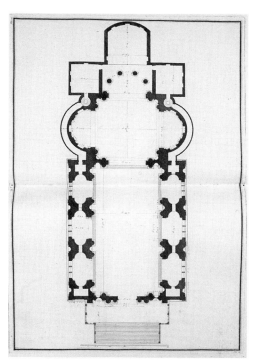

4-20 Plan of the Redentore according to Ottavio Bertotti Scamozzi. *M7616:4, 1786 Tavola*

4-21 Facade of the Redentore according to Ottavio Bertotti Scamozzi. *M7616:4, 1786 Tavola IV*

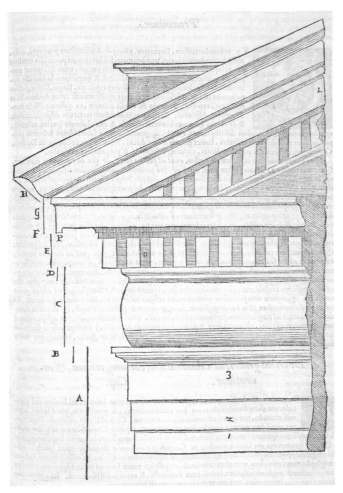

4-22 Drawing of the Ionic entablature in Barbaro's commentary on Vitruvius. *CCA, cage, NA44.V848 (W8778) c.2 p. 121*

would have been understood as a platonizing tendency in his time. This is particularly obvious in Palladio's formulation of the morphology of the Ionic entablature. Palladio's morphologies of the five orders are very similar to Barbaro's in terms of the Tuscan and Doric, but Barbaro had no influence on the Corinthian and Composite. The morphology of Palladio's Ionic corresponds to Barbaro's for the lower portions, but not for the entablature. This is not surprising with respect to proportions because Barbaro, unlike Palladio, believed that these should be subject to optical corrections. However, this does not explain the differences in the morphology itself.

Vitruvius and many of his Renaissance followers argued that mutules should not be placed above dentils since mutules represent primary rafters, dentils secondary rafters, and primary rafters cannot be placed above secondary ones. Vitruvius also dismissed the placement of dentils in the pediment, since secondary rafters cannot protrude from that part of the roof.[40] Barbaro treated this section in Vitruvius sympathetically, but in the end he did not take the instructions very seriously. He agreed that there should not be representations of conditions that cannot exist, but also added that in the case of dentils and mutules, practice had defeated Vitruvius's reasoning and that on ancient buildings they were often placed together. Such a combination, he noted, is successful, even though its tectonic interpretation makes no sense.[41] In the commentary, Barbaro included a drawing of the Ionic pediment with dentils clearly drawn and indicated (4-22). It is fair to conclude that, in Barbaro's opinion, the origin of the orders—what they imitate or represent—can not be taken as the guideline for their placement. A combination of elements can be successful even if it is historically or tectonically incorrect.

For Palladio, however, the tectonically correct use of the elements of the orders was very important. Chapter 20 of the first book of his treatise referred to departures from correct tectonic representation as "abuses." The chapter starts by explaining the tectonic origin of the elements of the orders and then makes a series of caustic attacks against their mannerist and tectonically incorrect use. Palladio included the use of *cartelli* or *cartucci*,

should accurately represent a possible disposition of interior columns. In this case, the orders are not merely an ornament; they enable the executed building to represent the ideal prototype. If an architectural form is to be manifest in a building, then the building must represent a structurally feasible combination of elements. Buildings, like all spatial objects, are reflections of forms of geometry; to reflect architectural forms, they must clearly express structural principles as well. In other words, the combination of ornaments on the facade must be tectonically credible.

The emphasis Palladio placed on the accuracy of tectonic representation in the use of the classical orders

breaking the pediments above doors and windows in the middle, cornices that are too big or project too much.[42] As for the canonical Ionic entablature, Palladio introduced, instead of dentils or modillions, a special kind of brackets, thus avoiding the Vitruvian strictures against combining dentils and mutules. Such brackets look like small cantilevers supporting the corona, and placing them in the pediment is tectonically acceptable: they do not look like representations of rafters protruding from the roof (4-23). These brackets appear regularly in Palladio's pediments, and this explains why his buildings with Corinthian columns so often lack canonical Corinthian entablatures.[43] At the same time, dentils appear in facades without pediments, at the Palazzo Schio, for example (4-24). Palladio obviously avoided applying his canonical Corinthian entablature (which has dentils) to facades with pediments. This concern can also be seen at the Villa Cornaro, where the upper loggia has Corinthian columns combined with a pediment. The entablature, which goes all around the central block of the house, has brackets without dentils. The two side wings are lower and they do not share the entablature of the central block. Since this cornice does not appear in the pediment, dentils are acceptable[44] (4-26). Similar reasoning seems to have determined the morphology of the two cornices of the rear facade of the Villa Foscari (Malcontenta): the upper cornice has dentils while the lower one, in the shape of the pediment, has brackets (4-25).

Conceived as a representation of a structural element belonging to the roof, and visible only from outside, dentils should not appear in interiors. Palladio used his canonical Composite entablature—which has double brackets and no dentils (4-27)—on the interior of his Venetian churches[45] (4-28). This restriction also explains the extremely unusual Doric entablature with no frieze in the interior of the Convento della Carità[46] (4-29). Using the correct Doric entablature in an interior would mean showing triglyphs inside the building. Triglyphs, as is known from Vitruvius, represent beams in the ceiling, which are not visible on the interior.[47] In contrast, Antonio da Sangallo the Elder incorporated both triglyphs and dentils on the entablature inside the Church of San Biagio in Montepulciano (4-30). For

4-23 Brackets on the Ionic entablature on the Rotonda.

Sangallo, these were obviously ornaments whose meaning did not inform their use. Finally, since triglyphs represent beams, it is legitimate to use them independently—to support a balcony, for example, as Palladio did on the Loggia del Capitaniato[48] (4-31).

During the Renaissance, the distinction between Barbaro's and Palladio's views on the importance of tectonic accuracy would have been interpreted by their contemporaries as the difference between Aristotelian and Platonist views on meaning and signification. When Barbaro said that tectonic interpretation ("meaning," as we would say today) is not essential for the aesthetic appreciation of a combination of mutules and dentils and

4-24 Entablature
at the Palazzo Schio.

4-25 Rear facade
of the Villa Foscari.

4-26 The cornice of the central block on Villa Cornaro has brackets because it appears below the pediment; the side wings, which are lower, have dentils.

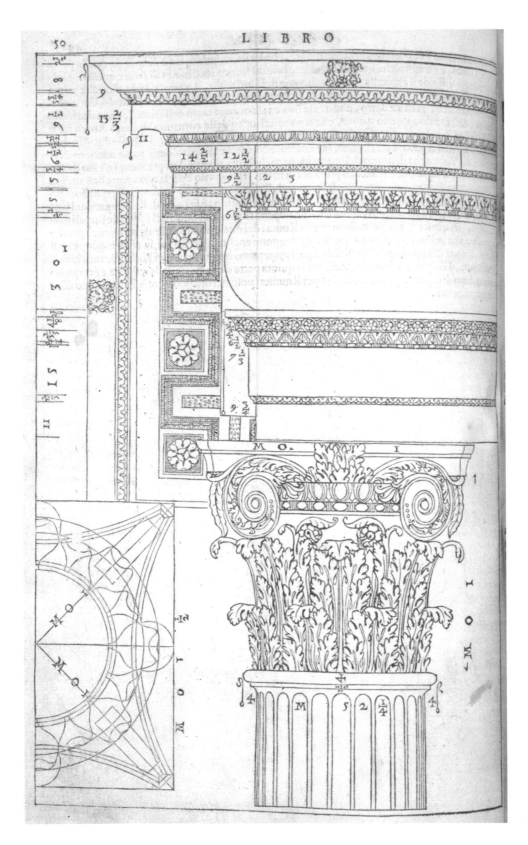

4-27 Presentation of the
Composite order in the
*Four Books. CCA,
NA44.P164 (88.B1843Cl, vol. 1,
p. 50)*

4-28 Interior entablature at San Giorgio Maggiore.

4-29 Interior entablature at Convento della Carità.
CISA, F0003306

that even a combination which makes no sense can still be aesthetically successful, he relied on the assumption that aesthetic judgments about shapes and spatial objects can be independent of the meanings ascribed to them. The assumption is that we can know what a certain shape (building or architectural detail) is like and we can think about it by imagining it from different sides without subsuming it under a concept such as "a representation of a structural element." Since we can visually contemplate formal properties of objects without ascribing meanings to them, it is plausible that we can also judge them aesthetically regardless of those meanings. This kind of view was well established in the Aristotelian cognitive psychology of the time, which provided the basis for understanding the human ability to think about shapes independently from concepts, and, consequently,

allowed the postulating of aesthetic judgments independently of the meanings ascribed to objects.[49]

However, Palladio need not have been aware of such niceties of Aristotelian philosophy, and even had he known about them, he would have considered them irrelevant. His architectural system is not concerned with the way things are perceived or thought about. But then, if the way buildings are thought about is irrelevant for the design principles his architectural system formulates, why would it be concerned with the meanings ascribed to architectural elements?

The question we face here is how to justify the canon of the five orders. The canon of the five orders cannot allow relativism. The very idea of a canon presupposes that certain dispositions and proportions of the elements are correct. But since it is normally

4-30 Interior entablature at Antonio da Sangallo the Elder's San Biagio (Montepulciano).

assumed that all meanings are social conventions, then it is hard to imagine how the interpretation of the elements would provide the justification of the canon. If every interpretation is relative to a system of conventions, the correct position of the elements of the five orders cannot be determined on the basis of their tectonic (or any other) interpretation. Every meaning is relative to the system of interpretation, while the canon of the five orders cannot allow relativism; therefore, there is no place for meanings in the formulation of the canon of the orders.

However, our contemporary view that all symbols and signs are cultural conventions is not necessarily a view that Renaissance theorists would have taken for granted. In fact, the difference between the view that meanings are conventional and the view that some meanings are in the nature of things (that signs can represent independently from human conventions, that things have "their real names," or that there are symbols that refer to certain things by their very nature) was regarded as one of the differences between Aristotelian and Platonist philosophy.

To summarize the argument presented so far: the canon of the classical orders cannot allow relativism. If the combinations of the elements the canon prescribes are justified by the meanings ascribed to the elements of the orders, and if these meanings depend on the context of interpretation, then the disposition and the size of the elements of the orders will depend on the context of their interpretation too. For this reason, every architectural theorist who relies on the theory of the classical orders must either assume that meanings ascribed to the elements of the orders possess no bearing on the formulation of the canon or claim that the elements of the orders have their meanings by themselves, and that these meanings determine their correct position. The latter approach is deeply incompatible with the views of modern science, so it is unlikely that it would be embraced by many theorists today. However, the view is fully compatible with the position of a number of twentieth-century critics of science and technology. Samir Younés, a contemporary theorist of classical architecture, developed this approach to the understanding of the principles of classical architecture in correlation with the critique of modern technological and scientific *Weltanschauung* based on the works of Jacques Ellul and Martin Heidegger.[50]

For a Renaissance architectural theorist, the distinction between the idea that meanings are conventional

4-31 Triglyphs
supporting the
balcony at the Loggia
del Capitaniato.

and that things can have meanings by their very nature was a distinction between the theories of meaning formulated in Aristotle's *De interpretatione* and Plato's *Cratylus*. Such a distinction is commonplace in Renaissance writings about language. Sperone Speroni and Benedetto Varchi, both of whom Barbaro knew as a student in Padua and Palladio would have met through his association with Trissino, referred in their writings to this distinction as the one between Platonist and Aristotelian views of language.[51] None of them, however, felt confident enough to take an independent stance on the problem. But Barbaro, in his *Commentaries on Porphyry*, clearly sided with the Aristotelian view and claimed that concepts were the same for all humans, but that the words that express them were arbitrary and conventional.[52] Such understanding of the concept of signification obviously goes hand in hand with Barbaro's stance regarding the relevance of tectonic interpretation. If meanings are relative to interpretation, they cannot be taken as decisive in the formulation of the canon of five orders. It is thus perfectly possible for a combination of the elements of the orders to be aesthetically successful and, at the same time, incorrect in the context of the standard Vitruvian interpretation of its parts. Barbaro's view of tectonic interpretation need not have even been consciously motivated by his Aristotelian views on meaning and signification. It is more likely that the way he understood such concepts as meaning, representation, and signification precluded the rigorous enforcement of tectonic arguments and made him open to tectonically incorrect and mannerist use of the classical elements.

Palladio's emphasis on accuracy of tectonic representation is thus a particularly good example of Platonist tendencies in his work. The point is not so much that he did not follow Barbaro through the implications of Aristotelian psychology. It is much more important that substantial aspects of his design procedures can only be explained by understanding the importance of the accuracy in tectonic representation that his detailing required. He took very seriously the idea that the elements of the classical orders should represent post-and-lintel structural systems and he made great effort to organize the canon around this understanding of the five

orders. If the way the elements are combined is to be deduced from their interpretation, then this interpretation cannot be just a convention: it is in the nature of dentils and mutules that they represent secondary and primary rafters. Their meaning, which is inherent in their nature, determines their correct placement. To the extent that Palladio's design principles rely on the assumption that built architecture is a reflection of eternal and immaterial architectural forms, the emphasis on the tectonic paradigm defines the distinction between such architectural forms and other Platonic forms, such as the forms of geometrical objects. Architectural forms are ultimately reducible to combinations of geometrical forms. But they are not just combinations of geometrical forms: what makes them architectural is the fact that they represent tectonic principles. Forms of geometry are reflected in any possible combination of spatial elements, while architectural forms are reflected through spatial elements that are organized in a tectonically correct way.

Palladio's application of the principles of tectonic representation in facade design is the most significant example of a narrative-driven approach to design in his oeuvre. Tectonic concerns strictly delimit which combinations of elements are acceptable in facade design. Nevertheless, the role of the tectonic paradigm (like any other narrative) in a design process can only be negative: it is there to prevent certain combinations of elements, for instance, those characterized as abuses. But no narrative can account for the totality of formal relationships on a spatial object. Once the forbidden combinations have been excluded from the repertoire, the tectonic paradigm provides no guidance as to how to compose the elements of a building into an aesthetically successful composition. Ultimately, the architect is left to his or her formal judgment.

PALLADIO AND PLATONISM

It could be argued that what is known about Palladio's education precludes the assumption of such Platonist tendencies. Palladio was trained as a stonemason and received humanist education only through his association with Trissino in his early thirties. The education he received could not have been extensive, and it is unrealistic to think that he would have understood much of the Aristotelian philosophy of his time. But between 1538 and 1540, when he probably spent considerable time with Trissino in Padua, he could well have been exposed to many different views. His understanding of Platonist philosophy could have been simple, but sufficient for the program of architectural design theory described here. It could have been limited to a number of very basic theses, including, for instance, the explanation that material things are perishable, but mathematical objects, such as numbers or geometrical figures are not. Just as mathematical entities are reflected in the material world, so other objects (including works of architecture) are perishable and imperfect reflections of higher reality. Beauty, like truth, can be reflected in the objects of the material world; it is independent of the human attitude to the reflections of eternal forms. In the same way that material objects can reflect ideal forms, so can all kinds of representations, including symbols and meanings of architectural elements. Such a highly predigested and simplified Platonism would have been sufficient to formulate the program of design theory we have just discussed. (It would be very difficult to formulate an equally predigested version of Aristotelian philosophy.) We should not expect Palladio to have read the complex writings of Renaissance Neoplatonists, such as Ficino. Trissino himself may not have had an interest in the more sophisticated philosophical arguments; he was a humanist and a man of letters, but his philosophical competencies seem to have been limited. Having led the life of a diplomat and a poet, he began showing an interest in philosophy only in his old age.[53] His studies of philosophy coincided with the period Palladio was with him in Padua. Even before that time, he was exposed to some Platonist views through Chalcondiles, under whom he studied in his youth. When he died in Rome in 1550 he left a large library consisting mainly of literary works with only a few philosophical volumes, including a manuscript version of Plato's works.[54]

At the same time, it is not Palladio's Platonism that matters here, but the Platonism of his system. The point is not whether and how the young Palladio was exposed to certain philosophical ideas. What matters is the internal consistency of his architectural system and the fact that Palladio's design theory exhibits a constant tendency to resolve theoretical problems by relying on a series of Platonist premises. This approach very often contradicts the Aristotelian mainstream to which he would have been exposed through Barbaro. In fact, it is remarkable that in his Platonist approach, Palladio confidently opposed the traditional Aristotelian reading of Vitruvius, including that represented by Barbaro.

Whether this allows us to talk about Palladio's Platonism is ultimately not a question we need to consider here. What should matter in the history of architectural theory is the analysis of principles and their mutual compatibility. A comparison with the methods of the history of philosophy may clarify this idea. The goal in the history of philosophy is to study the internal consistency of individual philosophical positions and discuss how they relate to the totality of a philosopher's views. What one person read or did not read is interesting biographical information; how his or her views constitute a consistent theory is what is important. Similarly, architectural theory elucidates how architecture should be made; it is concerned with the principles of design. Studying the internal consistency of systems of architectural theory through history means studying the mutual consistency of their design precepts. The approach of the historian of philosophy, applied to the history of architectural theory, thus reveals how consistent were the principles according to which individual buildings were designed. This approach is much more useful than the approach that studies the influences to which individual architects were exposed or tries to situate the narratives they produced within individual traditions. Unless we consider design principles and their mutual consistency, we cannot properly claim that we are discussing architectural theory as a systematic theory of architecture. Architectural works have their own spatial and visual properties; architects have to design these properties; studying the mutual consistency of the principles from which architects derive their design decisions means studying how these buildings were designed.

Corridor in a New
York apartment.
*John B. Murray
Architects; photo by
Durston Saylor, H.
Durston Saylor Inc.*

CHAPTER V

PALLADIANISM TODAY

CONTEMPORARY WRITINGS on architectural history and theory rarely if ever propose the study of works of the past in order to learn how to approach modern design. Throughout the twentieth century, the typical view was that the design methods of architects of the past were fundamentally irrelevant. Only in recent decades has there been a resurgence of interest in building in the classical style. The revival has caused a heated debate whose vehemence has become a cultural phenomenon worthy of study in its own right. Unfortunately, this passion has often precluded objective consideration of arguments in favor and against contemporary classicism—arguably a complex of theoretical problems with an extremely interesting and intellectually stimulating set of implications. The systematic study of these arguments can reveal a great deal about the background premises assumed (but often not stated) in the general argumentational framework of different positions in contemporary architectural theory.

The most elementary observation is the problematic status of the visual and formal that stands at the core of this debate. Modernist theorists never argued for a full break with the past; protagonists of Modernism have consistently emphasized that their architecture shares the same "principles" as the architecture of the past. "Principles" are understood here as narratives that can be applied, with equal success, to modern buildings and to a selected set of historical works. Such narratives typically reflect the cultural climate in which the author is writing. Since the 1970s, modernist architecture has been said to share the same ability to convey meanings as the great works of the past. In the years following World War II, narratives about proportions played a similar role, and before that, the claim that great works of architecture express the technology of their time. In contrast, the goal of contemporary classical architects is to produce buildings which share the same visual and formal properties (such as ornaments, spatial composition, or the orders) as great works of the past. It is the attitude towards the visual and formal properties of architectural works that distinguishes these architects from their modernist colleagues. To the extent that designing in the classical style today is a controversial idea, it is, in fact, the revival of certain visual and formal sensibility that causes so much debate. The usual argument is that visual and formal similarities with architecture of the past are literal and superficial, whereas one should search for deeper and more fundamental relationships—statements which all indicate the systematic anti-visual and anti-formal bias of their protagonists. Modernists have insisted that the formal is in a permanent state of flux, while there are other, non-visual properties of architecture (such as the expression of the technology of its time, the presence of certain proportions, or the ability to convey meanings) that are important, and which their architecture shares with the great works of the past. For almost a century, arguments of this kind have provided legitimacy rather than caused

5-1a and b Elevation and plan of
Villa Valdivia (Baja California, Mexico).
Marc Clemenceau Bailly, Architect.

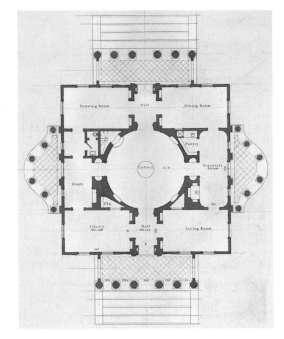

5-1a and b Elevation and plan of
Villa Valdivia (Baja California, Mexico).
Marc Clemenceau Bailly, Architect.

controversy. It is fair to conclude that those who are disturbed by modern classicism are not threatened by its relationship to historical architecture but by the visual and formal character of that relationship. Quite obviously, the visual and formal nature of this relationship will particularly anger those architectural historians who believe that their discipline is fully reducible to the study of narratives and that architectural works possess no formal or visual qualities worth acknowledging, let alone studying or emulating.

The differentiating line between the proponents and the opponents of modern classicism ultimately reflects the difference in the human ability to think visually and verbally. We are able to think about objects either by using concepts or by forming visual images (available through direct perception or in visual imagination). We can refer to and describe things that surround us and their properties in words or pictures. Visual imagery is far superior for describing the shape or color of an

object: saying that an object is curved or purple is less compelling than a drawing that faithfully represents its shape and color. However, visual thinking is incapable of specifying the historical origin, or providing a culturally derived interpretation, of a work of art (for instance, saying whether a mosaic is Roman or Byzantine—or whether certain architectural forms are "appropriate" to a certain epoch). The result is the debate about the extent to which our aesthetic judgments depend on visual or verbal properties of objects. For instance, it is impossible to visualize how an architectural work can "express its time," and this property can be thought about only conceptually and referred to verbally. Consequently, the tenet that "architecture should express its time" means that no aesthetic judgment can be purely formal and implies that all judgments of architecture are subject to verbal and conceptual considerations. Implicit differentiation between visual and verbal, formal and conceptual, runs

5-2 Juniper Hill. *Quinlan Terry*

PALLADIAN ARCHITECTURE
AND MODERN CLASSICISM

through the arguments for and against modern classicism. Its importance cannot be overstated, if we are to understand the full scope of the implications of the debate about building in the Palladian style today.

The application of Palladian design principles in modern classical architecture can be approached in a number of ways. It can pertain to the use of individual elements, combinations of elements, spatial compositions; the formal principles of Palladio's designs can be applied to residential architecture or used on structures built for purposes unknown in Palladio's time.

One approach would be to see in the application of Palladian design principles a renewal of the search for a more perfect expression of the ideal prototype, as is the case with Marc Bailly's Villa Valdivia (5-1 a and b). This version of the Rotonda replaces the side porticoes with curved colonnades, which convey representative aspects of the rooms behind. Here Bailly has followed Palladian rules for intercolumniations and the relationship of the columns and walls behind the facade. Robert A. M. Stern's house in California relates to Palladio's Villa Pisani in a similar way (5-3a and b). In this case, the correspondences are greater on the facade than in the plan, which has been adapted to modern life. Nevertheless, the plan reflects Palladian principles of spatial composition, particularly in the alignment of openings into visual axes.

Modern classical architects have drawn on elements of spatial composition, incorporating them in their projects in more or less liberal ways. No element of Palladian design theory has had greater impact than the pedimented portico. In modern works, pedimented porticos have been used both in residential architecture—

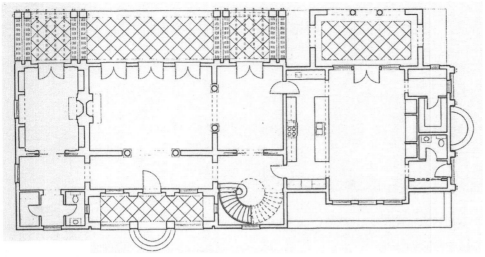

5-3a and b Plan and elevation of a villa in California. *Robert A. M. Stern Architects*

5-4 House in New York. *Fairfax and Sammons, Architects, P.C.; photograph by Durston Saylor, H. Durston Saylor Inc.*

5-5 New country house at Ascot. *Robert Adam*

a house in New York by Fairfax and Sammons, for example (5-4)—and in public buildings, such as Nashville's Symphony Hall by David Schwartz (5-6). Quinlan Terry's Juniper Hill and Robert Adam's country house at Ascot have explored this element of composition in a particularly refined way (5-2 and 5-5). In the Villa Vitruviana, Thomas Gordon Smith has revived the Palladian concept of a four-column vaulted sala in a way that is reminiscent of Villa Pisani in Montagnana (5-7). Peter Pennoyer has similarly incorporated the column-free staircase of the Convento della Carità in a project for The Mark Hotel (5-8), and John B. Murray has made the axial alignment of openings an important feature of a New York apartment (see page 170).

The use of the classical orders is another very complex source of inspiration. Among contemporary classical works, the buildings by John Blatteau are particularly notable for their refined classical detailing. While Blatteau's use of the orders tends to be inspired more by Vignola's than by Palladio's canon, his works certainly show the approach required to engage seriously with the use of the orders (5-9). Similar refinement in the use of the orders can be observed on a house in Florida by Ferguson and Shamamian (5-10). Orders can be used to define spatial composition, as Ionic columns were used by Dan Parolek in his design for the Millennium Gate in Washington, DC (5-11a and b). More typically, the orders will play a role in facade

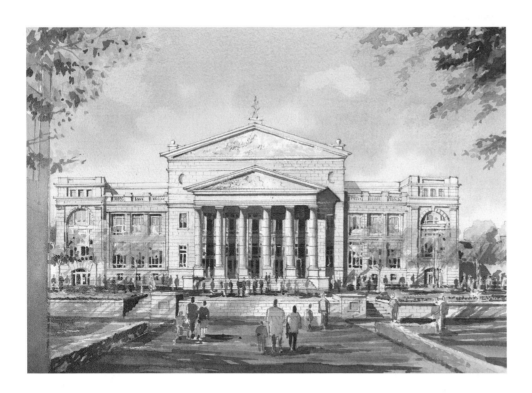

5-6 Schermerhorn
Symphony Hall
Nashville, TN.
David M. Schwartz/
Architectural Services, Inc.

5-7 Villa Vitruviana.
Thomas Gordon Smith;
photograph by Alan
McIntyre Smith

176

5-8 Staircase
in Mark Hotel
(New York City).
*Peter Pennoyer
Architects; photo-
graph by Peter Paige*

5-9 Riggs Bank.
John Blatteau

5-10 House in Florida, detail. *Ferguson and Shamamian Architects, LLP; photograph by Mick Hales*

compositions; they are more likely to be used to accentuate certain segments, as is the case with John Malick's Randolph Residence, William Baker's Krone Residence, and Jonathan Lee's Library in Michigan (5-12a and b, 5-13, and 5-14).

The works of modern classical and Palladian architects may be received with enthusiasm, but, ultimately, the question of the appropriateness of this approach today must be addressed. Is this work not—as modernist critics would say—full of nostalgic pastiche? Is it not absurd to use Doric or Ionic columns on buildings in modern times? How relevant can such an approach be to design today? Should modern architecture not express modern times? Is it not preposterous to advocate the use of architectural forms from the past in a world dominated by modern science and technology? These questions are legitimate, and they represent a concern and a theoretical problem that must be explored systematically.

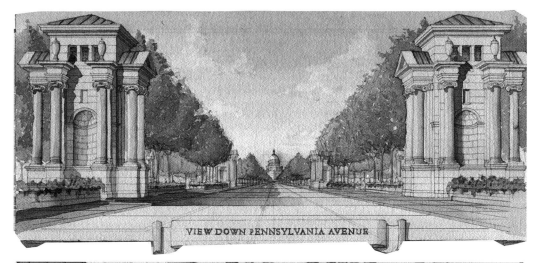

VIEW DOWN PENNSYLVANIA AVENUE

5-11a and b Millennium Gate (Washington DC).
Daniel Parolek, Opticos Design

PENNSYLVANIA AVENUE GATEWAY
BARNEY CIRCLE · WASHINGTON, D.C.

179

5-12a and b (left and opposite) Randolph Residence (San Francisco, California). *John Malick & Associates; designed by Stephen Sooter*

APPROPRIATENESS TO TIME

The impetus for modern classicism can be seen in the consensus about the aesthetic value of the works of architects of the past, including Palladio. It is plausible to argue that if formal design principles produce aesthetically pleasing results, then they should be used. One cannot say that our aesthetic sensibility has changed, because the argument is precisely that Palladio's architectural works are aesthetically successful by our own modern standards. Nor can one simply say that architects should not look to the past to find formal principles to apply to their work. Such a view would require a dismissal of all Renaissance architecture. So, if we agree about the aesthetic value of certain formal systems, why should we not use them? To insist on this, one must deny that a building designed today, on the basis of the same formal design principles which we find successful on, say, Renaissance buildings, will be aesthetically as successful. One explanation would be that an aesthetic judgment is never purely formal and that it always depends on the way buildings relate to our knowledge about the time when they were built. In other words, aesthetic judgments always depend on the way buildings "express their time," are "appropriate to their time," and so on. Even at a superficial level, this claim presents a number of difficulties. If modern architecture is to express modern times, what aspect of the era should it express? Should it

reflect the progress of science and technology? Was the twentieth century not marked by unprecedented horrors in its political history? Aren't the bare walls and unornamented facades of modernist architecture a celebration of the faceless and inhumane totalitarianisms the twentieth century produced? They certainly can be interpreted that way. Isn't it then morally reprehensible to design such buildings? The problem is that it is unclear how and by what criteria we are to decide what aspects of modern times modern architecture should express. Even if we could decide this and why it should be done, there is no guarantee that we could agree on how to do it. At most, we might produce architecture that some individuals would interpret as expressing our time.

The difficulty lies in the absence of clarity about how and by what criteria to decide which architectural shapes are "appropriate" to certain times. There is no logical process that will derive certain shapes from specific characteristics of individual epochs. The modernist movement argued that the system of shapes it advocated (bare walls without ornaments, flat roofs, asymmetry) was expressive of the modern age of science and technology. In fact, these formal properties were not new nor were they facilitated by technology. There is no logical connection between an architecture of bare walls and a modern scientific worldview. Asymmetry is characteristic of many medieval buildings. Flat roofs leak even with the most sophisticated materials. Mies van der Rohe

strove to develop ways of designing glass facades well before they were technologically possible; he did not derive his ideas from the technology that was available. In fact, it can be argued that modern technology provides great opportunities for classical architecture: the technologies of stone cutting today allow affordable mass production of classical elements. There is nothing contradictory in the use of modern technology in building modern classical buildings. Advocating building in the classical style today assumes construction costs within reasonable budgets, which implies the use of modern technology.

IF IT IS THE SAME, HOW CAN IT BE DIFFERENT?

It is a paradox that we agree about the quality of works of the past and formal principles of design that make them aesthetically successful, but at the same time we are also meant to believe that it is inappropriate to use these principles. The justification of this paradox in modernist writings has always been problematic. Le Corbusier's romantic fascination with the Parthenon in *Towards the New Architecture* stands in uneasy relationship with his principal message that classical forms should be abandoned in favor of simple, Modernist shapes. If Doric capitals can be admired, why should they not also be used?[1] If the Parthenon is indeed a wonderful building, why should it not be replicated? Are the nineteenth-century copies of the Parthenon not equally beautiful? It does not help to argue that Le Corbusier's critique targets nineteenth-century eclecticism for incompetence in proportioning and combining classical ornaments; his intention was not to advocate greater sophistication in the use of the classical orders, but to abolish it altogether.[2] Critics of modern Classicism are not complaining about the lack of consistent application of classicist design principles in modern works (in that case they would be arguing for more classicism!). They are attacking the contemporary use of classicist formal design principles, which, they agree, contributed substantially to the aesthetic value of the works of the past. The typical stance would be that formal identity need not be taken to guarantee aesthetic identity: the Parthenon's shapes are to be appreciated as the expression of the technology or spirit of their time. More generally, the claim is that no architectural form can be appreciated without knowledge about the cultural context in which it was created.

The question of whether formally identical buildings can be evaluated differently because they were built in different times is a version of a broader aesthetic problem. If we are presented with two identical shapes, and

5-13 A residence in Atlanta, GA.
William T. Baker & Associates, Atlanta, GA

5-14 Library in Michigan.
Jonathan Lee Architects

we agree about the aesthetic properties of one of them, under what conditions are we allowed to assume agreement about the aesthetic properties of the other? In twentieth-century aesthetic writings, this problem has been referred to as aesthetic supervenience, the principle that identical objects cannot be given different aesthetic evaluations. The principle seems plausible in certain cases, since it applies to a number of common artistic practices, such as performing and reproducing works of music. It seems reasonable that two identical performances of the same piece of music from the same compact disk under identical circumstances should be ascribed identical aesthetic value. Similarly, while original paintings typically have greater cultural value than reproductions because of their authenticity, it seems reasonable that reproductions share some aesthetic properties with the original.

Aesthetic debates about supervenience turn on the distinction between aesthetic properties ("elegant" or "grateful") and non-aesthetic properties (shape, color, material). This distinction originates from Frank Sibley's papers of the 1960s.[3] To put it simply, if supervenience is a valid principle in artistic evaluation, then the aesthetic properties of objects ("elegant") depend on their non-aesthetic properties ("polychromatic"). Two works of art that differ in their aesthetic properties must differ by some non-aesthetic property as well.[4] If aesthetic proper-

ties ("beautiful" or "cheerful") *supervene* on non-aesthetic properties ("circular" or "hard"), then two objects with identical non-aesthetic properties must have the same aesthetic properties. The set of non-aesthetic properties whose change will affect aesthetic properties is called the subvening base of aesthetic properties.

It is plausible to say that two identical etchings, produced at the same time by the same artist, will have the same aesthetic properties. But what about the Parthenon and its nineteenth-century copy? Even more complex is the case of the attribution of aesthetic properties to a building where the function has changed within the original envelope—a hospital converted into a school, for example. If we believe that the appropriateness of the building's shape to its function affects our aesthetic appreciation, then some or all of the aesthetic properties of a building will be changed by changing its function, even if it does not significantly change its shape.

The debate about the validity of supervenience in aesthetics was very lively in the late 1980s and the early 1990s. In 1988, John Bender argued that only physical and sensory properties of a work of art should be considered as non-aesthetic properties (i.e., be taken to constitute the subvening base of aesthetic properties).[5] Aesthetic supervenience, as he analyzed it, meant that if two works of art have precisely the same physical and sensory properties, they must also have the same aesthetic properties. Bender left no space for the claim that aesthetic properties, say, of a building, depend on the way we associate shapes of the building with the epoch when it was built. The critics of his thesis argued that an aesthetic property of a work of art cannot be specified outside of its historical categorization, which makes supervenience of little use in aesthetics.[6] For example, two objects may have the same physical and sensory properties, but some aesthetic properties could be ascribed to one and not to the other. Two identical mosaics, one Byzantine and the other Roman, can be judged differently; a Roman mosaic need not be organized in the context of Byzantine art. However, it has been pointed out that the latter argument only means that the subvening base should be expanded to include data about the origin and the categorization of the art-work.[7] In the context of the distinction between visual and verbal properties, the claim that no aesthetic properties can be ascribed to a work of art without considering its origin and cultural context means that no aesthetic judgment can be based solely on those properties of works of art that can be seen or imagined visually.

The thesis that all aesthetic properties always (at least in part) depend on those properties that can be thought of only conceptually and expressed verbally is very difficult to prove. We can think about objects and their formal properties visually, by imagining them, and there is no proof that we cannot derive pleasure purely from such contemplation of shapes. The claim that all aesthetic judgments always depend on verbal, conceptual thinking is simply not justified. It is plausible to believe that some aesthetic properties depend exclusively on verbal properties, others on a combination of formal and visual properties, and still others exclusively on formal properties. In the first case, the shape of the object is not important. A person with a penchant for things medieval may admire a Gothic church for historical reasons; for such a person, the actual shape of the church would be irrelevant. In the second case, aesthetic properties are attributed to a building depending on the way certain verbal properties can be ascribed to its visual properties—e.g., the building is appreciated because its shapes can be consistently interpreted in a certain way. A Doric temple may be ascribed certain aesthetic properties because it expresses consis-

tently tectonic principles; these properties will be denied to a Baroque church because of its broken pediments. Finally, some aesthetic properties could depend purely on formal properties, such as the composition of the facade, rhythm of interior spaces, and so on.

This insight can be taken as the starting point for the aesthetic position which the British aesthetician Nick Zangwill has referred to as "moderate formalism."[8] Zangwill argues that the wide diversity of aesthetic properties makes it impossible to generalize about non-aesthetic properties on which they depend. It is impossible to show that in the case of abstract paintings, for instance, some aesthetic properties may not supervene exclusively on the arrangement of lines, shapes, and colors. There is no proof that no aesthetic properties can be supervenient purely on the shape and color of the object. Zangwill distinguished between extreme formalism (all aesthetic properties are formal), extreme anti-formalism (none of them is formal), and moderate formalism (some aesthetic properties are formal while others are not).[9] Zangwill's critics would have to show that, in spite of the fact that we can visually contemplate works of architecture, shapes and colors thus contemplated can never alone be the subvening base of any aesthetic property whatsoever—a very difficult claim to prove.

Zangwill's analysis elucidates the full extent of the contradiction inherent in Le Corbusier's admiration of the Parthenon. The easiest solution would be to assume that the aesthetic properties of architecture must always depend on the appropriateness of architectural shapes to their time (or the technology of their time)—i.e., at least one verbal property. To dismiss the possibility of re-using the form of the Parthenon in modern times, Le Corbusier would have had to claim that no aesthetic properties can be ascribed purely on the basis of the visual contemplation of the building. In other words, Le Corbusier's view would have been what Zangwill has called an extreme anti-formalist position. The modernist position is not compatible with formalism, however moderate the latter may be. To sustain their critique of modern classicism, modernist critics must claim that aesthetic appreciation is always (at least partly) dependent on some properties of the building that can be thought of only conceptually and described only verbally. If purely formal aesthetic properties exist, then they would justify building new Parthenons in modern times.

Two problems follow from this: first, there is no proof that purely formal aesthetic judgments are impossible (and consequently that modernist criticism of modern Classicism is justified), and second, the level of dependence on verbal properties necessary to formulate this type of critique introduces dangerous relativism into the very foundations of the modernist program. If all appreciation of architectural works depends, for instance, on the way they express their time or the technology with which they were built, then works of modernist architecture will not be appreciated by those who have different associations about the time in which a building was created or know nothing about building technology. The problem is that such associations ("meanings") are always relative to individuals and sometimes, in part, to their cultural background. Sixteenth-century Platonists could have believed that some names, signs, or symbols have meanings by themselves; this strategy is equally available to our contemporary critics of technology and the scientific worldview. But it is not available to those architectural theorists who claim that their position is aligned with the spirit of modern technology and scientific *Weltanschauung*.[10]

Consequently, if buildings can be considered appropriate to modern times by one person but not another, then the criticism of modern Classicism as inappropriate to modern times is no more than an arbitrary statement of personal bias. Even worse, the agreement about the aesthetic value of modernist architecture becomes impossible. Le Corbusier may have wanted modernist architecture to please "the child, metaphysician, and the savage," but savages may fail to recognize the expression of modern times in a modernist building and are unlikely to be well informed about technology. Not everyone will necessarily recognize, let alone appreciate, such properties as the expression of modern times in the shapes of modernist architecture. In other words, if one allows for purely formal aesthetic properties, then one cannot dismiss the nineteenth-century replicas of the Parthenon. However, if one argues that all aesthetic judgments depend on conceptual properties in order to prevent endless reproduction of the Parthenon, it becomes impossible to agree about the inappropriateness of Classicism in modern times or about aesthetic qualities of modernist architecture.

PROBLEMS WITH RELATIVISM

Aesthetic relativism also presents a serious threat to the classicist program. To formulate the canon of the classical orders, it is necessary to claim that certain formal and proportional relationships are aesthetically more successful than others and to expect agreement about such judgments. Classicist architectural theory cannot allow aesthetic relativism because it must justify the system of the five orders. This does not necessarily mean that a certain disposition of the elements is unmistakably the right one. It is generally recognized that the orders gradually evolved over time through the experience of generations of architects. But in order to see gradual improvements in the development of the system of the five orders, it is necessary to claim that certain formal solutions are better than others and that such judgments can be expected to meet general agreement.

At the same time, aesthetic relativism is the dominant view in the contemporary understanding of aesthetic values, although it would be more accurate say that there is no answer to the question of whether some aesthetic judgments can be expected to be agreed upon. We simply do not know whether aesthetic judgments are always relative to individuals or cultures. In the future, cognitive science and knowledge about the functioning of the human brain may allow us to say whether the ability to derive pleasure from the contemplation of certain forms is inborn and perhaps constitutive of the human mind; at the moment any attempt to answer this question is mere speculation. While aesthetic relativism is certainly more widespread today than it was fifty years ago, this belief is a cultural phenomenon that cannot be taken as decisive in discussing a capacity of the human mind.

Frank Sibley provided an insightful discussion of this problem, suggesting that aesthetic judgments possess objective validity.[11] In his view, this claim can be justified by pointing to agreement about some settled and virtually indisputable cases, together with a procedure that offers a possibility of attaining a wider agreement in principle. The recognition of aesthetic properties in his view can be compared to the recognition of colors. While we normally assume a high level of agreement about colors, our color vision could have been much worse: we could have been fluctuatingly color-blind or possess only part-time color vision, e.g., after meals or until middle age. If this were the case, then differences in judging colors would be attributed to the viewer's physical condition. Color vision could be a rare ability: there might be a small minority that could see colors, the rest shading off in various degrees of color-blindness towards totally achromatic vision. Sibley suggested that this pattern, with a minority elite, ill-defined at the edges, but fairly constant over generations and identified by their performance, describes the situation in aesthetic matters. Most people, even with effort, do not notice similarities and differences they find others agreeing on. It is thus easy to reject aesthetic appreciation, as Sibley says, as "snobbish perpetuation of the bogus by means of dishonesty."[12] What impresses those who do agree is that they learn that critics through the ages have done so as well. Sibley emphasized the existence of transcultural agreements about some works of art, thus implying that it is possible to formulate a canon of architectural/art works that have been appreciated by individuals from different cultures because of their aesthetic value. It may take centuries to reach agreement about some works of art, partly because the possibility of error decreases as possible explanations of error become more obviously absurd: "we could not sensibly reject a consensus about *Oedipus* that has spanned centuries as being the result of personal bias, enthusiasm for a novel style, or passing fashions or fads."[13]

Sibley's papers clearly show how views about aesthetics have changed over the past forty years. Today, Sibley's belief in the possibility of the canon sounds almost eccentric. The immediate reaction is to dismiss his defense of the canon of transculturally appreciated works of art as a cultural construct of his time. The same applies to the idea of objective aesthetic judgments. But we have also to bear in mind that aesthetic relativism is equally a mark of our times and itself a cultural construct.

Nevertheless, Sibley did point out an important argument against the idea that all aesthetic judgments are relative to individuals or cultures. Generally valid aesthetic judgments can explain transcultural agreement about artworks where it genuinely exists. If all ascription of aesthetic properties were culturally relative, then it would be impossible to explain how some artworks could have elicited similar responses in widely diverse cultures. If one cannot describe, for each individual cultural context, how its cultural politics generated (claims of) the appreciation of *Oedipus*, then Sibley's explanation cannot be easily dismissed. The relativist argument against the canon is that attempts to formulate it are always culturally biased because our aesthetic appreciation is always culturally predetermined: this argument first assumes the validity of aesthetic relativism and then argues the impossibility of the canon. A defender of the canon, such as Sibley, will start from the historically documented, transcultural agreement about some artworks and argue that such agreement can only be explained by assuming the possibility of generally valid aesthetic judgments. As long as relativists have no explanation for each documented case of transcultural agreement, Sibley's case is stronger since he can point to a historical fact that the relativist theory cannot explain.

The debate about the possibility of agreement about aesthetic judgments is thus inconclusive. It would be methodologically wrong to assume that no transcultural agreement about aesthetic judgments is possible and then argue that agreement about formal principles of classical design is also impossible. A defender of Classicism could always invoke Sibley's argument and answer that since the forms of classical architecture were adopted by so many different cultures, therefore some aesthetic values must be transcultural.

PALLADIANISM AND FORMALISM

At the same time, if there are aesthetic judgments that are not relative to individuals (and their cultural background), these judgments must be formal. All aesthetic judgments that depend, partly at least, on conceptual properties of objects must be relative to individuals and their cultural backgrounds, unless one believes that some objects can have meanings by themselves. Such judgments are based on arbitrary, individual or culturally derived associations that we establish between shapes and concepts. This has two-fold implications for Modernism. On the one hand, saying that the aesthetic value of modernist architecture derives from its appropriateness to modern times is not a favorable thing to say, since it means that modernist architecture is a fad. On the other hand, relativism makes it impossible to formulate consistent criticism of modern Classicism. It is contradictory to endorse aesthetic relativism and at the same time assume the universal validity of judgments used to dismiss building in the classical style today.

The question remains whether a classicist architectural theory can be formulated in a way that does not contradict our modern worldview. Only purely formal aesthetic judgments can make a claim to transcultural validity. Since a classicist architectural theory cannot allow relativism in the formulation of the canon of the five orders, classicism can only be justified by formal aesthetic judgments. Saying that classical orders should be used (or should be used in a certain way) because their elements represent bodies or structural elements means also saying that they should not be used if these elements are not recognized to represent those elements. Since different individuals are likely to have different associations, the correct placement of the elements of the orders can be only justified by the visual properties of the five orders. Formalism is therefore the safest argumentational strategy in favor of the application of classicist design principles in contemporary architecture. The argument will be that certain formal relationships between parts, certain visual qualities, have been known for centuries to contribute to the aesthetic quality of architectural works. From this point of view, classical architects are simply using formal systems that have been developed and improved by generations of architects. The narratives traditionally associated with classical elements cannot play a role in the foundation of a classicist architectural theory or justification of modern Classicism.

However, formalism does have implications for the kind of Classicism that can be plausibly defended. If agreement about aesthetic judgments is to be possible at all, it will be possible only if it is exclusively based on properties that can be visually contemplated. This kind of formalist Classicism is much closer to Barbaro's theoretical position than Palladio's. The problem that seems to follow is that the kind of architecture that Barbaro's reading of Vitruvius is likely to give—with its conventionalist and relativist view about the meanings of elements—is Baroque and not Palladianism. It was Barbaro's commentary on Vitruvius that the early seventeenth-century Roman architects read. Their architecture was one of extreme formal refinement, but also one that ignored the idea of accurate representation of structural elements.

However, we must not forget that Palladianism is a segment of the classical tradition that was developed at a specific moment and, over time, it has been greatly admired for its formal aesthetic qualities. Some of its aspects originally arose from a strong concern for accurate tectonic representation. Rooted in Vitruvius, the tectonic paradigm was historically an extremely fruitful aspect of the classical tradition, and one that has proved very productive through the history of classical architecture. The paradigm is not credible today, but one should distinguish between the theoretical foundation, which explains and justifies the use of a certain formal system (such as the classical orders) and the reasoning that has led to the discovery (or formulation) of that formal system. We need not share Palladio's belief that the tectonic symbolism of certain ornamental elements is inherent in the structure of the universe in order to learn from him visually successful ways to proportion and combine these elements. The belief that certain elements of the classical orders represent structural elements is not essential for the theoretical foundation of the classicist program today. In other words, working within a tradition implies learning from the masters; modern classicists are likely to be interested in Palladio's methods of design, and Palladio's use of formal elements, but it is unlikely and unnecessary that they share his conceptual framework, his associations, or his cultural horizon. Ultimately, the goal is to make beautiful shapes, and if one agrees that a formal system of design principles produces such shapes, then it is contradictory to say that it should not be used. In visual arts—of which architecture is one—it is the visual and formal that matter.

AFTERWORD

"The mystery of the world is the visible, not the invisible," Oscar Wilde once wrote. "It is only shallow people who do not judge by appearances." Like so many of the Victorian aesthete's pronouncements, this opinion is worthy of serious consideration. Wilde's observation elegantly states the two underlying theses of this book: that visual and formal properties of architectural works are legitimate objects of study in architectural history and that if certain formal and visual design principles give aesthetically successful results, then we should use them in modern works. The importance of the distinction between visual and verbal, formal and conceptual, shape and its abstract properties, cannot be overemphasized when it comes to architecture. The intention of this book is not to argue the greater value of either, but merely to establish, from the example of Palladio's architecture, that architectural works have both. Sometimes, the formal decisions of an architect like Palladio may be affected by verbal properties ascribed to certain elements, but the architectural creative process is necessarily marked by formal and visual decisions that are ultimately not reducible to verbal, conceptual thinking.

Learning from Palladio means learning not only how to design, but also how to learn to design. It means learning to rely predominantly on formal considerations. Trying to summarize what is known about Palladio's design procedures also means trying to describe his design principles for those architects who want to follow them. It is not easy to dismiss this idea by appealing to judgments about the appropriateness of architecture to its time. "Appropriateness to one's time" is relative to individuals, and therefore a particularly unsuitable basis for any judgment requiring consensus. Certainly, architects can refuse to learn the formal treatment of design problems from the past, and they can try to design on the basis of their private associations with modern times, naively believing in the unquestionable rightness of these associations. But architecture derived from such an approach cannot simply expect people to agree that it has made the world more beautiful. Such a claim can be made only by an architecture that is genuinely formally motivated, and the important job of the architectural historian is to provide material for such an undertaking.

APPENDIX A

HORIZONTAL PROPORTIONS OF INTERIOR SPACES IN PALLADIO'S DESIGNS

Room Length/Width Ratios in the Plans of Palladio's Buildings Presented in the *Four Books* and Their Potential Proportional Interpretation

Room length/width ratios that appear more than once in a single plan (for instance, in the case of symmetrically placed rooms) have been listed only once. The list of rooms is based on a similar table published in Mitrović, "Palladio's Theory of Proportions," which in its turn was equivalent to a list published in Howard and Longair, "Harmonic Proportion," with the following additions:

Villa Pisani (Bagnolo): A room 30/18. The width of the room is given in the plan while Palladio says that the length/width ratio is 5/3.
Villa Thiene: The width of this room is given in the ground plan and its length in the elevation.
Palazzo Barbarano (Quinto): two rooms with dimensions 24/19 and 19/16. These rooms clearly appear in the left wing of the plan; the rooms in the right wing, which should be symmetrical with these, are

24/16 and 16/16. This would obviously result in an asymmetrical facade. In the text, Palladio says that the rooms on the right and the left side of the entrance have a length/width ratio of 3/2, but this must refer to the right wing room in the drawing (24/16). However, Palladio also wrote that the height of these rooms is 21 feet.

Numbers indicating room dimensions were not clearly printed in some copies of the first edition. For instance, in some copies, the length of the large rooms in the right and left wings of the Palazzo Chiericati (30) is not legible.

C1 indicates ratios close to 1.58 (or 1.6); C2 ratios close to 1.26. Ratios whose decimal value is less than 1.2 have been indicated because of their role in the discussion of chromaticism. Potential harmonic interpretation of ratios according to Wittkower has been omitted from the list.

TABLE 1

BOOK II PAGE NO.	BUILDING WITH ROOM DIMENSIONS	EQUIVALENT RATIO FROM PALLADIO'S LIST OF PREFERRED RATIOS	DECIMAL VALUE OF RATIOS THAT DO NOT CORRESPOND TO PALLADIO'S PREFERRED RATIOS	COMMENTARY
5	Antonini (Udine) 17/17 24/17 28/17 32/28 12½/8 12½/12¼	1:1 $\cong\sqrt{2}:1$ $\cong 5:3$ $\cong 1:1$	1.1428 1.5625	less than 1.2 C1
6	Chiericati (Vicenza) 18/12 18/18 30/18	3:2 1:1 5:3		
8	Porto (Vicenza) 30/20 20/20 20/9 9/7 30/30	3:2 1:1 1:1	2.2222 1.2857	exceeds 2/1 C2

BOOK II PAGE NO.	BUILDING WITH ROOM DIMENSIONS	EQUIVALENT RATIO FROM PALLADIO'S LIST OF PREFERRED RATIOS	DECIMAL VALUE OF RATIOS THAT DO NOT CORRESPOND TO PALLADIO'S PREFERRED RATIOS	COMMENTARY
11	Della Torre (Verona) 19/19 19/11 19/15 30/19 22½/18 19/17	1:1	 1.7227 1.2667 1.5789 1.25 1.1176	 √3/1 C2 C1 less than 1.2
13	Thiene (Vicenza) 20/20 56/20 34½/20 30/20	1:1 3:2	 2.8 1.725	 exceeds 2/1 √3/1
16	Valmarana (Vicenza) 20½/17½ 18/15 38/19	 2:1	1.1714 1.2	less than 1.2 less than 1.2
19	Rotonda (Vicenza) 26/15 15/11		1.7333 1.3636	√3/1
20	Capra (Vicenza) 27/17 13/13 32/32	 1:1 1:1	1.5882	C1
22	Barbarano (Vicenza) 12/7 41½/25 24/16 16/16 24/19 19/16 16/12	 ≅5:3 3:2 1:1 4:3	1.7143 1.2632 1.1875	√3/1 C2 less than 1.2
25	Atrio Toscano 20/20 60/40 25/20 38/30 28/20	1:1 3:2 ≅√2:1	 1.25 1.2667	 C2 C2
26	Atrio Toscano (Detail) 67½/45	3:2		
28	Atrio di 4 colonne 17½/16 53½/35	 3:2	1.0937	less than 1.2
30	Convento della Carità 26/26 54/40	1:1 ≅4:3		
34	Atrio Testugginato 27/18 36/18 21/18 20/18 36/36 72/36	3:2 2:1 1:1 2:1	 1.1667 1.1111	 less than 1.2 less than 1.2

BOOK II PAGE NO.	BUILDING WITH ROOM DIMENSIONS	EQUIVALENT RATIO FROM PALLADIO'S LIST OF PREFERRED RATIOS	DECIMAL VALUE OF RATIOS THAT DO NOT CORRESPOND TO PALLADIO'S PREFERRED RATIOS	COMMENTARY
35	Atrio Testugginato (Detail) 21/20 83⅓/50	5:3	1.05	less than 1.2
	Pisani (Bagnolo) 16/16 24/16 30/18	1:1 3:2 5:3		
48	Badoer (Fratta Polesine) 26½/16 16/16 32/16 16/8	≅5:3 1:1 2:1 2:1		
49	Zeno (Cesalto) 21½/14 14/12 14/14	1:1	1.5357 1.1667	C1 less than 1.2
50	Foscari (Malcontenta) 16/12 16/16	4:3 1:1		
51	Barbaro (Maser) 20/9 20/18 20/12 12/6	5:3 2:1	2.222 1.111	exceeds 2:1 less than 1.2
52	Pisani (Montagnana) 28/16 16/16 16/8½ 28/28	1:1 1:1	1.75 1.8823	√3/1
53	Cornaro (Piombino Dese) 32/27¼ 26½/16 16/10	≅5:3	1.1743 1.6	less than 1.2 C1
54	Mocenigo (Marocco) 16/16 16/10 26/16 32/32	1:1 1:1	1.6 1.625	C1
55	Emo (Fanzolo) 16/16 27/16 27/27	1:1 1:1	1.6875	
56	Finale (Saraceno) 26½/16 16/12	5:3 4:3		
57	Ragona (Ghizzole) 18/17 15/12 21¼/15	≅√2:1	1.0588 1.25	less than 1.2 C1

BOOK II PAGE NO.	BUILDING WITH ROOM DIMENSIONS	EQUIVALENT RATIO FROM PALLADIO'S LIST OF PREFERRED RATIOS	DECIMAL VALUE OF RATIOS THAT DO NOT CORRESPOND TO PALLADIO'S PREFERRED RATIOS	COMMENTARY
58	Pogliana (Pogliana) 30/17 18/17 30/18 30/30	 5:3 1:1	1.7647 1.0588	√3̅/1 less than 1.2
59	Valmarana (Lisiera) 12/12 15/15 15/12 27/17 32½/25	1:1 1:1 1:3	1.5882 1.3	C1
60	Trissino (Meledo) 18/14 18/12	3:2	1.2857	C1
62	Thiene (Cigogna) 18/18 36/36	1:1 1:1		
63	Angarano (Angarano) 13/10 22/18 36/18	2:1	1.3 1.2222	
64	Thiene (Quinto) 44/22	2:1		
65	Godi (Lonedo) 24/16 36/24	3:2 3:2		
67	Sarego (Santa Sophia) 24/24 18/24 24/10 36/20	1:1 4:3	2.4 1.8	exceeds 2/1
68	Sarego (La Miga) 27/16 40/20 16/16 16/12 24/9	2:1 1:1 4:3	1.6875 2.6667	exceeds 2/1
70	Villa antica 44½/44½ 40/6(16?)	1:1	2.5	exceeds 2/1
71	Unnamed 30/30 30/18 14/7 27/18 18/12 50/30 30½/16	1:1 5:3 2:1 3:2 3:2 5:3	1.9062	

BOOK II PAGE NO.	BUILDING WITH ROOM DIMENSIONS	EQUIVALENT RATIO FROM PALLADIO'S LIST OF PREFERRED RATIOS	DECIMAL VALUE OF RATIOS THAT DO NOT CORRESPOND TO PALLADIO'S PREFERRED RATIOS	COMMENTARY
72	Unnamed 30/20 20/16 20/8 40/24 20/20 34½/20 45/37½	3:2 5:3 1:1	 1.25 2.5 1.725 1.2	C1 exceeds 2/1 √3/1
74	Trissino (Vicenza) 23/20 20/18 20/15 14/8 20/15 40/20	 4:3 4:3 2:1	1.15 1.11111 1.75	less than 1.2 less than 1.2 √3/1
75	Angarano (Vicenza) 30/18 18/12	5:3 3:2		
76	Torre (Verona) 36/20 20/15 20/20	 4:3 1:1	1.8	
77	Garzadore (Vicenza) 20/18½ 18½/16 18½/12		1.0811 1.1562 1.5417	less than 1.2 less than 1.2 C1
78	Mocenigo (Brenta) 76/30 40/20 20/15	 2:1 4:3	2.53333	exceeds 2/1

Ottavio Bertotti Scamozzi's Surveys

Listed are those rooms in Bertotti Scamozzi's surveys for which there are grounds to believe that they were executed according to Palladio's plans. The first number in front of the name of the building stands for the volume of Bertotti Scamozzi's *Fabbriche*, the second number for the plate in the volume.

The data from modern surveys which I have managed to obtain are in parentheses. An asterisk indicates that they were calculated by restitution from drawings (i.e., they were not available in numerical form in the published version but had to be measured from in the drawing.)

C1 indicates ratios close to 1.58 (or 1.6); C2 ratios close to 1.26. Ratios whose decimal value is less than 1.2 have been indicated because of their role in the discussion of chromaticism.

	BERTOTTI SCAMOZZI'S SURVEY OF ROOM PROPORTIONS			
ROOM RATIO	L(m)	W(m)	L/W	INTERPRETATION
1.6 Isepo Porto (Vicenza) 29′2″/19′9″	10.413 (*11.54)	7.051 (*7.69)	1.47 (1.50)	1.5
20′7″/19′9″	7.348 (*8.02)	7.051 (*7.69)	1.04 (1.04)	1
20′7″/7′4″	7.348	2.618	2.80	more than 2

ROOM RATIO	L(m)	W(m)	L/W	INTERPRETATION
1.10 Chiericati (Vicenza)				
17'5.5"/17'3"	6.233	6.158	1.01	1/1
28'3"/17'4"	10.085	6.188	1.63	C1
55'2"/14'9"	19.695	5.266	3.74	more than 2
1.20 Valmarana (Vicenza)				
20'5"/13'3"	7.289	4.73	1.54	3/2
1.23 Thiene (Vicenza)				
35'6"/20'	12.674	7.14	1.77	$\sqrt{3}$/1
20'/19'7"	7.14	6.991	1.02	less than 1.2
20'/12'6.5"	7.14	4.478	1.59	C1
18'5"/18'5"	6.575	6.575	1	1/1
1.35 Civena (Vicenza)				
20'5"/16'3"	7.289	5.801	1.26	C2
11'3"/9'6"	4.016	3.392	1.18	less than 1.2
16'3"/11'3"	5.801	4.016	1.44	$\sqrt{2}$/1
1.43 Schio (Vicenza)				
10'1.5"/7'10"	3.615	2.797	1.29	C2
20'7"/7'10"	7.348	2.797	2.63	more than 2
24'7"/12'10"	8.776	4.582	1.91	2/1
2.1 Rotonda (Vicenza)				
24'4"/15'6"	8.687	5.534	1.57	C1
	(*8.68)	(*5.47)	(1.59)	
15'6"/12'4"	5.534	4.403	1.26	C2
	(*5.47)	(*4.34)	(1.26)	
15'9"/10'3.5"	5.623	3.674	1.53	3/2
	(*5.47)	(*3.77)	(1.45)	
R=29'10" (circular)	R=10.65			1/1
2.5 Pisani (Bagnolo)				
16'6"/16'	5.891	5.712	1.03	1/1
23'9"/16'	8.479	5.712	1.48	3/2
30'/17'6"	10.71	6.248	1.71	$\sqrt{3}$/1
10'9"/7'2"	3.838	2.559	1.5	3/2
2.9 Pisani (Montagnana)				
15'9"/15'9"	5.623	5.623	1	1/1
15'9"/8'4"	5.623	2.975	1.89	-
26'/15'9"	9.282	5.623	1.65	5/3
27'9"/26'	9.907	9.282	1.07	less than 1.2
2.13 Godi (Lonedo)				
23'7"/14'9"	8.419	5.266	1.60	C1
	(8.40)	(5.19)	1.62	
26'/15'5"	9.282	5.504	1.69	5/3
	(8.38)	(5.54)	1.52	
16'/15'5"	5.712	5.504	1.04	1/1
	(5.81)	(5.55)	1.05	
26'/17'3"	9.282	6.158	1.51	5/3
	(8.60)	(5.89)	1.46	
36'5"/23'7"	13.001	8.419	1.54	1/1
	(12.82)	(8.52)	1.50	
2.20 Poiana (Poiana Maggiore)				
30'4"/18'1"	10.829	6.456	1.68	5/3
17'4"/17'2"	6.188	6.129	1.01	1/1
29'8"/17'4"	10.591	6.188	1.71	$\sqrt{3}$/1

ROOM RATIO	L(m)	W(m)	L/W	INTERPRETATION
2.23 Saraceno (Finale)				
26'5"/16'3"	9.431	5.801	1.62	C1
16'3"/12'1"	5.801	4.314	1.34	4/3
2.29 Thiene (Quinto)				
21'2"/10'5"	7.557	3.719	2.03	2/1
21'10"/21'6"	7.795	7.557	1.03	less than 1.2
21'10"/21'2"	7.795	7.557	1.03	less than 1.2
21'6"/10'5"	7.676	3.719	2.06	2/1
2.33 Forni (Montecchio Precalcino)				
14'10"/9'2'	5.296	3.273	1.62	C1
18'8"/14'10"	6.664	5.296	1.26	C2
28'11"/15'5"	10.323	5.504	1.87	
15'2"/14'10"	5.415	5.296	1.02	1/1
18'10.5"/14'10"	6.739	5.296	1.27	C2
2.43 Caldogno (Caldogno)				
21'/17'10"	7.497	6.367	1.18	less than 1.2
22'3"/17'10"	7.943	6.366	1.25	C2
42'8"/26'8"	15.232	9.52	1.6	C1
22'1"/17'10	7.884	6.366	1.24	C2
17'10"/11'6"	6.366	4.106	1.55	3/2
22'3"/17'10"	7.943	6.366	1.25	C2
2.49 Gazotti (Bertesina)				
16'3"/8'3"	5.801	2.945	1.97	2/1
16'3"/16'1"	5.805	5.742	1.01	1/1
3.1 Foscari (Malcontenta)				
15'8"/9'9"	5.593	3.481	1.61	C1
	(5.60)	(3.44)	1.63	
15'9.75"/15'8"	5.645	5.593	1.01	1/1
	(5.60)	(5.60)	1	
23'1.75"/15'9.25'	8.263	5.63	1.47	3/2
	(8.27)	(5.60)	1.48	
3.12 Antonini (Udine)				
26'11"/15'11"	9.609	5.682	1.69	5/3
21'3"/15'11"	7.586	5.682	1.33	4/3
31'2"/26'11"	11.127	9.609	1.16	less than 1.2
15'11'/10'10"	5.682	3.868	1.47	√2/1
3.18 Emo (Fanzolo)				
26'9"/26'5"	9.55	9.431	1.01	1/1
	(9.45)	(9.33)	1.01	
15'10"/10'9"	5.653	3.838	1.47	3/2
	(5.66)	(3.80)	1.49	
26'9"/15'10"	9.55	5.653	1.69	5/3
	(9.44)	(5.66)	1.67	
15'10"/15'6"	5.652	5.534	1.02	1/1
	(5.66)	(5.62)	1.01	
3.20 Barbaro (Maser)				
43'/24'	15.351	8.568	1.79	
31'6.5"/15'6"	11.26	5.534	2.03	2/1
27'1"/10'2"	9.669	3.63	2.66	more than 2
11'7"/6'5"	4.135	2.291	1.80	
21'9.5"/11'7"	7.78	4.136	1.88	
18'9"/17'1"	6.694	6.099	1.10	less than 1.2
18'9"/10'3"	6.694	3.659	1.83	
18'/17'8"	6.426	6.307	1.02	1

ROOM RATIO	L(m)	W(m)	L/W	INTERPRETATION
17′8″/11′4″	6.307	4.046	1.56	3/2
19′5″/17′8″	6.932	6.307	1.10	less than 1.2
3.25 Zeno (Cessalto)				
30′5′/15′1′	10.859	5.385	2.02	2/1
19′9″/14′10′	7.051	5.296	1.33	4/3
13′9″/12′1′	4.909	4.314	1.14	less than 1.2
14′/13′9″	4.998	4.909	1.02	1/1
3.29 Cornaro (Piombino Dese)				
15′8″/8′8″	5.593 (5.6)	3.094 (3.0)	(1.86)	
15′8″/15′7″	5.664 (5.61)	5.563 (5.57)	1.02 (1.00)	1/1
26′6″/15′5″	9.461 (9.45)	5.504 (5.55)	1.72 (1.7)	√3/1
31′2″/25′6″	11.126 (11.13)	9.10 (9.05)	1.22 1.23	
3.41 Badoer (Fratta Polesine)				
31′8″/16′	11.305 (11.33)	5.712 (5.75)	1.98 (1.97)	2/1
16′/8′	5.712 (5.68)	2.856 (2.87)	2 (1.98)	1/1
14′10″/8′	5.296	2.856	1.85	
26′11″/16′3″	9.61 (9.57)	5.801 (5.72)	1.66 (1.67)	5/3
16′3″/16′	5.801 (5.68)	5.712 (*5.68)	1.01 (1)	1/1
3.47 Chiericati (Vancimuglio)				
10′3.5″/10′3.5″	3.674	3.674	1	1/1
16′3.5″/16′3.5″	5.816	5.816	1	1/1
26′6″/16′4.5″	9.461	5.846	1.61	C1
30′8.5″/28′8″	10.963	10.234	1.07	1/1

COROLLARY TO TABLES 1 AND 2

Approximations of Irrational Ratios

It is probable that Palladio used triangulation in his design procedures. The following plans in the *Four Books* include room length/width ratios that can be interpreted as triangulation-derived:

Building	Ratio	Decimal value
Torre (Verona)	19′/11′	1.7273
Thiene (Vicenza)	34′6″/20′	1.725
Barbarano	17′/12′	1.714
Pisani (Montagnana)	28′/16′	1.75
Poiana	30′/17′	1.7647

According to Bertotti Scamozzi's surveys, triangulation can be found in the following executed buildings:

Thiene (Vicenza)	35′6″/20′	1.77
Pisani (Bagnolo)	30′/17′6″	1.71
Poiana (Poiana Maggiore)	29′8″/17′4″	1.71
Cornaro (Piombino Dese)	26′6″/15′5″	1.72

Besides √2/1 and √3/1, two other ratios that appear in Palladio's work may stand for approximations of irrational ratios: 1.58/1 and 1.26/1. In the tables above, these ratios were marked with C1 and C2 respectively. In the *Four Books*, approximations of the ratio 1.58/1 appear in the following plans:

Antonini (Udine)	12′6″/8′	1.5625
della Torre (Verona)	30′/19″	1.5789
Capra (Vicenza)	27′/17′	1.5882
Cornaro (Piombino Dese)	16′/10′	1.6
Mocenigo (Marocco)	26′/16′	1.625
Valmarana (Lisiera)	27′/17′	1.5882
Garzadore (Vicenza)	18′6″/12′	1.5417

The same ratio can be also found in Palladio's executed buildings:

Chiericati (Vicenza)	28'3"/17'4"	1.63
Tiene (Vicenza)	20'/12'6.5"	1.59
Rotonda	24'4"/15'6"	1.57
Godi	23'7"/14'9"	1.60
Sarraceno	26'5"/16'3"	1.62
Forni	14'10"/9'2"	1.62
Caldogno	42'8"/26'8"	1.6
Foscari (Malcontenta)	15'8"/9'9"	1.61
Chiericati (Vancimuglio)	26'6"/16'4.5"	1.62

In the *Four Books* there are three rooms whose length/width ratio is close to 1.26/1:

Torre (Verona)	19'/15'	1.2667
Barbarano (Vicenza)	19'/16'	1.2631
Atrio Toscano	38'/30'	1.2667

This ratio also appears in Palladio's executed buildings:

Civena (Vicenza)	20'5"/16'3"	1.26
Schio (Vicenza)	10'1.5"/7'10"	1.29
Rotonda (Vicenza)	15'6"/12'4"	1.26
Forni (Montecchio)	18'8"/14'10"	1.26
	18'10"/14'10"	1.27
Caldogno (Caldogno)	22'3"/17'10"	1.25
	22'1"/17'10"	1.24
	22'3"/17'10"	1.25

VERTICAL PROPORTIONS OF INTERIOR SPACES IN PALLADIO'S DESIGNS

Palladio states that the height of a room with a vaulted ceiling should be the arithmetic, geometric, or harmonic mean between length and width. If the room is square, then its height should be 4/3 of one of its sides. Mathematically, if h_a, h_g and h_h are arithmetic, geometric, and harmonic means, respectively, and if 'w' is the width and 'l' is the length of a room while for the vaulted ceiling, then:

$$h_a = (w+l)/2$$
$$h_g = \sqrt{wl}$$
$$h_h = 2wl/(w+l)$$

Let us assume that 'l' is the length of a room, 'w' its width, and 'r' the ratio between 'l' and 'w'. Then:

$$r = l/w \qquad \text{i.e.} \qquad l = rw$$

(h_a, h_g, h_h are the heights of rooms calculated as the arithmetic, geometric, and harmonic means between the length and width of the room. h_q is the height of a square room calculated as 4/3 of the width of the room.)

If we replace l=rw in each of the first three formulas, we shall get:

$$h_a = (w+rw)/2 = w[(1+r)/2]$$
$$h_g = \sqrt{rw^2} = w(\sqrt{r})$$
$$h_h = 2wr/(1+r) = w[2r/(1+r)]$$

If we further assume that r (room length/width ratio) in these formulas is going to be one of Palladio's preferred room length/width ratios, √3/1, or one of the two ratios defining the Delian cubes, then we can reduce each of these formulas to the form:

$$h = wk$$

(i.e., express the height as the linear function of the width. "k" stands for k-factor here, the ratio between height and width (k=h/w). For instance, if r=4/3, then for the first of these equations we shall get:

$$h_a = w[(1+r)/2] = w[(1+4/3)/2] = wk \text{ where } k = 7/6$$

In other words:

$$h_a = w[(1+r)/2] = wk_a \qquad \text{where } k_a = [(1+r)/2]$$
$$h_g = w\sqrt{r} = wk_g \qquad \text{where } k_g = \sqrt{r}$$
$$h_h = w[2r/(1+r)] = wk_h \qquad \text{where } k_h = [2r/(1+r)]$$

We can now calculate k_a, k_g, and k_h by replacing r in each of these equations with ratios from Palladio's list of preferred ratios, or √3/1 or the Delian cubes. We shall then get the following values for k-factors:

Length/width Ratio	Type of Mean	k-factor Exact value	k-factor Decimal value
2:1	h_a	3/2	1.5
	h_g	$\sqrt{2}/1$	1.414 . . .
	h_h	4/3	1.333 . . .
5:3	h_a	4/3	1.333 . . .
	h_g	$\sqrt{5}/\sqrt{3}$	1.290 . . .
	h_h	5/4	1.25
3:2	h_a	5/4	1.25
	h_g	$\sqrt{3}/\sqrt{2}$	1.225 . . .
	h_h	6/5	1.2
4:3	h_a	7/6	1.166 . . .
	h_g	$^2\sqrt{3}/3$	1.154 . . .
	h_h	8/7	1.428 . . .
√2:1	h_a	$(1+\sqrt{2})/2$	1.207 . . .
	h_g	$\sqrt[4]{2}/1$	1.189 . . .
	h_h	$^2\sqrt{2}/(1+\sqrt{2})$	1.171 . . .
√3:1	h_a	$(1+\sqrt{3})/2$	1.366 . . .
	h_g	$\sqrt[4]{3}$	1.316 . . .
	h_h	$^2\sqrt{3}/(1+\sqrt{3})$	1.267 . . .
$(\sqrt[3]{2})^2$:1	h_a	$((\sqrt[3]{2})^2+1)/2$	1.294
	h_g	$\sqrt[3]{2}$	1.259. .
	h_h	$2(\sqrt[3]{2})^2/((\sqrt[3]{2}+1)$	1.227
$\sqrt[3]{2}$:1	h_a	$(\sqrt[3]{2}+1)/2$	1.129 . . .
	h_g	$\sqrt[6]{2}$	1.122 . . .
	h_h	$2\sqrt[3]{2}/(1+\sqrt[3]{2})$	1.115 . . .

The CCH rule requires that rooms with different l/w ratios should nevertheless have the same height, calculated as the arithmetic, geometric, or harmonic mean of length and width (or 4/3 of the width in the case of square rooms). Rooms in the same row tend to have at least one dimension in common. If two rooms have one dimension in common, then either the width of one room is equal to the length of the other, or they have equal widths or equal lengths. In the first case, it will be impossible to apply CCH rule. (If the height is calculated as a mean between the length and width, it is always a dimension greater than the width and shorter than the height. But, if 'w' is the width of one room and the length of another, then the height will at the same time have to be longer and shorter than 'w'.)

If the rooms have equal widths, and if their equal heights should be calculated as arithmetic, geometric, or harmonic means between lengths and widths, then the condition for the CCH rule will be that the k-factor of one room must be equal to the k-factor of the other:

$$k_1 = k_2$$

In other words, both rooms must have equal height/width ratios, since their heights and widths must be equal.

Alternatively, if their lengths are equal, then one could define k-factors as ratios between the room height and length ($k' = h/1$). In that case we shall get the following equations determining the relationship between k_a, k_g, k_h and k'_a, k'_g, k'_h:

$$k'_a = 1/k_h \qquad k'_g = 1/k_g \qquad k'_h = 1/k_a$$

The same way as the previous case, if two rooms have equal heights and lengths, then their height/length ratios must be equal as well.

The table above shows how two or more rooms can have equal height/width ratios (k-factors). Only in two cases is the condition precisely fulfilled: $k = 4/3$ and $k = 5/4$.

The inverted CCH rule is used when height/width ratio of one room equals length/width ratio of another room. For instance, the length/width ratio of the larger room in the Rotonda, according to the plan in the *Four Books* is $\sqrt{3}/1$, i.e.:

$$r_1 = 26/15 \cong \sqrt{3}/1$$

The height of this room was calculated as the arithmetic mean:

$$h_1 = (26 + 15)/2 = 21\tfrac{1}{2}$$

The corresponding height/width ratio (k-factor) is:

$$k_1 = h/w = 20.5/15 = 1.367 \ldots$$

At the same time, this is the length/width ratio of the smaller room next to this larger room:

$$r_2 = 15/11 = 1.364$$

In other words, the length/width ratio of one room is, at the same time, the height/width ratio of another room.

APPENDIX C

CHROMATICISM

Table 1 in Appendix A lists a substantial number of length/width ratios between 1/1 and 1.2/1 that cannot be interpreted as ratios from Palladio's list of preferred ratios. Also, few of them relate to the harmonic interpretation proposed by Wittkower. The ratios are:

Antonini	1.1428
Torre	1.11765
Valmarana	1.17143
Barbarano	1.1875
Atrio di 4 colonne	1.09375
Atrio Testiggiunato	1.16667
	1.11111
Zeno	1.16667
Barbaro	1.11111
Cornaro	1.17431
Ragona	1.05882
Poiana	1.05882
Trissino	1.15
	1.11111
Garzadore	1.08108
	1.15625

At the same time, musical chromaticism—a method of dividing tetrachords advocated by Barbaro in the commentary on Vitruvius—provides a great number of ratios between 1.2/1 and 1/1. The question is whether these ratios could provide a harmonic interpretation of the ratios from the above list.

According to Barbaro's account of chromaticism, there are three types of tetrachords, each encompassing one perfect fourth (4/3 ratio) and divided into three smaller intervals. Depending on this division, one can differentiate between diatonic, chromatic, and harmonic tetrachords. Here are Barbaro's explanations, translated into contemporary mathematical notation:

Harmonic
i.e.	1:	46/45	:	24/23	:	5/4
		1.02222 . . .		1.043478		1.0666

Chromatic can be organized in two ways:

chromatico molle;
i.e.	1:	28/27	:	15/14	:	6/5
		1.037037 . . .		1.071428		1.2.

chromatico syntono
	1:	22/21	:	12/11	:	7/6
		1.047619.		1.090909		1.16666. . . .

Diatonic can be organized in five possible ways, as follows:
molle:
	1:	8/7	:	10/9	:	21/20
decimal :		1.142857 . . .		1.11111 . . .		1.05

molle intento:
	1:	28/27	:	8/7	:	9/8
decimal :		1.037037 . . .		1.1428571		1.125

molle equale:
	1:	12/11	:	11/10	:	10/9
decimal :		1.090909		1.1		1.11111

sintonon:
	1:	16/15	:	9/8	:	10/9
decimal :		1.06666 . . .		1.125		1.1111 . . .

diatonon:
	1:	9/8	:	9/8	:	256/243
decimal:		1.125		1.125		1.0534979 . . .

In fact, Barbaro reworked Vitruvius's presentation of tetrachords according to Aristoxenus into Ptolemy's version (see Ptolemy, *De Musica*, 1.15.35, for enharmonic and chromatic genera; 1.15.87 and 1.16.40, for the diatonic). The result is the following list of ratios, which could serve for the interpretation of the unexplained length/width ratios:

1.02222
1.037037
1.04347
1.0476
1.05
1.066667
1.07143
1.0909
1.1
1.111111
1.125
1.142857
1.16667
1.2
105349

1.02857
1.03704
1.08482
1.125
1.14286
1.1852
1.25.

Another ancient source for the division of tetrachords, known in the Renaissance and mentioned by Gaffurio and others, is Architas, whose ratios have values different from Ptolemy's. Gaffurio *De harmonia*, 2.17, lists the following ratios in the presentation of Architas's system:

The answer to our question is generally negative. Very few ratios on the first list correspond to those of Barbaro in Gaffurio. It helps little to say that many of these ratios could be taken as approximations: chromaticism works with ratios between whole numbers and Palladio could have easily achieved exact ratios.

APPENDIX D

THE USE OF THE ORDERS

Intercolumniations in Palladio's Work: A Historical Survey

The table below presents intercolumniation-to-lower-column-diameter ratios on Palladio's facades. Unless indicated, these are front facade intercolumniations. The data were collected from different sources (Ottavio Bertotti Scamozzi, photographs, available modern surveys, the author's measurements) and compared. The accuracy is within 10–15%.

N/A=not applicable; S=side intercolumniation; C=central intercolumniation, GF=ground floor, TF=top floor

Table 1

Year	Building	∅ Intercolumniation	Order
1537	Godi (Lonedo)	N/A	
1540	Civena (Vicenza)	5.8	Corinthian
1541	Valmarana (Vigardolo)	N/A	
1541–1542	Forni (Montecchio)	N/A	
1542	Gazzotti (Bertesina)	6.6	Corinthian
1542–1545	Pisani (Bagnolo)	N/A	Doric, arcaded
1542–1546	Thiene (Vicenza)	courtyard upper story 5.0 facade upper story 4.5	Composite
1545	Saraceno (Finale)	N/A	
1545	Caldogno (Caldogno)	N/A	
1545–1546	Thiene (Quinto)	backside 3.45	Doric
1546–1549	Basilica (Vicenza)	N/A	
1548–1549	Poiana (Poiana Maggiore)	N/A	
1549	Iseppo Porto (Vicenza)	S 4, C 4.5	Ionic
1550	Chiericati (Vicenza)	GF: 2.8 TF: 4	Doric Ionic
1552	Pisani (Montagnana)	GF: S2.7, C3.8 TF: S.3.6, C 5.2	Doric Ionic
1553	Cornaro (Piombino Dese)	Front: GF: S 2.4, C 3.3 TF:S3.0, C 4 Back: GF: S2.4, C 3.3 TF: S3.0, C 4	Ionic Corinthian Ionic Corinthian

Year	Building	⌀ Intercolumniation	Order
1554	Chiericati (Vancimuglio)	S2.4, C2.7	Ionic
1554	Porto (Vivaro di Dueville)	S2.3, C2.8	Ionic
1556	Antonini (Udine)	Front: GF: S 2.3, C 3 TF: S 3, C4 Back: GF: S 2.3, C3 TF: S 3, C4	Ionic Corinthian Ionic Corinthian
1556	Badoer (Fratta Polesine)	S 2.3, C 3	Ionic
1557–1558	Barbaro (Maser)	4	Ionic
1559–1560	Foscari (Malcontenta)	S 2.5, C 3	Ionic
1560–1561	Convento della Carità (Venice)	GF 5.1 Middle Story 7.1 TF 7.8	Denticular Doric Ionic Corinthian pilasters
1562	Facade of S. Francesco della Vigna	S (central bay) 2.25	Corinthian
1562–1565	Palazzo Pretorio (Cividale)	4.23	Corinthian pilasters
1564	Emo (Franzolo)	S 2.7 C 3.1	Doric
1565	S. Giorgio Maggiore (Venice)	S 1.95, C 4.27	Composite w/ pedestals
1565	Valmarana (Vicenza)	S3.0	Composite
1565–1566	Schio (Vicenza)	5.6	Corinthian
1565–1571	Loggia del Capitaniato (Vicenza)	3.2	Composite
1566–1567	Rotonda (Vicenza)	S 2, C 2.5	Ionic
1569	Barbarano (Vicenza)	over 3 (intercolumniations not equal)	
1569	Sarego (S. Sofia)	3.8	Ionic
1570s	Porto in Piazza Castello	2.1	Corinthian
1576–77	Redentore (Venice)	S 2.2	Composite w/out pedestal
1580	Tempietto (Maser)	S 1.6 C 1.7	Corinthian

Palladio's Formulation of the Canonical Corinthian Entablature

The first column lists the elements of Palladio's canonical Corinthian entablature. The second column (bold) gives the proportions of these layers in relation to the lower-column diameter, as stipulated by Palladio. The same ratios are also stated in the top horizontal row (bold). The remainder of the table supplies size ratios between all the elements of the entablature. Those ratios that fall between 1 and 2 (i.e., the ratios that could correspond to the ratios of intervals within an octave) are indicated in bold. Among them, very few correspond to a musical interval (in bold and italics).

Element	xD	0.037	0.105	0.011	0.05	0.122	0.011	0.038	0.125	0.075	0.016	0.091	0.008	0.075	0.475	0.045	0.083	0.0333	0.175	0.0293	0.137	0.029	0.104
fillet	0.037	1	0.3554	3.3784	0.75	0.3074	3.3784	0.9643	0.3	0.5	2.2455	0.4091	4.5181	0.5	0.0789	0.8182	0.450	**1.1261**	0.2143	**1.284**	0.2727	**1.284**	0.3599
cyma recta	0.105	2.8147	1	9.5091	2.111	0.8652	9.509	2.7141	0.844	**1.407**	6.3203	**1.1514**	12.716	**1.407**	0.2222	2.3030	**1.266**	3.1696	0.6031	3.6147	0.7676	3.6147	***1.013***
fillet	0.011	0.296	0.1052	1	0.222	0.090	1	0.2854	0.088	0.148	0.6646	0.1210	1.3373	0.148	0.0233	0.2422	0.1332	0.3333	0.063	0.3801	0.080	0.3801	0.1065
cyma reversa	0.05	1.333	0.4739	4.5045	1	0.409	4.5045	**1.285**	0.4	0.6666	2.9940	0.5454	6.0241	0.6666	0.1052	**1.090**	0.600	***1.5015***	0.2857	**1.7123**	0.3636	**1.7123**	0.4798
fascia	0.122	3.2586	**1.158**	11.009	2.444	1	11.009	3.1422	0.9776	**1.629**	7.3173	***1.3330***	14.722	**1.629**	0.2572	2.6663	**1.466**	3.6696	0.698	4.1849	0.888	4.1849	**1.1727**
fillet	0.011	0.296	0.1052	1	0.222	0.090	1	0.2854	0.088	0.148	0.6646	0.1210	1.3373	0.148	0.0233	0.2422	0.1332	0.3333	0.063	0.3801	0.080	0.3801	0.1065
cyma reversa	0.038	**1.037**	0.3686	3.5036	0.7778	0.3187	3.5036	1	0.3111	0.5185	2.3287	0.4242	4.6855	0.5185	0.0818	0.848	0.4667	**1.167**	0.2222	**1.331**	0.282	**1.331**	0.3732
modillions	0.125	3.3333	**1.184**	11.213	2.5	**1.024**	11.261	3.2141	1	***1.666***	7.4850	**1.363**	15.060	***1.666***	0.2631	2.7274	***1.500***	3.7537	0.7142	4.280	0.909	4.280	***1.199***
ovolo	0.075	2	0.7109	6.7567	***1.5***	0.6147	6.7567	**1.928**	0.6	1	4.4910	0.8181	9.0361	1	0.1578	**1.636**	0.900	2.2522	0.4285	2.5684	0.5454	2.5684	0.7197
fillet	0.016	0.4453	0.1582	**1.504**	0.334	0.1368	**1.504**	0.4294	0.1336	0.2226	1	0.1821	2.0120	0.2226	0.0351	0.3643	0.200	0.5015	0.0954	0.5719	0.1214	0.5712	0.1602
dentils	0.091	2.4445	0.868	8.2585	**1.833**	0.7513	8.2585	2.3571	0.7333	**1.222**	5.4892	1	11.044	**1.222**	0.1929	2.000	**1.100**	2.7528	0.5238	3.1393	0.6666	3.1393	0.8797
fillet	0.008	0.2213	0.0786	0.7477	0.166	0.068	0.7477	0.2134	0.066	0.1106	0.4970	0.090	1	0.1106	0.0174	0.1811	0.099	0.2492	0.0474	0.2842	0.060	0.2842	0.0796
cyma reversa	0.075	2	0.7109	6.7567	***1.5***	0.6147	6.7567	**1.928**	0.6	1	4.4910	0.8181	9.0361	1	0.1578	**1.636**	0.900	2.2522	0.4285	2.5689	0.5454	2.5684	0.7197
frieze	0.475	12.666	4.5023	42.792	9.5	3.8934	42.792	12.213	3.8	6.3333	28.443	5.1816	57.228	6.3333	1	10.364	5.7002	14.264	2.7142	16.267	3.4545	16.267	4.5585
fillet	0.045	**1.222**	0.4344	4.1288	0.9166	0.3756	4.1288	**1.1785**	0.3666	0.6110	2.7443	0.4999	5.5216	0.6110	0.096	1	0.5499	**1.376**	0.2618	**1.569**	0.3333	**1.569**	0.4398
cyma reversa	0.083	2.2221	0.7898	7.5072	**1.666**	0.683	7.5072	2.1427	0.6666	**1.1111**	4.9898	0.909	10.039	**1.1111**	0.1754	**1.818**	1	2.5024	0.4761	2.8537	0.606	2.8537	0.7997
astragal	0.033	0.888	0.3159	3.0027	0.6666	0.2732	3.0027	0.8570	0.2666	0.4444	**1.995**	0.3635	4.0156	0.4444	0.0701	0.7272	0.3999	**1.000**	0.1904	**1.1414**	0.2424	**1.1414**	0.3198
upper fascia	0.175	4.6666	**1.658**	15.765	3.5	**1.434**	15.765	4.4998	**1.4**	2.3333	10.479	**1.909**	21.084	2.3333	0.3684	3.8184	2.1000	5.2552	1	5.9931	**1.272**	5.9931	**1.679**
astragal	0.029	0.7786	0.2767	2.6306	0.584	0.2393	2.6306	0.7508	0.2336	0.3893	**1.748**	0.3185	3.5180	0.3893	0.0614	0.6371	0.3504	0.8768	0.1668	1	0.2123	1	0.280
middle fascia	0.137	3.6666	**1.303**	12.387	2.75	**1.127**	12.387	3.5356	**1.1**	**1.833**	8.2335	***1.499***	16.566	**1.833**	0.289	3.000	**1.650**	4.1291	0.7857	4.7089	1	4.7089	**1.319**
astragal	0.029	0.7786	0.2767	2.6306	0.584	0.2393	2.6306	0.7508	0.2336	0.3893	**1.748**	0.3185	3.5180	0.3893	0.0614	0.6371	0.3504	0.8768	0.1668	1	0.2123	1	0.280
lower fascia	0.104	2.778	0.9876	9.3873	2.084	0.8541	9.3873	2.6793	0.8336	**1.389**	6.2395	**1.1367**	12.554	**1.389**	0.2193	2.2736	***1.250***	3.1291	0.5954	3.5684	0.7578	3.5684	1

END NOTES

EPIGRAM

1. Jorge Luis Borges, "Un poeta del siglo xiii," in Jorge Luis Borges, *Selected Poems*, Penguin Books (Harmondsworth, 1999), 176. Author's translation.

> ¿Habrá sentido que no estaba solo
> Y que el arcano, el increíble Apolo
> Le había revelado un arquetipo . . . ?

INTRODUCTION

1. The classic work on Palladio's biography is Ackerman, *Palladio*. More recent works are Boucher, *Andrea Palladio* and Tavernor, *Palladio and Palladianism*. For specific dates in Palladio's life, see also Puppi, *Palladio*, especially 512–13.
2. For Trissino's biography, see Morsolin, *Trissino*.
3. The seminal study of Barbaro's life is Laven, *Daniele Barbaro*.
4. For a full list of Barbaro's publications, see the bibliography.
5. For Palladio's relationship with Barbaro, see Forssman, "Palladio e Daniele Barbaro." See also Barbaro, *I dieci*, 64.
6. This difficulty has been summarized by Robison, "Structural Implications." In the second book of his treatise, Palladio provided a drawing showing the size of half of the Vicentine foot he used for the plans in that volume. That measurement would be 35 cm. However, this was certainly not the measure that appeared in the original woodcuts. In the process of printing, the size of the wooden plates would change slightly so the printed size is not the same as the engraved size. Robison lists solutions to this problem suggested by different scholars: Zurko 35.7 cm, Favero 34.75 cm, Burns, Fairburn, and Boucher 35.4 cm. The smallest size proposed is 34.7 cm, proposed by Deborah Howard and Malcolm Longair ("Harmonic Proportions," 129). The biggest difference between these measures is about 3 percent, which would not result in a significant error when converting the surveys into the metric system. In this context, it is important to remember Palladio's insistence on excessive precision when defining the elements of the classical orders.
7. The assumption that all dimensions given in the treatise are in Vicentine feet is more likely to be valid for the presentation of Palladio's own buildings in the second book, than for the archaeological surveys in the fourth book. The illustrations of the second book were prepared for publication in the late 1560s and it is reasonable to expect that the dimensions in these drawings were consistently expressed in the same foot size, whatever this size may have been (see note 6). There is, however, no guarantee that the standard measurement in the second book is the same one that Palladio used to measure the Roman temples in the early 1550s. In fact, Lewis pointed out that the unpublished drawings of Palladio's archaeological surveys occasionally combine measures in Roman and Veronese feet (*Drawings*, 61). It is neither certain, nor even probable, that in the process of preparing his old surveys for publication in the late 1560s, Palladio recalculated all the measurements of his old surveys into Vicentine feet.
8. See, for instance, Lavin, "The Crisis."
9. Forssman, *Palladios Lehrgebäude*, 127–28.
10. Tafuri, "Committenza," 127.
11. Puppi, *Palladio*, 383.
12. I am indebted to Charles Burroughs's article "Palladio and Fortune" for drawing my attention to the explicit statements by Forssman, Puppi and Tafuri. This article is one of the most significant attempts to establish an alternative, narrative-based approach to Palladio. In the opening footnote, Burroughs critically referred to the fact that "an often impressive current of scholarship tended to restrict discussion of the symbolic and semiotic resonances in Palladio's work," and stated that his intention was to oppose this kind of methodological formalism. Burroughs's extensive and learned study then made the attempt to reconstruct the systems of meanings that determined the design of the Rotonda. He discussed in detail Palladio's reconstruction of the sanctuary of Fortune in Palestrina (Palladio there drew a building with Rotonda's facade), pointed out that Leandro Alberti wrote about *Roma quadrata*, that some ancient sources referred to Roman fortune, that Paolo Almerico (the patron of the Rotonda) made a successful career in Rome and not in his native Vicenza. But if we are meant to conclude that the Rotonda was conceived as a temple of Fortune, then it is hard to understand why a Catholic priest (and a "man of the Church" as Palladio described Almerico in the *Four Books*) would commission a pagan temple. Palladio was certainly aware of the similarities of the Rotonda with his reconstruction of the sanctuary in Palestrina, and Almerico may have seen the relevant drawings as well. The decision to apply the form of a pagan sanctuary on the house of a Catholic priest and the *referendario* of two Popes must have thus included the act of divorcing that form from its symbolic connotations. Forssman, Tafuri, and Puppi are fundamentally right: the motivation to apply this shape must have been formal, and no amount of research about semantics, symbolism, and meanings can bridge this gap. Burroughs complained that the evidence he assembled is not conclusive (60), but in fact it is fully conclusive in the opposite direction from the point he wanted to make. His thorough research clearly illustrates the point made by Forssman, Tafuri, and Puppi.

CHAPTER 1

1. Palladio, *Four Books*, 1.52 and 2.3; see also Carboneri, "Spazi," 166–70.
2. For villas in the Renaissance, see Ackerman, *Villa*, and "The Influence of Antiquity."
3. Palladio, Four Books, 1.76.
4. Prinz, "La 'sala di quattro colonne.'"
5. Pellechia, 377.
6. Ibid., 379.
7. *Four Books*, discussion of the palazzi Torre (2.11), Thiene (2.12), Barbarano (2.22), and Garzadori (2.77).
8. Antonini, Chiericati, Torre (Verona, the two side wings, but not the back section), Thiene (actually a square around a courtyard, with all rooms of equal width), Rotonda, Zeno, Pisani (Montagnana), Cornaro, Mocenigo (Marocco), Emo, Repeta, Sarego, the unidentified building on page 72, Angarano, Torre (Verona), Mocenigo (Brenta).
9. Iseppo Porto, Barbarano (right wing), Foscari (Malcontenta), Thiene, Angarano, unidentified building illustrated on page 71, and Trissino (Vicenza).
10. Palladio described the procedure in *Four Books*, 1.55; see also Forssman, *Lehrgebäude*, 26.
11. Palladio, *Four Books*, 1.52.
12. March, "Foreword" in Belli, *On Ratio and Proportion*, 11.
13. Nicomachus, *Introduction*, 2.22–2.28.
14. One may try to calculate wall thicknesses on the basis of some indications provided in plans. For instance, if a plan has a sala 26 feet long and to this sala correspond three little rooms in another part of the building, each 8 feet wide, then it is possible to say that Palladio assumed wall thickness of 1 foot. (There are two walls between three rooms and 8+1+8+1+8=26.) Howard and Longair ("Harmonic Proportion") have found 16 plans in which wall thicknesses can be calculated in this way and the results they found vary between 0 and 2 feet. It is thus reasonable to conclude that the plans in the second book of *Four Books* do not rely on a consistent set of assumptions about wall thicknesses.
15. 24/17 in the Palazzo Antonini, 28/20 in the drawing of a Tuscan Atrium, and 21¼ /15 in the Villa Ragona.
16. Robison, "Structural Implications," 180. Robison has found three wall thicknesses in the Villa Poiana as it was built (roughly approximating 50, 60, and 70 cm) and pointed out that these thicknesses correspond to the number of brick-derived-units in an individual wall: for instance, the wall with thickness 50 cm stands for a brick-and-a-half thick wall, whereas 60 cm wall stands for a two-brick thick wall. The variation between different brick-and-a-half thick walls on the Villa Poiana is 8 cm, which equals almost one quarter of the Vicentine foot Palladio used to measure his buildings. The reason for such high variation is probably in different thicknesses of mortar joints and stucco coverings. The precision with which walls can be executed ultimately determines the precision which to expect in Palladio's plans. While Robison's observation pertains to the executed version of the Villa Poiana, it is nevertheless reasonable to assume that such considerations would have influenced Palladio in defining room dimensions in the second book of his treatise. Indeed he did not rely on dimensions smaller than one quarter of a foot in defining brick masonry work.
17. See Zorzi, "L'interpretazione" and "Errori."
18. Howard and Longair, "Harmonic Proportion," 129.
19. See Spinadel, "Triangulature," and Wassell, "Mathematics," for a discussion of Palladio's methods for approximating $\sqrt{3}$.
20. Vitruvius, *De arch.*, 1.2.4; 6.2.1.
21. Ibid., 6.3.3.; 4.1.11.
22. Vitruvius, *De arch.*, 9.P.5; Plato, *Meno* 82.
23. For Barbaro on the importance of proportions, see Barbaro, *I dieci*, 34 and 108 (for the use of modules); see also page 29 for the identification of symmetry with what we call commensurability today.
24. Palladio, *Four Books*, 4.9.
25. Serlio, *Tutte*, 1.15; Martini, *Trattati*, vol. 2, 349.
26. Feinstein, *Der Harmoniebegriff*, 105–7
27. Alberti, *De re.*, 7.8.8.
28. Pacioli, *De Divina Proportio*. In "Palladio's Theory of Proportions" I referred to Zloković's "Divina Proportio ≠ Sectio Aurea" in which it was denied that Pacioli's *Divina Proportio* was the Golden Section. I have since had access to both editions of the book, and I now have no doubt that Pacioli knew how to formulate the Golden Section and that he also knew it was the ratio between the side and the diagonal of a pentagon. Chapter VII of *Divina Proportio* gives the definition of the Golden Section; Chapter XVIII explains this ratio on pentagon.
29. Barbaro, *Pratica*, 25. As mentioned, Golden Section is the ratio of the diagonal to the side of a pentagon; if this simple fact is known, then drawing a regular pentagon with a given side, is easy. One should be careful not to confuse the construction of a regular pentagon with a given side (which is the kind of problem Barbaro systematically presents for a large number of polygons in the mentioned chapter) with the inscription of a pentagon into a given circle. The solution of the latter problem is to be found in Serlio (Serlio, *Tutte*, 1.14L).
30. Barbaro, Marciana lat.5446, 276. (The second manuscript version preserved in Marciana has illustrations from the printed edition. Marciana lat.5447.) This chapter of the *Pratica* is dedicated to the construction of regular polygons, and Barbaro was obviously heavily drawing on Dürer, whom he cited as the source for the construction of the regular polygon with 17 sides (Barbaro, *Pratica*, 26). Naredi-Rainer (*Architektur und Harmonie*, 198) says that the probable source of the approximative method for the construction of a regular pentagon in Dürer is Roritzer's *Geometria Deutsch*. He also remarked that Dürer failed to mention the Golden Section in relation to the construction of a regular pentagon (Ibid., 198; see also Schröder, *Dürer*, 2).
31. Vatican, MS Vat. Lat., 7246.
32. Vitruvius, *De arch.*, 5.P.3,4.
33. Euclid, *Elementa*, 6.9 and 6.13.
34. Palladio, *Four Books*, 1.53.
35. If the edge of a cube is a, then its volume is V = a³. For a cube with twice that volume, the edge will be a³√2. On the other hand, if we try to find two mean proportionals of numbers $\overline{1}$ and 2, they are ³√2 and (³√2)². From this it follows that for a given cube, with an edge *a*, the edge of $\overline{a}$ cube with a double volume is equal to the smaller of the two mean proportionals between *a* and *2a*.
36. Heath, *A History*, vol.1, 245.
37. Marsden, *Greek and Roman*, 40.
38. Vitruvius, *De arch.*, 9.P.14
39. Barbaro, *I dieci*, 360.
40. For a general survey of different solutions, see Heath, *A History*, vol. 1, p. 244 . . . ; the most comprehensive survey is by Breidenbach, *Das Delische Problem*.
41. Foscari (Malcontenta), Poiana, Pisani (Bagnolo), Iseppo Porto, Torre (Verona), Pisani (Montagnana), Thiene (Cicogna), Zeno, and Angarano (Vicenza).
42. Arithmetic: Palazzo Chiericati and villas Rotonda, Foscari (Malcontenta), Cornaro, and Mocenigo (Marocco), as well as the two unidentified buildings illustrated on pages 71 and 72 of the treatise; Geometric: Palazzo Torre and villas Zeno and Pisani (Montagnana); Harmonic: Palazzo Iseppo Porto and villas Zeno, Garzadore, and Trissino.
43. In the Palazzo Trissino, the height of the large rooms to the right and left of the entrance (each 20 by 40 feet) is 27 feet, a harmonic mean even though the rooms have flat ceilings. In the same building the height of one pair of smaller rooms (each 20 by 18 feet) was determined as equal to the width of the room, although they have vaulted ceiling. In the Villa Garzadore, there are rooms with vaulted ceilings whose height is equal to their width (h=w=16 feet).
44. Palladio, *Four Books*, 1.54.
45. In an executed building, it is necessary to work with approximations. Since

the walls are not fully parallel, the corresponding lengths and widths are not always equal. Average lengths are about 9.45 meters, widths 5.55 meters, and heights 7.17 meters. Palladio's statements about these dimensions in the *Four Books* are contradictory; the illustration presents the length/width ratio as $26^{1/2}/16 = 1.656\ldots$ whereas in the text he states this ratio as $7/4 = 1.75$. None of these ratios plays an important role in his proportional considerations elsewhere, and triangulation provides a much better explanation in this case. Palladio also says that the height was calculated as the arithmetic mean of the length and width but this would give 7.5 meters as the height of the room, whereas the geometric mean gives 7.24 meters.

46. If the length/width ratio of a room is $\sqrt{3}$ and if its height is calculated as the geometric mean, then the height/width ratio will be 1.31, a reasonably good approximation for 4/3.

47. If we have two rooms with equal widths, whose length/width ratios are $r_1 = l_1/w$ and $r_2 = l_2/w$ and whose height/width ratios are $k_1 = h_1/w$ and $k_2 = h_2/w$, the inverted CCH rule means that $r_2 = k_1$.

48. Alberti, *De re.*, 1.13.1.

49. Palladio, *Four Books*, 1.60–66.

50. Mielke, "Die Treppen," 170 and 173.

51. Palladio, *Four Books*, 1.54.

52. Mielke "Die Treppen," 168.

53. Palladio, *Four Books*, 1.64, translation Tavernor and Schofield.

54. See Prinz, *Schloß Chambord*, esp. "Der Treppenraum," 23–27, for a description of the staircase in Chambord. See also Plate 16, illustration 26, for the internal space of this staircase, which is substantially different from the way Palladio presented it.

55. Mielke, "Die Treppen," 171, cites Blodnel's *Course d'architecture* (1698 edition, 676); Leoni Jacques *Architecture de Palladio*, The Hague 1726; Johann Jakob Schübler *Sciagraphia artis Tignariae*, Nuremberg 1736, plate 42.

56. Mielke, "Die Treppen," 172.

57. Mielke, "Die Treppen," 174–75; Bassi, "La scala," 89.

58. Palladio, *Scritti*, 1.61.

59. Ibid., 1.61.

60. Goethe refers to this staircase as "die schönste Wandeltreppe der Welt," *Italienische Reise*, 63–64.

61. Bassi, "La scala."

62. For the history of elliptical staircases in the late sixteenth and early seventeenth century, see Waddy, *Seventeenth-Century Roman Palaces* 212–17 and 321–39 for the problem of authorship of the staircase in Palazzo Barberini.

CHAPTER 2

1. Wittkower, *Architectural Principles*. For the influence of the book see Millon, "Rudolf Wittkower" and Payne, "Rudolf Wittkower." The most important critique of Wittkower's book in recent decades was formulated by George Hersey; see Hersey and Freedman, *Possible Palladian Villas*.

2. Wittkower, *Architectural Principles*, 111.

3. Alfons Kiene defended a dissertation at Hanover University in 1950 with similar ideas and probably uninfluenced by Wittkower's; whereas a circle of musical theorists around Hans Kayser in Switzerland were working at the same time on similar issues.

4. Plato, *Republic*, 616–17.

5. Macrobius, *In somnium Scipionis*, 2.1.3 and 2.4.13.

6. Ptolemy, *De Musica*, 3.3–3.7; 3.9; 3.10.3.15

7. Palisca, *Humanism*, 167.

8. Gaffurio, *De harmonia*, 4.12; 4.14; 4.15; 4.17; 4.18; 4.19.

9. Wittkower, *Architectural Principles*, 137; see also Zarlino, *Supplementi*, 179 and 288.

10. Tafuri, *Venice*, 121, 114.

11. Zarlino, *Istituzioni*, 12–18; 101; 27.

12. Alberti, *De re.*, 9.5.14; 9.5; and 9.6.

13. See 'Francesco Giorgi's Memorandum for San Francesco della Vigna,' Wittkower, *Architectural Principles*, 154–57.

14. Barbaro, *I dieci*, 124.

15. Ibid., 282, 244.

16. Ibid., 23 and 367.

17. Barbaro, *I dieci*, 38. "Fucato" is a sixteenth-century term that meant "false, painted with *fuco*"; the word originates from Latin "fucatus" which in its turn was derived from "fucus," a kind of algae that was used in coloring textiles (Battisti, *Dizionario etimologico*, vol. III, 1728). See also Tommaseo, *Dizionario*, vol. 3, 947 and Battaglia, *Grande dizionario*, vol. 6, 415.

18. Barbaro, *M. Vitruvii*, 12.

19. Barbaro, *I dieci*, 21.

20. Tafuri, "Norma e programa," xvi.

21. Barbaro, *I dieci* (1556), 82.

22. Venetian authorities were generally reluctant to send those arrested for heresy to Rome for trial. However, on at least one occasion, Barbaro intervened in order to ensure the extradiction of a person accused of heresy to the Roman Inquisition. The accused was Guido da Fano, a priest who returned from England in 1537 with a number of heretical books. He ran into trouble with the Inquisition in 1545 and had to flee to England, where he stayed for four years. In 1561, he was arrested for heresy by the Venetian authorities, who refused to send him to Rome and finally released him from prison towards the end of the year. He was arrested again in 1566, and this time, at the intervention of Daniele Barbaro, he was sent to Rome for trial. We learn this in a letter from the papal nuncio in Venice to cardinal Alessandrino. See Paschini, *Venezia e l'inquisizione*, 131. Barbaro's motives are unknown. It may be that he was simply trying to ingratiate himself with the *curia*.

23. Palladio, *Scritti*, 123.

24. Vignola, *Regola*, Preface. This is the third plate in the first (1563) edition and the second plate in the second (1572) edition.

25. Barbour, *Tuning*, 5.

26. Levarie and Levy, *A Study*, 20.

27. $(5/3)(5/4)(1/2)$ The multiplication of ratios is equivalent to the addition of intervals and consequently this is a sixth plus a third minus an octave.

28. Howard and Longair, "Harmonic Proportion," 122–23.

29. Ibid., 135.

30. Wittkower, *Principles*, 108.

31. Lindley, "Early 16th Century." Note Lindley's observation that by the year 1588 only one person (a certain Girolamo Roselli) is known to have advocated the adoption of equal temperament in keyboard instruments.

32. Walker, *Studies*, 10.

33. Ptolemy, *De musica*, 1.10.24, Theon, *Expositio*, 2.8, Euclid, *Sectio Canonis*, 169.

34. Gaffurio, *De harmonia*, 101, Vicentino, *L'antica*, 146.

35. Through the sixteenth century, theorists supporting equal temperament were rare. Mark Lindley has managed to trace the beginnings of the use of equal temperament back to the late fifteenth century (Lindley, *Lutes*, 19–31). Among Renaissance theorists, it was the secretary of Cesare Borgia, Carlo Valgulio, who first defended the idea of equal temperament, but during the sixteenth century, only a few supported it, such as Cardano (Palisca, *Humanism*, 97).

36. Euclid, *Elementa*, 6.9 and 6.13; Palisca, *Humanism*, 242.

37. Fogliani, *Musica*, 3.2, fol.36r. See also Lindley, *Lutes*, 19.

38. Zarlino, *Istituzioni*, 94–96

39. Ibid., 94.

40. Barbaro, *I dieci*, 227. It is impossible to say whether he had actually read Aristoxenus before the publication of the Latin translation in 1562; what Barbaro says about Aristoxenus is what he could have learned from other sources, for instance, Ptolemy and/or Boethius. For the greater part of the

Renaissance, Aristoxenus was mostly known only from secondary sources. Palisca remarked: "The name of Aristoxenus came up frequently in the literature about music theory . . . yet he remained a phantom author throughout most of the Renaissance. His *Harmonic Elements* did not attract much attention, partly because it was incomplete (only three books survive), partly because it was extremely technical, but mostly because it contradicted Pythagorean doctrine" (Palisca, *Humanism*, 48). If Barbaro had read Aristoxenus, this was probably from the manuscript that once belonged to Cardinal Bessarion and is today Marciana Graecus 257. (This manuscript came to Venice only in 1470, after Bessarion's death, so it is not mentioned in the donation list from 1468, published by Omont in *Inventaire* in 1896. It can be found, however, in Labowski, *Bessarion's Library*, 166, 174, 185.) It seems that by Barbaro's time this was the only copy of Aristoxenus available in Venice. In any case, Gogava, who published the first printed Latin translation of Aristoxenus in Venice in 1562 complained in the Preface that he could get a hold of only one copy, though he had searched in both Rome and Venice. But a few decades earlier, there had indeed been two copies of Aristoxenus in Venice—another one belonging to Giorgio Valla, after whose death it passed to Alberto Pio of Carpi and is now in Naples, Biblioteca Nazionale, MS III C2. It is thus reasonable to assume that the only manuscript of Aristoxenus that Barbaro could have had in his hands was the one from Bessarion's library.

41. Barbaro, *I dieci*, 242; See also 232.
42. Ibid., 349.
43. This passage is identical in the Italian editions from 1556 and 1567 (Barbaro, *I dieci . . .* , 349; *I dieci . . .* , (1556), 202). The Latin edition from 1567 lacks the first sentence (starting with "Puo ben essere . . .), but it contains the remaining explanation about the diagonal of a square (Barbaro, *M. Vitruvii Polionis*, 268). All three editions of the commentary on Vitruvius also include a drawing of a square whose side is 5 and the diagonal clearly indicated as 7 $^1/_{14}$ (Barbaro, *I dieci*, 351; *I dieci* (1556), 202; *M. Vitruvii Polionis*, 270).
44. An example is in Bologna, Civ. Mus. B.26, fols. 1r-20r; see also Moyer, *Musica Scientia*, 185.
45. Barbaro, *I dieci*, 229, 230.
46. Berger, *Theories*, 56.
47. Ibid., 5.
48. Forssman, "Palladio e Daniele Barbaro," 75.
49. Macrobius, *In somnium*, 2.4.13.
50. Ptolemy, *De musica*, 1.16.
51. For a discussion of commercial interests behind the rise of Modernist ideology in the late 1940s and early 1950s, see Mitrović, "Modernists against Modernity."
52. Banham, "The New Brutalism," 361; A.V. (?), "The Abstraction of History."

CHAPTER 3

1. See general discussion of the problem in Thoenes and Günther, "Gli ordini architettonici."
2. Barbaro discussed the theory of the classical orders in two of his books: the commentary on Vitruvius (*I dieci*) and the treatise on perspective (*Practica*, including the Latin manuscript version *Scenographia pictoribus et sculptoribus*.) A few manuscript versions of both works are preserved in the Marciana, some of them with interesting marginal notes in Barbaro's hand.
3. Tafuri, "La norma," xiv.
4. The two printed Italian versions of the commentary on Vitruvius supply the theory of the classical orders in the commentary on Vitruvius's Book Three. This does not conform to Vitruvius's organization of the material. Vitruvius described the Ionic order in Book Three, and the Doric and Corinthian in Book Four; Barbaro rearranged this, placing his descriptions of the Tuscan, Doric, Ionic, and Corinthian as a separate section in the commentary on Book Three. In Book Four, Barbaro provided the translation of Vitruvius's text accompanied by much shorter comments. Only in the Latin version of the commentary do Barbaro's explanations of the classical orders stand next to the Vitruvian descriptions to which they pertain. *Practica*, in turn, summarizes the theory of orders presented in the commentary on Vitruvius.

5. Vitruvius, *De arch.*, 'dorico genere,' 4.3.1, 'dorico more,' 4.3.3.
6. Cesariano, *Di Lucio Pollione Vitruvio*, 60.
7. Barbaro, *I dieci*, 163, 170, 171.
8. Serlio, *Tutte l'opere*, 4.126, 4.127, 4.139, 4.158, 4.170. See Powels, "Les origines," for the view that it was Serlio who codified the system of the orders as we know it today.
9. "*dispensatione*" of "*cose pari & dispari, eguali & diseguali*," Barbaro, *I dieci*, 28.
10. Ibid., 1.15–49.
11. Vitruvius, *De arch.*, 3.3.10.
12. In fact, these ratios already had a contradictory position in Vitruvius, who left undefined what kind of intercolumniation was appropriate if the column-height-to-lower-diameter ratio was less than eight.
13. Their collaboration could not have started before Barbaro returned from his ambassadorship in England in late spring 1551, while designs for Palazzo Chiericati seem to have been completed by March 1551. For Barbaro's biography, see Lavin, *Daniele Barbaro*; for Chiericati, see Puppi, *Palladio*, 281–286.
14. For Chiericati, see Puppi, Palladio, 281–86. There are three drawings that seem to represent pre-1550 design works (not archaeological surveys) with intercolumniations of less than 3D.

1) *Devonshire Collections, RIBA, Chiswick 27*, (Lewis, Drawings, #32) is a study of a two-story colonnade. Lewis dates this drawing c. 1540 on the basis of its similarity to a preparatory drawing for the Palazzo Civena (*RIBA: Palladio*, XIII-10, Lewis, *Drawings*, #7). But the Civena drawing has intercolumniations of almost 5D while this drawing, as Lewis rightly notes, "shows a much greater mastery than Trissino and Serlio of correct Ionic proportions, and rather surprisingly presents a Doric order that is almost Bramantesque in its sobriety and power, and strongly reflects Sanmicheli in its sculptural richness." There are thus strong stylistic grounds, besides the intercolumniation width, to date this drawing at least ten years later. Nevertheless, it is impossible to preclude the possibility that this was an extremely precocious exploration of the correct proportions of intercolumniations, motivated by the study of Vitruvius and early trips to Rome.

2) *RIBA, Palladio, XVII-16*, (Lewis, *Drawings*, #45): a villa project, possibly the Villa Pisani (Bagnolo), dated 1539/40, shows a colonnade of freestanding columns with intercolumniations of 3D. There are good stylistic reasons for this dating, since columns framing windows and distinct from the overall system of orders, generally atypical for Palladio, do appear in other drawings from the period (*RIBA, Palladio, XVII-26* and *RIBA, Palladio, XVII-19*, see illustrations 3-12 and 3-13). However, these are freestanding columns, and in this case Palladio could have been motivated by the structural concerns mentioned by Vitruvius.

3) *RIBA, Palladio, XVII-21*, (Lewis, *Drawings*, #68) dated in 1547–48. This is a very small villa, which is extremely difficult to relate to any known commission. The composition of the portico and the placement of the columns resembles the palazzo Chiericati, which could justify dating the drawing a couple of years later. (For unexplained reasons, Lewis also dates the Chiericati project to 1548.) (Lewis, *Drawings*, 118.)

15. The seminal account of the un-Palladian aspects of the Villa in Maser is Huse's "Palladio und Villa Barbaro" But some of Huse's arguments are not well supported. For instance, he claims that fireplaces and doors in the Villa in Maser are atypical for Palladio's work without providing a survey of these elements on other Palladio's villas that could substantiate the claim (109, 110). Huse also makes the mistake of identifying the broken

entablature on the Villa in Maser with *frontespizi . . . spezzati*, which Palladio criticized in the chapter on abuses in the first book (113). Palladio's authorship of the villa has been particularly questioned on the basis of the execution of the internal decoration. For the summary of this debate, see Lewis, "Palladio's Painted Architecture." See also Ackerman, *Palladio*, 43; Wolters, "Andrea Palladio e la decorazione," and Oberhuber, "Gli affreschi."

16. We know from Vasari that Palladio provided the model of this building. Even Puppi, who is inclined to argue that Palladio's model was "completely realized" admits "un'esecuzione maldestra dell'idea" (Puppi, *Palladio*, 357–58). Beltramini's judgment that the building was executed without much concern for Palladio's original model is probably much more accurate (*Atlante*, 211).

17. According to Bertotti Scamozzi's survey.

18. Colossal orders appear much earlier in his designs of palazzo courtyards.

19. Since it is difficult to obtain accurate measurements of wall thicknesses, it is often easier to state the lateral shift (i.e. the distance between the column edge and wall edge).

20. I am indebted to Professor Wolfgang Wolters for drawing my attention to the problematic placement of columns on the Rotonda.

21. Mitrović, "Palladio's Theory of the Classical Orders," 120–121.

22. See Puppi, *Palladio*, 296–97.

23. This is the drawing RIBA XVI/20A recto.

24. Goedicke, Slusallek and Kubelik, "Thermoluminescence Dating," 405. At the same time, in his *Architectura* (vols. 1, 12), Muttoni himself expressed the opinion that the columns were placed in the position detached from walls by Vincenzo Scamozzi.

25. CISA R0000451 and R0000452.

26. The modern survey suggests that the position of columns in the Palazzo Chiericati was defined by aligning their axes with the surfaces of walls.

27. Palladio, *Four Books*, 2.53. The survey carried out in summer 2003 by the author together with Stephen Wassel, Melanie Bourke, and Tim Ross confirms this statement.

28. The Villa Foscari (Malcontenta) is particularly interesting. Since the modern surveys published by Erik Forssman have confirmed the accuracy of Bertotti Scamozzi's old surveys, proportional relationships on this villa can be discussed with confidence (see Forssman, *Visible Harmony*.) An important problem is, however, that Forssman provided the room dimensions in the form of table. The table does not give each individual dimension for each individual room or element; for instance Forssman simply stated "the thickness of the column," assuming that that the builders managed to insure that all columns have the same thickness. Similarly, the dimensions of rooms are based on the assumption that symmetrical rooms have identical dimensions.

29. This is according to the surveys published by Forssman (see note 154). However, Forssman did not state the exact value of the smaller width of the sala; it has been assumed here (on the basis of the restitution from the drawings he provided) that this dimension is about 560 cm. (This is plausible, since in that case the smaller width of the sala would be equal to the width of the larger rooms, or the side of the square rooms, or half of the larger width of the sala.) In any case, the mentioned lateral shift (50 cm) is what follows if the restitution is correct and the smaller width of the sala is 560 cm.

30. An interesting attempt to reconstruct the history of the writing of the *Four Books* is in Zorzi, *I Disegni*, 147–56. Barbaro mentioned in his 1556 version of the commentary that Palladio was working on a treatise about architecture (*I dieci*, (1556), 178, 306) and Zorzi has tried to relate some of the early drawings and manuscripts preserved in RIBA and Museo Correr to this early project and to the final version of the text of the first of the *Four Books*. Zorzi ascribed the handwriting of these chapters to Palladio's son Silla.

31. See Mitrović, "Palladio's Theory of the Classical Orders," for a full comparison of ratios stipulated by individual authors.

32. For example, the thickness of the bottom astragal of the Doric capital: in Barbaro, it is three-and-a-half thicknesses of the annulet (Barbaro, *I dieci*, 145) but only three annulets in Palladio (Palladio, *Four Books*, 1.26).

33. In his description of the Attic base, Barbaro stated its thickness as D/2, while the plinth is D/3. (Barbaro, *I dieci*, 144.) The implication is that the part above the plinth is only D/6, which is absurd, because it would mean that the plinth is thicker than the rest of the base. All other ratios are deduced by dividing this upper segment following Vitruvius's precepts. However, Vitruvius and all Renaissance authors except Barbaro stated the thickness of the base as D/2, and said that *the area above the plinth was* D/3 (i.e. the plinth is 1/6 *of the base*). In the translation, Barbaro correctly rendered this passage from Vitruvius (Vitruvius, *De arch.*, 3.5.2., Barbaro, *I dieci*, 155). Had Barbaro's description in the commentary on Book Three said "grossezza della basa" instead of "grossezza della colonna," then all the ratios he supplied would agree with those of Vitruvius and Palladio (Palladio, *Four Books*, 48). Yet the same formulation that renders the plinth twice as big as it should be is found in all editions of the commentary (Barbaro, *I dieci* (1556) 99; *M. Vitruvii Pollionis*, 113). Two additional arguments suggest that we may be dealing with a slip of the pen. Ratios in the drawing Barbaro supplied in the commentary are not indicated in numbers, but if we measure the sizes we arrive at the ratios prescribed by Vitruvius and Palladio. Moreover, Vitruvius did not state the sizes of the trochilus and its adjacent fillets, but both Barbaro and Palladio divide the total thickness of the trochilus with fillets into six parts and assign one to each fillet. They thus agreed about the way of proportioning the Attic base, and Barbaro's seemingly different ratios are due to a slip of the pen. Vignola's ratios differ significantly. Alberti and Serlio, on the other hand, divide the trochilus-with-fillets segment into seven parts, assigning one part to each fillet, and five to the trochilus (Vignola, *Canon*, plate 31, Serlio, *Tutte*, 4.139, Alberti, *De re*, 7.7.3).

34. In Barbaro's commentary, *apophysis* is first mentioned in the description of the Tuscan base, and here it refers to the fillet on the top of the base (*I dieci*, 142). Vitruvius did not say that the Tuscan base should have a fillet on the top, but an *apophysis*, and stated the thickness of the torus and apophysis together (*De arch.* 4.7.3). However the relevant drawings from Palladio's *Four Books* and Barbaro's commentary both show a fillet there and they state D/16 as its thickness. Palladio says that this fillet [*listello*] is also called *cimbia*; he did not use the term *apophysis* (Palladio, *Four Books*, 1.19). Barbaro often directly identified Vitruvius's *apophysis* as a fillet. ("Apofige, o cimbia che si dica," "cimbia detta apofige," Barbaro, *I dieci*, 142). Also, he distinguished *apofige* from the hollow curve of the column: "bastone, con quella parte, che si chiama apofige, & apothesi; che sono certe piegature dalle teste de i fusti delle colonne, che danno gratia mirabile, quando sono ben fatte"(142). *Apofige* here refers to the fillet, *apothesi* to the curve above. In Barbaro's treatise on perspective, the fillet on the top of the base is indicated as "*cimbia*, called *apophygis*, or *listello*" (Barbaro, *Pratica*, 131), and the name *apophysis* for this fillet also appears in the corresponding drawings of the Attic and Ionic bases in the same treatise (Ibid., 133 and 134). The drawings of the Tuscan, Attic, and Ionic bases in which the fillet above the torus labelled 'apophigis' appear also in the *Scaenographia pictoribus* (the Latin manuscript version of the treatise on perspective, Marciana, Lat. VIII, 41, 3069, 53ᴸ, 54ᴸ, and 55ᴸ). In the same manuscript, the fillet under the astragal of the Tuscan capital is also labelled 'apophigis,' and Barbaro explains in the text that 'apophygis' comes immediately under the astragal ("collarinum . . . sub quo est apophigis uel Apophisis," Ibid., 57ᴿ).

Barbaro was not fully consistent in interpreting *apophysis* that way; the drawing of the Attic base in the Latin version of the commentary on Vitruvius designates the fillet as *quadra apophygys* whereas the curved part of the column is marked as *apophigis* (*M. Vitruvii Pollionis*, 113).

35. Vitruvius said that the Tuscan capital should be divided into three parts, the lowest of which should be assigned to "hypotrachelio cum apophysi" (Vitruvius, *De arch.* 4.7.3). He similarly divided the Doric capital into three parts, the lowest segment being the *hypotrachelium* — in the case of the Doric, no *apophysis* was mentioned (Ibid., 4.3.4). Pierre Gros remarked that the exact meanings of both *apophysis* and *hypotrachelium* in Vitruvius are unclear, though *hypotrachelium* seems to designate the

lower section of the capital, in the form of a neck or cylinder (Gros in Fleury, ed: Vitruve: *De l'architecture*, vol. 4, 188). In regards to the Doric capital, Gros explains Vitruvius's *hypotrachelium* as the upper ring of the column, which is part of the capital (Ibid., 130).

Barbaro's use of the term *hypotrachelium* is also occasionally contradictory. In his description of the Tuscan capital in the commentary, he says that the thickness of the fillet under the echinus is one-sixth of the *hypotrachelium*, while the *hypotrachelium* has twice the thickness of the subechinal fillet ("...listello, che ua sotto l'ouolo [che è alto la sesta parte di quella che ua all'hipotrachelio] . . . lo Hipotrachelio, o sottogola, si fa al modo che si fa l'Apofige: & è alto il doppio listello sotto l'ouolo" Barbaro, *I dieci*, 144.) The *hypotrachelium* of the Tuscan capital here refers at the same time to the bottom astragal and the entire lower third of the capital. The illustration in Barbaro's commentary has the letters H (the area below the subechinal fillet), I (the astragal), K (the fillet below the astragal), and L (the hollow curve below the fillet) described together as "Hypotrachelium con Apofigi. cioè parte contratta alla sottogola, con la cimbia" (Barbaro, *I dieci*, 144). The lowest third is called *hipotrachelio & apofigi* in the text (Ibid., 142) and Barbaro says that the lowest part consists of *hypotrachelio, o collarino, & apophyge* and that the fillet under the echinus is one third of the thickness of the *hypotrachelium* (Ibid., 142). In his treatise about perspective and its Latin version, the manuscript *Scaenographia pictoribus*, Barbaro supplied a drawing of the Tuscan capital where hypotrachelium is the part between the annulet and the astragal, i.e., the entire lower third of the capital (Barbaro, *Pratica . . .* , 139; Scaenographia pictoribus, Marciana, Lat. VIII, 41, 3069, 57^R). In the *Pratica* (139) Barbaro labels the area between the annulet and the astragal as "collarino detto hypotrachelium."

36. Vitruvius, *De arch.*, 4.3.5. Vitruvius's Doric module is half of the lower column diameter; the triglyph width in this case is 1 module, the height 3/2 modules, which is also the width of the metopes (Ibid., 4.3.5). Half of the module thus makes 1/3 of the metope width.

Vitruvius says that the front of a *diastyle tetrastylos* should have 27 modules at the bottom level. (Ibid., 4.3.3.) The central intercolumniation should have three and the side intercolumniations two triglyphs. The total number of triglyphs thus comes to 11; between them there are 10 metopes. Altogether this makes 26 modules. The overall width of a diastyle tetrastylos was defined as 27, and, if the temple at the bottom were as wide as the frieze is long, then the side metopes would have to be half a module each, i.e., 1/3 of the normal metope size. (It seems plausible that the frieze cannot be longer than the temple is wide at the bottom level.) A similar calculation can be made for *diastyle hexastylos*, *systyle tetrastylos*, and *hexastylos*, the result being always 1/3 metope at the corners.

However, these calculations imply that the frieze length is equal to the temple width at the column base level. If the frieze is somewhat shorter, this would affect the size of corner semi-metopes. Thus the corner metope can be 1/3 of the normal metope size, or less. Knell states 1/6 of the lower column diameter, or 9/2 of the metope width as the solution, and Gros remarks that this is also the most common understanding of the majority of exegetes (Knell, *Vitruvs Architekturtheorie*, 90–91; Gros, in Fleury, ed: *Vitruve IV*, 134).

37. Barbaro, *I dieci*, 173.
38. Palladio, *Four Books*, 1.43.
39. The side of a metope is about 67 cm on the Palazzo Chiericati and 66 cm on the Basilica; the respective semi-metopes are 16.5 cm and 16 cm.
40. Barbaro, *I dieci*, 198.; Palladio, *Four Books*, 1.43.
41. The Composite entablature was similarly undefined, but it was much less used.
42. Hesberg, *Konsolengeisa*, 18.
43. Alberti, *De re.*, 7.9.11.
44. Bruschi, "L'Antico," 48.
45. See Marchini, *Il Duomo*, 57–71.
46. Angelini, *Mauro Codussi*, plate 85 for the portico of the Palazzo Zorzi a S. Severo and plate 98 for palazzo Vendramin-Calergi. For the latter entablature, see also Howard, "Exterior Orders," particularly 189.
47. Vitruvius, *De arch.*, 4.2.5.
48. Serlio, *Tutte*, 3.54, 3.99, 3.112, 4.170. I am indebted to an anonymous reviewer of *Architectural History* for drawing my attention to these passages during the preparation for publication of my article "Palladio's Theory of the Classical Orders." Serlio used the term 'mensole' and from illustrations it is clear that he meant 'modillions,' as Hart and Hicks render it in their translation.
49. Martini, *Trattati*, (1967), vol.2, f.36v, tav.226.
50. "...i mutuli, o modioni....rappresentano gli sporti de i canterij sotto le cornici...," Barbaro, *I dieci*, 169. Barbaro actually supplied a drawing representing the Doric entablature, where mutules are referred to as "modioni" (Ibid., 170).
51. Vignola, *Canon*, plate 14, caption. This caption does not appear in the version of the 1563 edition of the *Regola*, which was reprinted in the Polifilo, but it is found in the more widely spread version of the same edition, equivalent to the one in the Vatican, Cicogn.VIII 416. It also appears in the second edition, Rome, 1572.
52. Mitrović, "Palladio's Theory of the Classical Orders," 124.
53. Vitruvius, *De arch.*, 3.5.10.
54. Boucher, "Nature."
55. Ibid., 301.
56. I am indebted to Professor John Stamper of the University of Notre Dame, for this observation.
57. Jones, "Designing."
58. While this discussion concentrates on the relationship of Palladio's published surveys of Roman temples with his canonical Corinthian entablature, it is still important to mention entablatures from other buildings which may have influenced Palladio's formulation of the canon. In particular, the morphology of the entablatures from the Arch of Titus, the Arch of Constantine, and the Baths of Diocletian can be said to possess the standard morphology. For entablatures of the Arch of Titus and the Baths of Diocletian, see Mauch, *Die Architektonischen Ordnungen*, VIII edition (Berlin 1896), plates 50 and 51. For the Arch of Constantine, see Ibid., but VII edition (Berlin, 1875), plate 22. Palladio's survey drawings of the entablatures on the Arch of Titus and Diocletian's Baths have been preserved; these are respectively drawings D10v and D15r in Vicenza's *Museo Civico*. See also Puppi, *Corpus*, #19 and #27 and #27bis; for the Arch of Constantine see also RIBA, *Palladio*, XVII-5verso.

All three entablatures show substantial morphological similarities to Palladio's and Vignola's canonical Corinthian. Any morphological differences pertain to very small details. However, they still differ more from Palladio's standard Corinthian entablature than the entablatures on the temples of Venus Genetrix, Vespasian or Castor and Pollux. If we compare the proportions of these entablatures with Palladio's, we can see that none of them could have been the precedent from which Palladio derived the proportions of his canonical Corinthian entablature. The following table shows this well (data according to Mauch):

	ARCHITRAVE	FRIEZE	CORNICE
Vignola	0.75D	0.75D	1.042D
Palladio	0.638D	0.475D	0.768D
Arch of Titus	0.767D	0.741D	1.03D
Baths of Diocletian	0.741D	0.733D	0.85D
Arch of Constantine	0.75D	0.667D	0.975D

59. The nine relevant entablatures are those from the Basilica of Maxentius in Rome (4.14), Temple of Mars Ultor in Rome (4.20), Temple of Minerva

on Nerva's Forum, two entablatures (4.28 and 4.29), Temple of Castor and Pollux in Rome (4.69), Temple of Vespasian on the Roman Forum (4.72), Temple of Castor and Pollux in Naples (4.97), Temple in Pola (4.109), Maison Carrée in Nimes (4.116), and Temple of Venus Genetrix in Rome (4.132). The entablature from the Temple of Castor and Pollux in Naples was destroyed in an earthquake in 1688. Similarly, the part of the entablature above the architrave of the Temple of Mars Ultor had already disappeared when Cresy and Taylor made their surveys in the nineteenth century (Cresy and Taylor, *The Architectural Antiquites*, 50). According to Serlio's description, the section of this entablature above the architrave was already missing in the early sixteenth century (Serlio, *Tutte l'opere*, 3, 88v). Both Palladio and Labacco, however, present this entablature in its full height, implying that all its parts were sufficiently preserved to be measured (Labacco, *Libro*, 12; Palladio, *Four Books*, 4.20). While they present entablatures with similar morphology, the proportions of the major elements are different.

60. Pierre Gros noted that the only reliable published surveys of Roman entablatures are those produced by Toebelmann in 1923 (Gros, *Aurea Templa*, 252. The reference is to Toebelmann, *Römische Gebälke*). Since he made this statement, he and Robert Amy have published a survey of the Maison Carrée, but that survey presents only the dimensions of the largest elements (architrave, frieze and cornice) of the entablature (Amy and Gros, *La Maison Carrée*). Tobelmann's surveys include only two entablatures from the list in note 56, those from the Forum of Nerva (4.29) and Basilica of Maxentius (4.14). Even if we disregard Gros's warning about the accuracy of older surveys, we shall not find many published surveys of Roman entablatures. Desgodetz' surveys cannot be used for the purpose of establishing the accuracy of Palladio's, since the measurements he provided were not stated as size measurements, but as ratios of the lower column diameter. However, nineteenth-century surveys by Cresy and Taylor of the temples of Vepasian in Rome. Castor and Pollux in Rome, and Minerva on Nerva's Forum in Rome are presented in a way that can be eyed and have been used here.

61. Where mistakes occur, they are far greater than 3 percent and exceed the possible error, which could have been generated by converting Palladio's data into the metric system. See Mitrović, "Palladio's Corinthian."

62. Total heights are not legible in three cases: the entablature from the Temple of Vesta in Tivoli (4.93) and two entablatures from the Pantheon (4.80 and 4.83). In the case of one entablature from Nerva's Forum (4.29) comparison is not possible because the lower column diameter is not known.

63. According to Antolini, "Palladio fu ingannato" (Antolini, *Il tempio di Minerva*, 16). See also Boucher, "Nature," for a discussion of this comparison.

64. The Temple of Castor and Pollux in Rome (2.52D), the Temple of Serapis on the Quirinal (2.43D), the Maison Carée (2.57D), and the Temple in Pola (2.37D).

65. Palladio, *Four Books*, 7.15

66. See Mitrović, "Aesthetic Formalism."

67. Ibid., 335–338.

68. Alberti, *De re.*, 9.8.3.; 9.5.3; 9.8.5.

69. Vignola, *Regola*, Table 2 of the 1562 edition and Table 1 of the 1572 edition.

CHAPTER 4

1. See Assunto, "Introduzione," and Boucher, "Nature," for a discussion of the role of nature in Palladio's aesthetic views.

2. See Goethe, *Italienische Reise*, 47–48, and Hugo von Hofmannsthal, "Sommerreise."

3. One could argue that the works on the Rotonda were probably initiated with the intention to expand the platform later, that the underground staircases were a subsequent addition by Vincenzo Scamozzi, and that they are merely a functional resolution of the problem created by the excessive cost of completing the platform would require. But one can also present the counterargument that the expense would have been clear from the beginning. For a discussion of the history of these staircases, see Kubelik, Goedike, and Susallek, "Primi resultati" and "Thermoluminescence Dating."

4. Zorzi, "La interpretazione," 97. For a systematic comparison of differences between the plans in the *Four Books* and Palladio's executed buildings, see also Kubelik, "Per una nuova lettura." From Zorzi's text it is not clear whether he meant that all illustrations were made relatively independently of Palladio or only those of Palladio's own designs presented in the second book. Also, some of Zorzi's premises, used in order to argue against the relevance of the illustrations in the *Four Books* seem patently wrong. He claimed that, with some exceptions, all Palladio's works in existence today, were executed during his lifetime and under his supervision (99). Starting from this assumption, Zorzi further argued that the study of executed buildings provides us with the safest and most authentic access to the original idea and Palladio's intention (104). However, the list of buildings Palladio did not finish during his lifetime is long and distinguished, including the Basilica, San Giorgio Maggiore, Redentore, the Rotonda, Villa Cornaro, to mention only a few.

5. Barbieri, "Il Valore." Barbieri convincingly argued that Palladio's impulsive late style is in great opposition to the serenity of the buildings presented in the treatise and cannot be taken as the explanation of discrepancies between the published and built work. Barbieri's judgment coincides with the view of other scholars. Bruce Boucher, for instance, writing unrelated to this debate, stated that "the treatise [the *Four Books*] is heavily weighted toward his [Palladio's] earlier architectural style" (Boucher, *Palladio*, 235).

6. Barbieri, "Il valore dei *Quattro libri*," 69.

7. Ibid., 76 and 77.

8. Boucher, *Palladio*, 198. Throughout Palladio's biography there are occasions in which his unwillingness to sacrifice an ideal-formal solution to the realities of the site resulted in losing major commissions, such as the project for the Rialto bridge, the facade of San Petronio, the project for the Ducal Palace (Ibid., 258).

9. Wittkower, in *Architectural Principles*, insisted on deriving the origin of musical proportions in Palladio from the *Timaeus*. Boucher, in his *Palladio*, talks about Palladio's drawings in the *Four Books* as representations of architectural ideas (220), the presentation of the Palazzo Barbarano in the treatise as "ideal version of his creation" (223), and expressed the view that in the *Four Books* Palladio "felt that he was responding to a higher truth by presenting designs that corresponded to his own system rather than the accidental state of an existing architecture" (247). See also similar views in Assunto, "Introduzione," Rupprecht "Prinzipien" and Fagiolo "Palladio e il significato" and "Contributo all'interpretazione."

10. Panofsky, *Idea*.

11. Vitruvius, *De arch.*, 3.5.8–9; 3.3.11; 3.3.12–13

12. Alberti, *De re.*, 7.6.6.–7.6.7.

13. Vignola, *Canon*. This statement is in the third plate of the first edition (1562) and the second plate of the second edition (1572).

14. Barbaro, *I dieci*, 159; 133.

15. Ibid., 133.

16. Ibid., 256.

17. Barbaro, *Pratica*, 14.

18. Lomazzo, *Trattato*, 246.

19. Plato, *Sophist*, 236a.

20. Alberti, *De re.*, 2.1.4.

21. Raphael (?), "Lettera a Leone X," in Bruschi, Maltese, Taffuri, Bonelli (eds.), *Scritti*, 481.

22. Barbaro, *La pratica*.
23. Vitruvius, *De arch.*, 1.2.2.
24. Giocondo, *M. Vitrvvivs*, 4v.
25. Barbaro, *I dieci*, 32.
26. Barbaro, *M.Vitrvii Polionis...*, 19.
27. Barbaro, *M.Vitruvii Polionis...*, 19; Barbaro, *I dieci*, 29–30.
28. Barbaro, *I dieci*, 30, 256; *Pratica*, 14.
29. Barbaro, *I dieci*, 30.
30. Bernhard Rupprecht, "Prinzipien," 15 and 32. See also the Italian version of the article "Proiezione."
31. Rupprecht, "Prinzipien," 35.
32. Ibid., 43.
33. Frommel, "Roma," 146.
34. Gioseffi, "Il disegno," 61.
35. Fagiolo, "Le facciate palladiane," 53–54.
36. Wittkower, *Architectural Principles*, 89–98.
37. The current facade of San Giorgio probably does not correspond to Palladio's original design, but it is nevertheless an application of Palladio's solution to the church facade problem. See Guerra, "Movable Facades," and Cooper, "La facciata." I am indebted to Professor Andreas Beyer for drawing my attention to this problem.
38. Wittkower, *Architectural Principles*, 89–98.
39. Larsen, "Palladio's Redentore."
40. Vitruvius, *De arch.*, 4.2.5.
41. Barbaro, *I dieci*, 171 and 154.
42. Palladio, *Four Books*, 1.69.
43. It would be wrong to simply identify the entablatures with brackets with Palladio's Ionic entablatures and think that Palladio in such cases followed Vitruvius's recommendation to use the Ionic entablature with the Corinthian order. This recommendation was indeed repeated by Barbaro (*I dieci*, 155) and Serlio (*Tutte*, 4.170)—although the latter also proposed his own version of the Corinthian entablature. But Palladio and Vignola made efforts to suggest their own versions of the Corinthian entablature; in the *Four Books* Palladio stated that the difference between the Ionic and the Corinthian entablature was in the cornice.
44. The wings were completed only in 1590. Lewis ("La datazione" and "Girolamo II Corner's Completion") thinks that they were completed according to Palladio's plans. See also Bruce Boucher, *Andrea Palladio*, 136.
45. There are two cases where the placement of the dentils contradicts their tectonic interpretation: the ceiling of the ground floor loggia of the Palazzo Valmarana and the ceiling of the portico of the Palazzo Chiericati. In the case of the Palazzo Chiericati, these dentils were placed during Giovanni Miglioranza's repair works of 1853–55. See Barioli, "Ristauro" and Barbieri, "Palazzo Chiericati," 33–43, esp. 39. I am indebted to Ms. Daniela Tovo from Centro Internazionale di Studi di Architettura in Vicenza for the help in resolving this question. The Palazzo Valmarana was heavily damaged in World War II and extensively repaired afterwards. See Guiotto "Recenti." I have not been able to establish whether these dentils are original.
46. Entablatures without frieze and cornice appear also in other cases where columns are used in combination with vaults or arches—e.g., on the Basilica and inside the Villa Pisani (Montagnana).
47. The soffit of the internal entablature at the Carità has what we call mutules today. Palladio did not identify mutules with modillions, the way it was the case with many of his Renaissance predecessors. But there is no indication that he recognized mutules in the soffit ornamentation which we call "mutules' today. In the description of the Doric order in the *Four Books* he only used the term *goccie*.
48. Such massive protruding beams appear elsewhere in Palladio's work, e.g. on the back loggia of the Palazzo Valmarana.
49. See Mitrović, "Aesthetic Formalism."
50. Younés, "Architecture and Language" and "Poetic Order" in Younés, *The True*.
51. Speroni (*I dialoghi*) discussed language theory in two of his dialogues: "Delle lingue" (105–31) and "Della retorica" (131–61) but left the issue of conventionalism versus anti-conventionalism undecided. In the former dialogue, he compared Italian to Latin and Greek; the claim that Greek is particularly suitable for learning is justified by reference to Plato's *Cratylus*, the view that no language can have the privilege of expressing the concepts of the human soul is defended by referring to Aristotle (74). Benedetto Varchi discussed the problem in his dialogue, *L'Ercolano*, and also left it unresolved (Varchi, *Opere*, 55). Varchi says that according to Plato names were natural; a similar view was shared by the Jews, who called their science of names *Cabala*. But Aristotle, who believed that names were arbitrary, dismissed this view. Varchi also refrained from expressing his own judgment.
52. Barbaro, *In Porphirium*, C1.
53. Morsolin, *Trissino*, 242–260.
54. Ibid., 246–247 and 524.

CHAPTER 5

1. Le Corbusier, *Towards*, 133–48 and 203–23.
2. In that case, a critic of Le Corbusier could easily simplify the argument and ask whether a seventeenth-century Doric column, executed faithfully following Vignola's precepts, is aesthetically equivalent to its twentieth-century clone.
3. Sibley, "Aesthetic."
4. For different definitions, see Levinson, "Aesthetic Supervenience."
5. Bender, "Supervenience."
6. Wicks, "Criticism."
7. Zangwill, *Metaphysics*, 43–51; see also "Long Live Supervenience."
8. Zangwill, *Metaphysics*, 55–81; see also "Feasible Aesthetic Formalism."
9. Zangwill defined formal aesthetic properties as those which are determined solely by (supervene on) sensory or physical non-aesthetic properties. He referred to physical and sensory properties as "narrow properties," as opposed to the "broad" non-aesthetic properties which cover everything else, including the history of the production of the artwork, meanings historically associated with it, and so on. In the context of the distinction between visual and verbal non-aesthetic properties, visual non-aesthetic properties fall entirely within the category of Zangwill's narrow properties. For the sake of simplicity, it has been assumed here that Zangwill's "narrow properties" can be fully identified with visual properties. This is a simplification, since when it comes to architecture, Zangwill's narrow properties would include visual properties plus the building material. Our knowledge about the material is always verbal: we perceive the surface, color and texture, but in order to name the material, we must use words.
10. It may be difficult to say which architectural forms are appropriate for modern times, but there is much less confusion about the appropriateness of theoretical positions. The belief in signification independent from human conventions cannot be reasonably upheld without embarking on a radical revision of the modern scientific worldview, whose most elementary premise is that all signs are conventional. If names, signs, symbols could be part of the natural order of the world, then the outcome of an experiment would depend on the words used to name the objects used in the experiment.
11. Sibley, "Objectivity."
12. Ibid, 44.
13. Ibid., 50–51.

BIBLIOGRAPHY

BIBLIOGRAPHICAL STUDIES

Ackerman, James. "Gli studi palladiani degli ultimi trent'anni," in Chastel and Cevese (eds.), *Andrea Palladio*, 122–26.

Ferrari, Giorgio. "Schede di bibliografia palladiana dal 1955." Bollettino del Centro Internazionale di Studi di Architettura "Andrea Palladio" 3 (1961): 163–71; 7 (1965): 363–91.

Howard, Deborah. "Four Centuries of Literature on Palladio." Journal of the Society of Architectural Historians 39 (1980): 224–41.

Puppi, Lionello and Daniela Battilotti. "Bibliografia" in Puppi. *Palladio*, 529–553.

Timofiewitsch, Wladimir. "Die Palladio Forschung in den Jahren von 1940 bis 1960." Zeitschrift für Kunstgeschichte 23 (1960): 1974–181.

SOURCES BEFORE 1900

Alberti, Leon Battista. *De re aedificatoria*. Translated by Giovanni Orlandi as *L'architettura*. Milan: Edizioni Il Polifio, 1966. Translated by Joseph Rykwert, Robert Tavernor, and Neil Leach as *On the Art of Building*. Cambridge, MA: MIT Press, 1988.

Antolini, Giovanni. *Il tempio di Minerva in Assisi confrontato colle tavole di Andrea Palladio architetto di Vicenza*. Milan, 1803.

Aristoxenus. *Elementa harmonica*. Translated by Antonio Gogava as *Aristoxeni musici antiquiss. Harmonicorum elementorum libri III, Cl. Ptolemaei Harmonicorum seu de musica lib. III*. Venice, 1562. Translated by Henry Stewart Macran as *The Harmonics of Aristoxenus*. Hildesheim and New York: Olms, 1974.

Barbaro, Daniele. *Exquisitae in Porphirium commentationes Danielis Barbari*. Venice, 1542.

_____. *In tres libros Rhetoricorum Aristotelis commentaria*. Lion, 1544.

_____. *I dieci libri dell'architettura tradotti et commentati*. Venice, 1556 and 1567; Facsimile of the second edition Milan: Edizioni Il Polifilo, 1987. The Italian manuscript is in the Biblioteca Marciana, Venice, codici Italiani: IV, 37, 5133 and IV, 152, 5106.

_____. *M. Vitruvii Polionis de Architectura libri decem cum commentariis Danielis Barbari*. Venice, 1567.

_____. *La pratica della perspettiva di Monsignor Daniele Barbaro eletto patriarca d'Aquileia, opera molto prodittevole a pittori scvltori, et architetti*. Venice, 1569; Facsimile, Sala Bolognese: A. Forni, 1980. The Biblioteca Marciana holds manuscripts of the treatise both in Italian and Latin: Codici Latini, VIII, 41, 3069; Codici Italiani, IV, 39, 5446 and IV, 40, 5447.

_____. *Dialogo della eloquenza*. Venice, 1557. Reprinted in Bernard Weinberg, ed., *Trattati di poetica e retorica del cinquencento*. Bari, G. Laterza, 1970.

Barbaro, Daniele, ed. *I Dialoghi di Messer Sperone Speroni*. Venice, 1542

_____. *Compendium ethicorum librorum Hermolai Barbari*. Venice, 1544.

_____. *Hermolai Barbari Patritii Veneti Compendium scientiae naturalis, ex Aristotle*. Paris, 1547.

Belli, Silvio. *Della Proportione, et Proportionalità, Communi Passioni del Quanto, Libri Tre*. Venice, 1573. Translated with commentary by Stephen R. Wassell and Kim Williams as *On Ratio and Proportion: The Common Properties of Quantity*. Forward by Lionel March. Florence: Kim Williams Books, 2002.

Bertotti-Scamozzi, Ottavio. *Le fabbriche e i disegni di Andrea Palladio*. Venice, 1786. CD version with English translation by Howard Burns, Vicenza: Centro Internazionale di Studi di Architettura, 1998.

Cesariano, Cesare. *Di Lucio Pollione Vitruvio de architectura libri decem*. Como, 1521; Facsimile, Milan: Edizioni Il Polifilo, 1981.

Desgodetz, Antoine. *Les Èdifices antique de Rome*. Paris, 1682.

Dürer, Albrecht. *Unterweysung der messung*. Nuremberg, 1525; Nordlingen: Uhl, 1983.

Euclid. *Elementa*. Translated by Thomas L. Heath as *The Thirteen Books of Euclid's Elements*. New York: Dover Publications, 1926.

_____. *Sectio Canonis*. Translated by Andre Barbera as *The Euclidean Division of the Canon*. Lincoln: University of Nebraska Press, 1991.

Fogliani, Ludovico. *Musica Theorica*. Venice, 1529. Bologna: A. Forni, 1970.

Gaffurio, Franchino. *De harmonia musicorum instrumentorum opus*. Venice, 1518. Rome: American Institute of Musicology, 1977.

Giocondo, Giovani. M. *Vitruvius per Iocondum solito castiqvatior factvs cum figvris et tabvla*. Venice, 1511.

Goethe, Johann Wolfgang. *Italienische Reise (Reisen. Aufsätze und Abhandlungen)* in *Werke* Vol. 7. Bergen: Müller & Kiepenhauer, 1948.

Labacco, Antonio. *Libro d'Antonio Labacco appartinente a architettvra nel qual si figurano alcvne notabili antiquità di Roma*. Rome, 1559; Cremona: Il Polifilo, 1992.

Letarovilly, Paul Marie. *Edifices de Rome moderne*. Paris, 1840; New York: Princeton Architectural Press, 1984.

Ligorio, Pirro. *Delle Antichita di Roma circi* [sic], *theatri, amphitheatri con numerose tavole e la pianta cinquecentesca di Roma*, Daniela Negri, ed. Rome: E & A Editori Associati, 1989.

Lomazzo, Giovan Paolo. *Trattato dell'arte della pittura, scoltura et architettura*. Milan, 1585; Rome: S. Del-Monte, 1844.

Macrobius, Ambrosius Aurelius Theodosius. *Commentarii in Somnium Scipionis*. Translated by William Harris Stahl as *Commentary on the Dream of Scipio*. New York: Columbia University Press, 1952.

Martini, Francesco di Giorgio. *Trattati di architettura ingegneria e arte militare*. Corrado Maltese, Livia Maltese De Grassi, eds. Milan: Edizioni Il Polifilo, 1987.

Mauch, Johann Mathaus von. *Die architekonischen Ordnungen Griechen und Römer*, VII edition. Berlin: Ernst & Korn, 1875; VIII edition. Berlin: Wilhelm Ernst & Sohn, 1896. Reprinted as *Parallel of the Classical Orders of Architecture*. New York: Acanthus, 1998.

Morsolin, Bernardo. *Giangiorgio Trissino, monografia d'un gentiluomo litterato nel secolo XVI*. Florence, 1894.

Muttoni, Francesco. *Architectura di Andrea Palladio Vicentino di nuovo ristampata con le osservazioni dell'architetto NN*. Venice, 1740.

Omont, Henri Auguste. *Inventaire des manuscrits grecs et latins donnés à Sait-Marc de Venise par le cardinal Bessarion (1468)*. Paris, 1894.

Pacioli, Luca. *Divina proportione: opera a tutti glingegni perspicaci e curiosi necessaria oue ciascun studioso di philosophia; pro spectiva; pictura; sculptura; architectura; musica; e altre mathematice; suavissima sottile; e admirabile doctrina consequira; e delectarassi co varie questione de secretissima scientia*. Venice, 1509; Como: Maspero & Fontana, 1967. Manuscript in the collection of the Biblioteca Anbrosiana, Milan (ms. 170. sup.). Facsimile. Milano: Silvana, 1982.

Palladio, Andrea. *L'antichità di Roma*. Venice, 1554. Translated in Peter Murrey, ed. *Five Early Guides to Rome and Florence*. Farnborough: Gregg, 1972.

_____. *Descritione de le Chiese*. Venice, 1554. Translated by E.D. Howe as *The Churches of Rome*. Binghamton: State University of New York at Binghamton, 1991.

_____. *I quattro libri dell'architettura*. Venice, 1570. Facsimile. Milan: Ulrico Hoepli Editore, 1990. Translated by Richard Schofield as, *The Four Books on Architecture*. Cambridge, MA: MIT Press, 1997.

_____. *Sctitti sull'architettura (1554-1597)*. Lionello Puppi, ed. Vicenza: Neri Pozza, 1988.

Plato. *Republic*.

_____. *Sophist*.

_____. *Meno*.

Ptolemy. *De musica*. Translated by Ingemar Düring as *Die Harmonielehre*. Hildesheim and Zurich: Olms, 1982. Translated by Jon Solomon as *Harmonics*. Leiden: Mnemosyne, 2000.

Roritzer, Matthaus. *Geometria Deutsch*. Regensberg, 1486. Wiesbaden: Presler, 1999.

Sanzio, Raphael. "Lettera a Leone X," in Bruschi, Maltese, Taffuri and Bonelli (eds.), *Scritti*, 459–85.

Serlio, Sebastiano. *Tutte l'opere d'architettura et prospetiva*. Venice, 1619. Translated by Vaughan Hart and Peter Hicks as *Sebastiano Serlio, "On Architecture."* New Haven and London: Yale University Press, 1996.

Speroni, Sperone. *I dialoghi*. Venice, 1542.

Taylor, George Lidwell and Edward Cresy. *The Architectural Antiquities of Rome*. London, 1874.

Varchi, Benedetto. *Opere*. Trieste, 1858.

Vignola, Giacopo Barozzi da. *Regola delli cinque ordini*. Rome, 1563 and 1572. For modern reprints of the first edition see Christof Thoenes, ed. *Regola delli cinque ordini di M. Iacomo Barozzio da Vignola*. Vignola: Casa di risparmio di Vignola, 1974 and Elena Bassi, ed. *Trattati*. Milan: Edizioni Il Polifilo, 1985. Second edition translated by Branko Mitrović as *Canon of the Five Orders of Architecture*. New York: Acanthus, 1999.

Vincentino, Nicola. *L'antica musica ridotta alla moderna pratica*. Venice, 1555.

Vitruvius. *De Architectura*. Translated by Frank Granger as *On Architecture*. Cambridge, MA: Harvard University Press, 1983. Also translated by Morris Hickey-Morgan as *The Ten Books on Architecture*. New York: Dover, 1960, and by Ingrid Rowland as *Ten Books on Architecture*. New York: Cambridge University Press, 1999. See also important Renaissance editions, translations, and commentaries by Fra Giocondo, Cesare Cesariano, and Daniele Barbaro. An important collection of modern commentaries on individual books is *Vitruve: "De l'architecture,"* Phillipe Fleury, ed. Paris: Les Belles Lettres, 1969–92. This collection includes Pierre Gros's commentaries on Books Three and Four, cited in this book.

Zarlino, Gioseffe. *Le istitutioni harmoniche*. Venice, 1558; Ridgewood, NJ: Gregg Press, 1966.

_____. *Dimostrationi harmoniche*. Venice, 1571; Ridgewood, NJ: Gregg Press, 1966.

_____. *Sopplementi musicali*. Venice, 1588; Ridgewood, NJ: Gregg Press, 1966.

SOURCES AFTER 1900

Ackerman, James. *Palladio*. Harmondsworth: Penguin, 1966.

_____. "Palladio's Vicenza: A Bird's Eye Plan of ca. 1571," in *Studies in Renaissance and Baroque Art Presented to Anthony Blunt*. London: Phaidon, 1967.

_____. "The Tuscan/Rustic Order: A Study in the Metaphorical Language of Architecture." *Journal of Architectural Historians* 42 (1983): 15–34.

_____. *The Villa: Form and Ideology of Country Houses*. Princeton: Princeton University Press, 1990.

_____. *Distance Points: Essays in Theory and Renaissance Art and Architecture*. Cambridge, MA: MIT Press, 1991.

_____. "Palladio e lo sviluppo della concezione della chiesa a Venezia." *Bolletino del Centro Internazionale di Studi di Architettura "Andrea Palladio"* 19 (1977): 9–26.

_____. *Origins, Imitation, Conventions*. Cambridge MA: MIT Press, 2002.

Ackerman, James and Rhys Carpenter. *Art and Archaeology.* Englewood Cliffs, NJ: Prentice-Hall, 1963.

Adam, Robert. *Classical Architecture: A Comprehensive Handbook to the Tradition of Classical Style.* New York: Harry N. Abrams, 1991.

Adroni, Bruno, Christoph Luitpold Frommel, Christof Thoenes, and Richard Tuttle, eds.. *Jacopo Barozzi da Vignola.* Milan: Electa, 2002.

Amy, Robert and Pierre Gros. *La Maison Carrée de Nimes.* Paris: C.N.R.S., 1979.

Angelini, Luigi. *Le opere in Venezia di Mauro Codussi.* Milan: Edizioni d'Arte E. Bestetti, 1945.

Angelis d'Ossat, Gugliemo de. "Palladio e l'antichità." Bollettino del Centro Internazionale di Studi di Architettura "Andrea Palladio." 15 (1973): 29–42.

Argan, Giulio Carlo. "L'importanza di Sanmicheli nella formazione del Palladio," *Venezia e l'Europa. Atti del 18° congresso internazionale di storia dell'arte.* Venice: Arte Veneta, 1950, 387–89.

_____. "Palladio e la critica neoclassica." L'arte 1 (1930): 327–46.

Asquini, Licia and Massimo Asquini. *Andrea Palladio e gli Antonini: un palazzo 'Romano' nella Udine del Cinquecento.* Mariano di Friuli: Edizioni della Laguna, 1997.

Assunto, Rosario. "Introduzione all'estetica del Palladio." Bollettino del Centro Internazionale di Studi di Architettura "Andrea Palladio" 14 (1972): 9–26.

A.V. (the author's name stated only in initials): "The Abstraction of History." Oppositions 15/16 (1979): 129.

Banham, Reynar. "The New Brutalism," Architectural Review 118 (1955): 355–61.

Barbieri, Franco. *Architetture Palladiane.* Vicenza: Neri Pozza Editore, 1972.

_____. "Il valore dei *Quattro Libri.*" Bollettino del Centro Internazionale di Studi di Architetture "Andrea Palladio" 14 (1972): 63–79; reprinted in Barbieri, *Architetture,* 135–45.

_____. *Il museo civico di Vicenza.* Vicenza: Fondazione Giorgio Cini, 1962.

Barbour, James Murray. *Tuning and Temperament.* New York: Da Capo Press, 1972.

Baroli, Gino "Ristauro di una fabbrica Palladiana." Prospettive 26 (1963): 16–24.

Bassi, Elena. *Il Convento della Carità (Corpus Palladianum VI).* Vicenza: Centro Internazionale di Studi di Architettura "Andrea Palladio," 1971.

_____. "La scala ovata del Palladio nei suoi precedenti e nei suoi consequenti," Bollettino del Centro Internazionale di Studi di Architettura "Andrea Palladio" 20 (1978): 89–111.

Battaglia, Salvatore. *Grande dizionario della lingua Italiana.* Turin: Unione tipografico-editrice torinese, 1961.

Battilotti, Daniela. "Per il Palazzo di Iseppo da Porto del Palladio: un documento inedito e una nota." Antichità Viva 20 (1981): 40–45.

Battisti, Carlo. *Dizionario etimologico Italiano.* Florence: Barberà, 1952.

Battisti, Eugenio. "Le tendenze all'unità verso la metà del cinquecento." Bollettino del Centro Internazionale di Studi di Architettura "Andrea Palladio" 10 (1968): 127–46.

_____. "La lotta culturale durante il cinquecento e le avanguardie." Bollettino del Centro Internazionale di Studi di Architettura "Andrea Palladio" 10 (1968) 147–52.

_____. "Un tentativo di analisi strutturale del Palladio tramite le teorie musicali del cinquecento e l'impiego di figure rettoriche." Bollettino del Centro Internazionale di Studi di Architettura "Andrea Palladio" 15 (1973): 211–32.

Bauer, Herman, ed. *Wandlungen des Paradiesischen und Utopischen: Studien zum Bild eines Ideals.* Berlin: De Gruyter, 1966.

Beltramini, Guido and Pino Guidolotti. *Andrea Palladio Atlante delle architetture.* Venice: Marsilio, 2001. Translated as *Andrea Palladio: The Complete Illustrated Works.* New York: Universe, 2001.

Bender, John. "Supervenience and the Justification of Aesthetic Judgments." Journal of Aesthetics and Art Criticism 46 (87–88): 31–40.

Bentmann, Reinhard and Michael Müller. *Die Villa als Herrschaftsarchitektur.* Frankfurt am Main: Syndikat, 1970.

Berger, Karol. *Theories of Chromatic and Encharmonic Music in Late Sixteenth-Century Italy.* Ann Arbor: UMI Research Press, 1980.

Bieganski, Piotr. "I problemi della composizione spaziale delle ville palladiane." Bolletino del Centro Internazionale di Studi di Architettura "Andrea Palladio" 7 (1965): 23–34.

_____. "Spazi e planimetrie nella villa palladiana." Bollettino del Centro Internazionale di Studi di Architettura "Andrea Palladio" 14 (1972) 151–64.

Bordignon Favero, Giampaolo. *La Villa Emo di Fanzolo, (Corpus Palladianum V).* Vicenza: Centro Internazionale di Studi di Architettura "Andrea Palladio," 1972.

Boucher, Bruce. "The Last Will of Daniele Barbaro," Journal of Warburg and Courtauld Institutes 42 (1979): 277–82.

_____. *Palladio.* New York: Abbville Press, 1994.

_____. "Nature and the Antique in the Work of Palladio." Journal of the Society of Architectural Historians 59 (2000): 296–311.

Breidenbach, Walter. *Das Delische Problem.* Leipzig: Teubner, 1952.

Bruschi, Arnaldo. "L'Antico e il processo di identificazione degli ordini nella seconda metà del Quattrocento," in Guillaume, *L'emploi des ordres dans l'architecture de la Renaissance,* 11–58.

Brushi, Arnaldo, Corrado Maltese, Manfredo Taffuri, and Renato Bonelli, eds. *Scritti rinascimentali di architettura.* Milan: Il Polifio, 1978.

Burns, Howard. "The Lion's Claw: Palladio's Initial Project Sketches." Daidalos 5 (1982): 73–80.

Burns, Howard, Lynda Faibairn, and Bruce Boucher. Andrea Palladio: *The Portico and the Farmyard.* London: Art Council of Britain, 1975.

Burroughs, Charles. "Palladio and Fortune: Notes on the Sources and Meaning of the Villa Rotonda." Architectura 18 (1988): 59–91.

Carboneri, Nino. "Spazi e planimetrie nel palazzo palladiano." Bollettino del Centro Internazionale di Studi di Architettura "Andrea Palladio" 14 (1972): 165–86.

Carboz, André. "L'articolazione verticale degli spazi nelle ville palladiane." Bollettino del Centro Internazionale di Studi di Architettura "Andrea Palladio" 20 (1978): 129–43.

Carpenter, Rhys. See Ackerman, James and Rhys Carpenter.

Carpo, Mario. *L'architettura dell'eta della stampa.* Milan: Jaca Books, 1998. Translated by Sarah Benson as *Architecture in the Age of Printing.* Cambridge, MA: MIT Press, 2001.

Cevese, Renato. "La casa del notaio Pietro Cogollo, detta volgarmente 'casa del Palladio,'" in Chastel and Cevese (eds.), *Andrea Palladio,* 73–82.

Chastel, André and Renato Cevese, eds. *Andrea Palladio: nuovi contributi.* Milan: Electa, 1989.

Ciaponi, Lucia. "Il *De Architectura* di Vitruvio nel primo umanesimo." Italia mediviale e umanistica 3 (1960): 59–99.

Cocke, Richard. "Veronese e Daniele Barbaro." Journal of Warburg and Courtauld Institutes 35 (1972): 226–46.

Cooper, Tracy. "La facciata commemorativa di S. Giorgio Maggiore," in Chastel and Cevese (eds.), *Andrea Palladio,* 136–45.

De Fusco, Renato, and Maria Luisa Scalvini. "Significanti e significati della Rotonda Palladiana." Op.cit 16 (Sept. 1969): 5–26.

Fagiolo, Macello. "Palladio e il significato dell'architettura." Bollettino del Centro Internazionale di Studi di Achitettura "Andrea Palladio" 14 (1972): 27–41.

———. "Contributo all'interpretazione dell'ermetismo in Palladio." Bollettino del Centro Internazionale di Studi di Architettura "Andrea Palladio" 14 (1972): 357–80.

———. "Le facciate palladiane: la progettazione come proiezione sul piano spazi dietro spazi." Bollettino del Centro Internazionale di Studi di Architettura "Andrea Palladio" 20 (1978): 47–70.

Fagiolo, Marcello, ed. Roma e l'antico nell'arte e nella cultura del Cinquecento. Rome: Istituto della Enciclopedia Italiana, 1985.

Feinstein, Diego. Der Harmoniebegriff in der Kunstliteratur und Musiktheorie der italienischen Rennaissance, Ph.D diss., Freiburg University, 1977.

Forssman, Erik. Dorisch, ionish, korintisch. Studen über den Gebrauch der Säulenordnungen in der Architektur des 16. bis 18. Jahrbunderts. Stockholm: Almquist & Wiksel, 1961.

———. Palladios Lehrgebäude. Stockholm: Almquist & Wiksell, 1965.

———. "Palladio e Daniele Barbaro." Bolletino del Centro Internazionale di Studi di Architettura "Andrea Palladio" 8 (1966): 68–81.

———. Visible Harmony: Palladio's Villa Foscari at Malcontenta. Stockholm: Sveriges arkitekturmuseum, 1973.

———. "Palladio e le colonne." Bolletino del Centro Internazionale di Studi di Architettura "Andrea Palladio" 20 (1978): 71–87.

Forster, Kurt. "Is Palladio's Villa Rotonda an Architectural Novelty?" in Forster and Kubelik, Palladio, 27–34.

Forster, Kurt and Martin Kubelik. Palladio: Ein Symposium. Rome: Sweizarisches Kunstinstitut, 1980.

Forster, Kurt and Richard Tuttle. "Giulio Romano e le opere vicentine del Palladio." Bollettino del Centro Internazionale di Studi di Architettura "Andrea Palladio" 15 (1973): 107–19.

Foscari, Antonio and Manfredo Tafuri. L'armonia e i conflitti: la chiesa di San Francesco della Vigna nella Venezia del '500. Turin: G. Einaudi, 1983.

Frascari, Marco. Monsters of Architecture: Anthropomorphism in Architecture. Savage, MD: Roman & Littlefield, 1990.

Frommel, Christoph Luitpold. "Bramantes Nimphäum in Genazzano." Römisches Jahrbuch fur Kunstgeschichte 12 (1969): 139–60.

———. "Roma e la formazione architettonica del Palladio," Chastel and Cevese (eds.). Andrea Palladio, 146–162.

———. "Reflections on the Early Architectural Drawings," Millon and Lampugnani (eds.) The Renaissance, 101–103.

Gioseffi, Decio. "Il disegno come fase progettuale dell'attività palladiana." Bollettino del Centro Internazionale di Studi di Architettura "Andrea Palladio" 14 (1972): 45–62.

———. "Palladio e l'antico." Bollettino del Centro Internazionale di Studi di Architettura "Andrea Palladio" 14 (1972): 45–62.

Gros, Pierre. Aurea Templa. Recherches sur l'architecture de Rome à l'époque d'Auguste. Rome: École Français de Rome, 1976.

Gruenter, Rainer, ed. Vierhunderjahre Andrea Palladio. Heidelberg: Carl Winter Universitätsverlag, 1982.

Guerra, Andrea. "Moveable Facades: Palladio's Plan for the Church of San Giorgio Maggiore in Venice and its Successive Vicissitudes." Journal of the Society of Architectural Historians 61 (2002): 276–295.

Guillaume, Jean, ed. L' emploi des orders dans l'architecture de la Renaissance. Paris: Picard, 1992.

Guiotto, Mario. "Recenti ristauri di edifici palladiani." Bollettino del Centro Internazionale di Studi di Architettura "Andrea Palladio" 6/2 (1964): 70–88.

Günther, Hubertus. "Palladio e gli ordini di colonne," Chastel and Cevese eds. Andrea Palladio, 182–197.

Günther, Hubertus, and Christof Thoenes. "Gli ordini architettonici: Rinascita o invenzione," in Fagiolo, ed. Roma e l' antico, 272–310.

Hale, J.R. "Andrea Palladio, Polybius and Julius Cesar." Journal of the Warburg and Courtauld Institutes 9 (1977): 240–55.

Hart, Vaughan, and Peter Hicks, eds. Paper Palaces. The Rise of the Renaissance Architectural Treatise. New Haven and London: Yale University Press, 1998.

Heath, Thomas Little. A History of Greek Mathematics. Oxford: Clarendon Press, 1921.

Hersey, George and Richard Freeman. Possible Palladian Villas. Cambridge, MA: MIT Press, 1992.

Hersey, George. Pythagorean Palaces: Magic and Architecture in the Italian Renaissance. Ithaca: Cornell University Press, 1976.

Hesberg, Henner von. Konsolengeisa des Hellenismus und der frühen Keiserzet. Mainz: Philipp von Zabern, 1980.

Hofer, Paul. Palladio's Erstling: die Villa Godi Valmarana in Lonedo bei Vicenza. Basel: Birkhäuser, 1969.

Hofmannstahl, Hugo von. "Sommerreise" in Prosa, vol. 2. Frankfurt (M): Fischer, 1959, 64–74.

Howard, Deborah. "Exterior Orders and Interior Planning in Sansovino and Sanmicheli," in Guillaume (ed.) L'emploi des ordres, 183–92.

Howard, Deborah and Malcolm Longair. "Harmonic Proportion and Palladio's Quattro Libri." Journal of the Society of Architectual Historians 41 (1982) 116–43.

Huse, Nobert. "Palladio und die Villa Barbaro in Maser. Bemerkungen zum Problem der Autorschaft. Arte Veneta 28 (1974): 106–22.

Isermayer, Christian Adolf. "Le chiese del Palladio in rapporto al culto." Bollettino del Centro Internazionale di Studi di Architettura "Andrea Palladio" 10 (1968): 42–58.

———. "La concezione degli edifici sacri palladiani." Bollettino del Centro Internazionale di Studi di Architettura "Andrea Palladio" 14 (1972): 105–35.

———. "Die Villa Rotonda von Palladio." Zeitschrift für Kunstgeschichte 30 (1967): 207–21.

Jones, Mark Wilson. "Designing the Roman Corinthian Capital." Papers of the British School of Rome 59 (1991): 89–150.

———. Principles of Roman Architecture. New Haven and London: Yale University Press, 2001.

Knell, Heiner. Vitruvs Architekturtheorie. Darmstadt: Wissenschaftliche Buchgesellschaft, 1985.

Kruft, Hanno Walter. Geschichte der Architekturtheorie. Munich: C. H. Beck, 1986. Translated by Ronald Taylor as History of Architectural Theory. New York: Princeton University Press, 1994.

Kubelik, Martin. "Gli edifici palladiani nei disegni del magistrato Veneto dei Beni Inculti." Bollettino del Centro Internazionale di Studi di Architettura "Andrea Palladio" 16 (1974): 445–75.

———. Die Villa im Veneto. Zur typologischen Entwicklung im Quattrocento. Munich: Süddeutscher Verlag, 1977.

———. "Per una nuova lettura del Secondo Libro di Andrea Palladio." Bollettino del Centro Internazionale di Studi di Architettura "Andrea Palladio" 21 (1979) 177–97.

Kubelik Martin, with Christian Goedicke and Klaus Slusallek. "Thermoluminescence Dating in Architectural History: The Chronology of Palladio's Villa Rotunda." Journal of the Society of Architectural Historians 45 (1986): 396–407.

_____. "Primi resultati sulla datazione di alcune ville palladiane grazie alla termolumniscenza." Bollettino del Centro Internazionale di Studi di Architettura "Andrea Palladio" 22 (1980): 97–118.

Labowski, Carlota. _Bessarion's Library and Biblioteca Marciana._ Rome: Edizioni di storia e litteratura, 1978.

Larsen, Sinding S. "Palladio's Redentore: A Compromise in Composition." The Art Bulletin 47 (1965): 418–37.

Laven, P. J. _Daniele Barbaro, Patriarch-Elect of Aquileia,_ Ph.D. dissert., University of London, 1957.

_____. "The 'Causa Grimani' and Its Political Overtones." Journal of the Religious History 4 (1966): 184–205.

Lavin, Irving. "The Crisis of 'Art History.'" The Art Bulletin 78 (1996): 13–16.

Le Corbusier. _Towards the New Architecture._ New York: Dover, 1986.

Levarie, Siegmund and Ernest Levy. _A Study in Musical Acoustics._ Westport, CT: Greenwood Press, 1980.

Levinson, Jerrold. "Aesthetic Supervenience." Southern Journal of Philosophy 22 (1984): Supplement, 93–111.

Levy, Ernest. See Levarie, Siegmund.

Lewis, Douglas. "La datazione della villa Corner a Piombino Dese." Bollettino del Centro Internazionale di Studi di Architettura "Andrea Palladio" 14 (1972): 381–93.

_____. "Girolamo II Corner's Completion of Piombino with an Unrecognized Building of 1596 by Vincenzo Scamozzi." Bollettino del Centro Internazionale di Studi di Architettura "Andrea Palladio" 17 (1975): 401–5.

_____. _The Drawings of Andrea Palladio._ Washington D.C.: International Exhibitions Foundation, 1981.

Lindley, Mark. "Early 16th Century Keyboard Temperaments." Musica Disciplina 18 (1974): 129–51.

_____. _Lutes, Viols, and Temperaments._ Cambridge: Cambridge University Press, 1984.

Losito Maria. "La ricostruzione della voluta ionica vitruviana nei trattati del rinascimento." Mélange de l'Ècole française de Rome 105 (1993): 133–75.

Lotz, Wolfgang. "La Rotonda, edifizio civile con cupola." Bollettino del Centro Internazionale di Studi di Architettura "Andrea Palladio" 4 (1962): 69–73.

_____. "Palladio e Sansovino." Bollettino del Centro Internazionale di Studi di Architettura "Andrea Palladio" 9 (1967): 83–94.

Loukomsky, Georgii Kreskentevich. _Les villas des doges de Venice._ Paris: Morance, 1927.

Lykoudis, Michael, ed. _Modernism, Modernity, and the Other Modern_ (in press). New York: W. W. Norton & Company.

Marchini, Guiseppe. _Il Duomo di Prato._ Milan: Electa, 1957.

Margolin, Jean Claude, ed. _Platon et Aristote a la renaissance._ Paris: Librairie Philosophique J. Vrin, 1976.

Marsden, Eric William. _Greek and Roman Artillery._ Oxford: Clarendon Press, 1969.

Meiss, Millard, ed. _The Renaissance and Mannerism._ Princeton: Princeton University Press, 1963.

Mielke, Friedrich. "Die Treppen im Werk Andrea Palladios." Bollettino del Centro Internazionale di Studi di Architettura "Andrea Palladio" 22 (1980): 167–86.

Millon, Henry. "Rudolf Wittkower, Architectural Principles in the Age of Humanism: Its Influence on the Development and Interpretation of Modern Architecture." Journal of the Society of Architectural Historians 31 (1972): 83–91.

Millon, Henry and Vittorio Magnago Lampugnani, eds. _The Renaissance from Brunelleschi to Michaelangelo: The Representation of Architecture._ New York: Rizzoli, 1994.

Mitrović, Branko. "Palladio's Theory of Proportions and the Second Book of the _Quattro Libri dell'architettura._" Journal of the Society of Architectural Historians 49 (1990): 279–92.

_____. "Objectively Speaking." Journal of the Society of Architectural Historians 52 (1993): 59–67.

_____. "Paduan Aristotelianism and Daniele Barbaro's Commentary on Vitruvius' _De architectura._" The Sixteenth Century Journal 29 (1998): 667–88.

_____. "Palladio's Theory of Classical Orders in the _First Book of I Quattro Libri dell'architettura._" Architectural History 42 (1999): 110–40.

_____. "A Palladian Palinode: Reassessing Rudolf Wittkower's _Architectural Principles in the Age of Humanism._" architettura 31 (2001): 113–31.

_____. "Palladio's Canonical Corinthian Entablature and the Archaeological Surveys in the Fourth Book of _I quattro libri dell'architettura._" Architectural History 45 (2002): 113–27.

_____. "Aesthetic Formalism in Renaissance Architectural Theory," Zeitschrift für Kunstgeschichte 66 (2003), 321–39.

_____. "Modernists against Modernity" in Lykoudis (ed.) _Modernity, Modernism, and the Other Modern._ New York: W. W. Norton & Company, in press.

Morresi, Maria. "Le due edizioni dei commentary di Daniele Barbaro 1556–1567." Introductory article to Barbaro's _I dieci._ Milan: Edizione Il Polifilo, 1987.

Moyer, Ann. _Musica Scientia: Musical Scholarship in the Italian Renaissance._ Ithaca: Cornell University Press, 1992.

Naredi-Rainer, Paul von. _Architektur und Harmonie._ Cologne: Du Mont, 1982.

Oberhuber, Konrad. "Gli affreschi di Paolo Veronese nella Villa Barbaro." Bollettino del Centro Internazionale di Studi di Architettura "Andrea Palladio" 10 (1968): 188–202.

Onians, John. _Bearers of Meaning: The Classical Orders in Antiquity, the Middle Ages, and the Renaissance._ Princeton University Press, 1988.

Pagello, Elisabetta. "Un motivo ricorrente nell'architettura palladiana: il fregio pulvinato." Bollettino del Centro Internazionale di Studi di Architettura "Andrea Palladio" 21 (1979): 315–33.

Palisca, Claude. _Humanism in Italian Renaissance Musical Thought._ New Haven: Yale University Press, 1985.

Panofsky, Erwin. _Idea: A Concept in Art Theory._ New York: Harper & Row, 1968.

Paschini, Pio. "La nomina del patriarca di Aquileia." Rivista di storia della Chiesa in Italia 2 (1948): 63–69.

_____. _Eresia e riforma cattolica._ Rome: Facultas Theologica Pontificii Athenaei Lateriansis, 1951.

_____. "Gli scritti religiosi di Daniele Barbaro." Rivista di storia della Chiesa in Italia 5 (1951): 340–49.

_____. _Venezia e l'inquisizione Romana da Giulio III a Pio IV._ Padua: Antenore, 1959.

_____. "Daniele Barbaro: Letterato e prelato veneziano nel Cinquecento." Rivista di storia della Chiesa in Italia 15 (1962): 73–107.

Pasquali, Susanna: "Francesco Algarotti, Andrea Palladio e un frammento di marmo di Pola." Annali d'architettura 10/11 (1998–99): 159–66.

Pauwels, Yves. "Les origins de l'ordre composite." Annali d'architettura 1 (1989): 29–46.

Payne, Alina A. "Rudolf Wittkower and Architectural Principles in the

Age of Modernism." Journal of the Society of Architectural Historians 53 (1994): 322–42.

_____. The Architectural Treatise in Italian Renaissance. Cambridge: Cambridge University Press, 1999.

Pellecchia, Linda. "Architects Read Vitruvius: Renaissance Interpretations of the Ancient House." Journal of the Society of Architectural Historians 51 (1992): 377–416.

Prinz, Wolfram. "La 'sala di quattro colonne' nell'opera di Palladio." Bollettino del Centro Internazionale di Studi di Architettura "Andrea Palladio" 11 (1969): 370–85.

_____. "Appunti sulla relazione ideale tra la villa Rotonda e il cosmo, nonché alcune osservazioni su un mascherone posto al centro del pavimento." Bollettino del Centro Internazionale di Studi di Architettura "Andrea Palladio" 22 (1980): 279–87.

_____. Schloß Chambord und die Villa Rotunda in Vicenza. Berlin: Gebr. Mann Verlag, 1980.

Puppi, Lionello. Alvise Cornaro e il suo tempo. Padua: Comune di Padova, 1980.

_____. "Un litterato in villa: Giangiorgio Trissino a Cricoli." Arte Veneta 25 (1971): 72–91.

_____. La Villa Badoer in Fratta Polesine (Corpus Palladianum, VIII). Vicenza: Centro Internazionale di Studi di Architettura "Andrea Palladio," 1972.

_____. Palladio. Milan: Electa, 1973.

_____. Palladio: Corpus dei disegni. Milan: Berenice, 1989.

Rackusin, B. "The Architectural Theory of Luca Pacioli." Bibliothèque d'Humanisme et Renaissance 39 (1977): 479–502.

Robison, Elwin, C. "Structural Implications in Palladio's Use of Harmonic Proportions." Annali d'Architettura 10/11 (1988–99): 175–82.

Rowe, Colin. "The Mathematics of the Ideal Villa." Architectural Review 101 (1947): 101–4.

Rupprecht, Bernhard. "Palladios Projekt für den Palazzo Iseppo Porto in Vicenza." Mitteilungen des Kunsthistorischen Institutes in Florenz 10 (1971): 289–314.

_____. "Proiezione e realtà architettonica nei disegni dei 'Quattro libri.'" Bollettino del Centro Internazionale di Studi di Architettura "Andrea Palladio" 21 (1979): 159–75.

———. "Prinzipien der Architekturdarstellung in Palladios I quattro libri dell'architettura" in Gruenter, Vierhundertjahre, 11–45.

Rykwert, Joseph. Dancing Column. Cambridge, MA: MIT Press, 1997.

_____. The Palladian Ideal. New York: Rizzoli, 1999.

_____. The Villa: From Ancient to Modern. New York: Harry N. Abrams, 2000.

Schiller, P. Sapiens dominabitur astris. Studien über den Zusammenhang von'Architektur und Himmelskunde bei Andrea Palladio, Ph.D. diss., Freiburg University, 1985.

Schröder, Eberhard. Dürer, Kunst und Geometrie. Dürers Künstlerisches Schaffen aus der Sicht seiner "Unterweysung." Basel, Boston, and Stuttgart: Birkhäuser, 1980.

Semanzato, Camillo. La Rotonda di Vicenza (Corpus Palladianum I.). Vicenza: Centro Internazionale di Studi di Architettura "Andrea Palladio," 1968.

Sibley, Frank. "Aesthetic and Nonaesthetic." The Philosophical Review 74 (1965): 135–59.

_____. "Objectivity and Aesthetics." The Aristotelian Society 42 (1968): 31–54.

_____. "Particularity, Art, and Evaluation." The Aristotelian Society Supplementary volume, 48 (1974): 1–21.

Smith, Christine. Architecture in the Culture of Early Humanism: Ethics, Aesthetics, and Eloquence, 1400–1470. New York: Oxford University Press, 1992.

Smith, Robert. "A Matter of Choice: Veronese, Palladio, and Barbaro." Arte Veneta 43 (1977): 60–71.

Spielman, Heinz. Andrea Palladio und die Antike. Munich: Deutscher Kunstverlag, 1966.

Spinadel, Vera de. "Triangulature in A. Palladio." Nexus Network Journal 1 (1999): 117–20.

Streitz, Robert. La Rotonde et sa géometrie. Lausanne and Paris: Bibliothèque des Arts, 1973.

Summers, David. The Judgment of Sense: Renaissance Naturalism and the Rise of Aesthetics. Cambridge University Press, 1987.

Tafuri, Manfredo. Teorie e storia dell'architettura. Bari: Laterza, 1968.

_____. "Commitenza e tipologia delle ville palladiane." Bollettino del Centro Internazionale di Studi di Architettura "Andrea Palladio" 11 (1969): 120–69.

_____. "Sansovino 'versus' Palladio." Bollettino del Centro Internazionale di Studi di Architettura "Andrea Palladio" 15 (1973): 149–65.

_____. "Discordant Harmony from Alberti to Zuccari." Architectural Design 49 (1979): 36–44.

_____. Venezia e il Rinascimento: Religione, Scienza, Architettura. Turin: Einaudi, 1985. Translated by Jessica Levine as Venice and the Renaissance. Cambridge, MA: MIT Press, 1989.

_____. "Il norma e il programma: Il Vitruvio di Daniele Barbaro." Introductory article to Barbaro's I dieci. Milano: Il Polifilo, 1987, XI–XL.

_____. Ricerca del Rinascimento: Principi, città, architetti. Turin: Einaudi, 1985.

Tavenor, Robert. Palladio and Palladianism. London: Thames and Hudson, 1991.

Thoenes, Christof. Sostegno e adornamento: Saggi sull'architettura del rinascimenta. Milan: Electa, 1998.

———. Opus incertum. Italienische Studien aus duei Jahrzehnten. Munich: Deutscher Kunstverlag, 2002.

Timofiewitsch, Wladimir. Die Sakrale Architektur Palladios. Munich: Fink, 1968.

_____. La chiesa del Redentore (Corpus Palladianum III). Vicenza: Centro Internazionale di Studi di Architettura "Andrea Palladio," 1969.

Töbelmann, Fritz. Römische Gebälke. Heidelberg: C. Winter, 1923.

Tommaseo, Niccolò. Dizionario della lingua Italiana. Turin: Unione tipografico-editrice, 1916.

Turrini, Giancarlo. "Aspetti costruttivi e strutturali nell'opera di Andrea Palladio," in Chastel and Cevese (eds.), Andrea Palladio: nuovi contributi. Milan: Electa, 1989, 127–35.

Waddy, Patricia. Seventeenth Century Roman Palaces: Use and the Art of Plan. New York: Architectural History Foundation; Cambridge, MA: MIT Press, 1990.

Walker, Daniel Pickering. Studies in the Musical Science in the Late Renaissance. London: Warburg Institute, 1978.

Wassell, Stephen. "Mathematics of Palladio's Villas." Nexus Network Journal 1 (1999): 121–28.

Wicks, Robert. "Criticism and Counterthesis: Supervenience and Aesthetic Judgment." Journal of Aesthetics and Art Criticism 46 (1988): 509–11.

_____. "Supervenience and the 'Science of the Beautiful.'" Journal of Aesthetics and Art Criticism 50 (1992): 322–25.

Wilinski, Stanislaw. "La finestra terminale nelle ville di Andrea

Palladio." Bollettino del Centro Internazionale di Studi di Architettura "Andrea Palladio" 11 (1969): 207–21.

_____. "La serliana di villa Poiana a Poiana Maggiore." Bollettino del Centro Internazionale di Studi di Architettura "Andrea Palladio" 10 (1968).

Wittkower, Rudolf. *Architectural Principles in the Age of Humanism.* London: Warburg Institute, 1949; Alec Tiranti, 1962.

Wolters, Wolfgang. "Andrea Palladio e la decorazione dei suoi edifici." Bollettino del Centro Internazionale di Studi di Architettura "Andrea Palladio" 10 (1968): 255–67.

_____. "Sebastiano Serlio e il suo contributo alla villa veneziana prima del Palladio." Bollettino del Centro Internazionale di Studi di Architettura "Andrea Palladio" 11 (1969): 83–94.

_____. *Architektur und Ornament.* Munich: Beck, 2000.

Younés, Samir. *The True, the Fictive, and the Real: The Historical Dictionary of Architecture of Quatremère de Quincy.* London: Andreas Papadakis, 1999.

Zangwill, Nick. "Long Live Supervenience." Journal of Aesthetics and Art Criticism 50 (1992): 319–22.

_____. "Supervenience Unthwarted: Rejoinder to Wicks." Journal of the Aesthetics and Art Criticism 52 (1994): 466–69.

_____. "Feasible Aesthetic Formalism. Nous 33 (1999): 610–29.

_____. *The Metaphysics of Beauty.* Ithaca: Cornell University Press, 2001.

Zloković, Milan. Divina Proportio ≠ Sectio Aurea. Pregled arhitekture 4/5 (1954).

Zocconi, Mario. Costanti e variazioni nelle misure degli spazi palladiani." Bollettino del Centro Internazionale di Studi di Architettura "Andrea Palladio" 14 (1972): 187–221.

_____. "I cortili degli edifici palladiani." Bollettino del Centro Internazionale di Studi di Architettura "Andrea Palladio" 16 (1974): 467–81.

Zorzi, Giangiorgio. *Disegni delle antichità di Andrea Palladio.* Venice: Nero Pozza, 1959.

_____. "Errori, deficienze e inesattezze de 'I quattro libri dell'architettura' de Andrea Palladio.'" Bollettino del Centro Internazionale di Studi di Architettura "Andrea Palladio" 6 (1960): 143–48.

_____. *Le opere pubbliche e i palazzi di Andrea Palladio.* Venice: Nero Pozza, 1965.

_____. *Le chiese e i ponti di Andrea Palladio.* Venice: Nero Pozza, 1966.

_____. "L'interpretazione dei disegni Palladiani." Bollettino del Centro Internazionale di Studi di Architettura "Andrea Palladio" 10 (1968): 97–111.

_____. "La datazione delle ville palladiane." Bollettino del Centro Internazionale di Studi di Architettura "Andrea Palladio" 11 (1969): 137–48.

INDEX